Books in Motion

Contemporary Cinema   2

Contemporary Cinema is a series of edited volumes and
single-authored texts focusing on the latest in film culture, theory,
reception and interpretation. There is a concentration on films
released in the past fifteen years, and the aim is to reflect important
current issues while pointing to others that to date have not been
given sufficient attention.

Books in Motion

Adaptation, Intertextuality, Authorship

Edited by

Mireia Aragay

Rodopi

Amsterdam - New York, NY 2005

Institutional support:
The Department of Theatre, Film and Television Studies at the
University of Wales-Aberystwyth

The paper on which this book is printed meets the requirements
of "ISO 9706:1994, Information and documentation - Paper for
documents - Requirements for permanence".

ISBN: 90-420-1957-3
ISSN: 1572-3070
©Editions Rodopi B.V., Amsterdam - New York, NY 2005
Printed in the Netherlands

For Víctor, Tomàs and Òscar

CONTENTS

Contexts, Intertexts, Adaptation

Beyond Adaptation

List of Illustrations

Acknowledgements

This book is the result of a long-standing interest in the hybrid, interstitial field of adaptation studies. Salzburg Seminar Session 403, 'From Page to Screen: Adapting Literature to Film', helped crystallise that interest. My warmest thanks to the Session's Faculty—Steven Bach, Peter Lilienthal, Gerald Rafshoon, Richard Schickel and David Thacker—and Fellows—some of whom have contributed to this volume—for their inspiration and stimulus. The Facultat de Filologia at the University of Barcelona provided funding towards my visit to the British Film Institute Library in London. I wish to thank the staff there, especially Head Librarian David Sharp, for their generous help during my stay. My gratitude also to editor Stephen Schneider for his unstinting trust and support during the completion of this volume. Mònica Miravet proofread the final draft with her usual efficient diligence. My family, friends and colleagues have kept me going, sane and in good spirits—to them all, my deepest gratitude.

Mireia Aragay
Barcelona, 2005

Introduction

Reflection to Refraction: Adaptation Studies Then and Now

Mireia Aragay

Even though, as has often been noted, the history of adaptation is as long as the history of cinema itself, the critical and theoretical debate about adaptation was not established in the academy until the mid-twentieth century. Critics as diverse as Graeme Turner (1993: 39), Imelda Whelehan (1999: 17), Robert B. Ray (2000: 44-5) or Barbara Hodgdon (2002: v) have underlined the importance of the institutional history of film studies for an understanding of the different shapes adaptation theory has taken since its inception. Film departments, and the field of film and literature, began to emerge in the United States and the United Kingdom in the 1960s and 1970s out of English literature departments, inheriting the main assumptions of the dominant New Criticism and liberal humanism. These hinged on a view of the literary work as unitary and self-contained, and of meaning as immanently inhering in the words on the page, an immutable essence to be apprehended by the (fundamentally passive) reader. Such assumptions depended, in their turn, on an as yet unchallenged faith in the sovereign Author as source and centre of the reified text—as, ultimately, what careful, indeed 'reverential' close reading would reveal in the literary work. The words on the page, emanating from the Author-God, were sacrosanct—witness the hostility to translation (Ray 2000: 45) and the downgrading of the element of performance (Marsden 1995: 9; Worthen 1998: 1094) within the New Critical and liberal humanist paradigms. In this context, while not necessarily alluding to Walter Benjamin's 1936 essay 'The Work of Art in the Age of Mechanical Reproduction', first published in English in 1968, adaptation studies up to the late 1970s resonated with Benjamin's argument that mechanical reproduction, most pre-eminently film technology, obliterates the 'aura'—i.e. the authenticity, authority,

originality, uniqueness—of the work of art, thus bringing about a
'liquidation of the traditional value of the cultural heritage' (Benjamin
1968: 223-4).[1] More crudely, Virginia Woolf's 1926 rhetoric of
cinema as a rapacious animal of prey or parasite devouring 'its
unfortunate victim', literature (Woolf 1966: 269-70), was equally
pervasive within the discourse of adaptation until relatively recent
times. Adaptation studies also appeared to be haunted by the history of
the new medium itself. The earliest Anglo-American academic
monograph on literature and film, George Bluestone's hugely influential *Novels into Film* (1957), opened with the statement that 'the film
in recent years has become more and more insistent on its claim to
serious recognition' (1957: vii), a legitimacy the early film industry,
considered to be a low-brow, popular form of entertainment, had
originally sought through adaptation, that is, by turning to 'presold
product' (Ray 2000: 43), the older and more 'respectable' art of
(canonical) literature, with a view to enlarging its audience beyond the
working-class by appealing to the middle class's taste for realistic
narratives and classic drama (Ray 2000: 42-3; Rothwell 2004: 1-26).

The conjunction of the factors delineated above resulted in a
binary, hierarchical view of the relationship between literature and
film, where the literary work was conceived of as the valued original,
while the film adaptation was merely a copy, and where fidelity
emerged as the central category of adaptation studies. The discourse
of fidelity has exercised a firm, persistent grip within the field of
adaptation studies. George Bluestone's 1957 *Novels into Film*,
mentioned above, is a case in point. As is made clear in the preface
and opening chapter, Bluestone offers a strong medium-specific
approach to adaptation based on what Kamilla Elliott (2003: 9-13)
describes as a categorical distinction between novel and film, according to which the two media are essentially different in that the novel is

---

[1] However, in Benjamin's dialectical approach the role of film is not seen in entirely
negative terms. Mechanical reproduction, he claims, 'can put the copy of the original
into situations which would be out of reach for the original itself' (1968: 222), and 'in
permitting the reproduction to meet the beholder ... in its own particular situation, it
reactivates the object reproduced' (1968: 223)—two statements which, over and
beyond the overt rhetoric of 'original' vs. 'copy/reproduction', anticipate some of the
central claims of recent adaptation studies, as will be seen below. Benjamin's insight
into the potentially transformative, dialogic power of film (adaptation) is all the more
striking if one bears in mind that it was written at a time when film had not yet shed
its originary stigma as popular entertainment for the masses.

linguistic, conceptual and discursive, while film is primarily visual, perceptual and presentational (1957: viii-ix). In contrast with the dominant tendency at the time to judge adaptations on the basis of an impressionistic fidelity criterion (Cardwell 2002: 45), Bluestone argues that the view that 'the novel is a norm and the film deviates at its peril' (1957: 5) reveals a lack of awareness of the radical difference between the two media—'changes are *inevitable* the moment one abandons the linguistic for the visual medium' (1957: 5 [emphasis in original]); novels and films are 'different aesthetic genera' (1957: 5) or 'autonomous' media (1957: 6). Adaptations, that is, should be judged on their own merits *as* films—no doubt a bold claim to make at a time when, as Bluestone himself points out (1957: vii), film was still struggling for serious recognition as art.

However, as soon as Bluestone focuses on the 'unique and specific properties' of each medium (1957: 6), it becomes obvious that his discussion is underpinned by a continued belief in the intrinsic superiority of literature. The novel, he claims, is 'more complex' than film (1957: 7); the fact that it is a linguistic—hence symbolic— medium means that it is more self-conscious and self-reflexive, far more deeply steeped in metaphor, far better equipped to render thought and other mental states. Film, as a primarily visual medium, can only aspire to metaphor 'in a highly restricted sense' (1957: 20)— mainly through the uniquely cinematic technique of editing, Bluestone claims (1957: 27)—and is singularly inadequate when it comes to rendering thoughts and feelings (1957: 48). Such technological determinism (Cardwell 2002: 46) and disregard for the fact that, as Kamilla Elliott points out, novels and films interpenetrate each other—words are present in films as much as images and 'image-effects' pervade novels (Elliott 2003: 12-13)—lead Bluestone to claim that novel and film are mutually 'hostile' (1957: 2) or 'antithetical' media (1957: 23), and that adaptation is, in the last instance, an impossibility (1957: 57).[2] However, he paradoxically goes on to devote the rest of his monograph to six case-studies of adaptation which, unsurprisingly by this stage given his valorisation of the novel over film, of words over images, invoke the integrity and centrality of

---

[2] Bluestone did try to broaden his focus by discussing audiences, censorship and modes of production, and by looking at film and literature as separate institutions rather than simply different media (1957: 31-45). His overall argument, however, leans heavily towards technological determinism and indeed formalism.

Authorial meaning and the fidelity criterion—the 1940 MGM *Pride and Prejudice*, Bluestone claims, 'render[s] the quality of Jane Austen's intentions' and 'do[es] not alter the meanings of Jane Austen's novel' (1957: 136)—even as they (unwittingly) undermine the earlier argument about the fundamental incommensurability of the two media. In fact, the incongruity is both built into and foreshadowed by Bluestone's methodology as described in his preface:

> The method calls for viewing the film with a shooting-script at hand. During the viewing, notations of any final changes in the editing were entered on the script. After the script had become an accurate account of the movie's final print, it was then superimposed on the novel [...] Before each critical evaluation, I was able to hold before me an accurate and reasonably objective record of how the film differed *from its model*. (1957: xi [my emphasis])

Even allowing for the absence of video and DVD equipment, Bluestone's methodology, based on 'converting' the film into a written record of itself, is obviously at odds with his strong medium-specific thesis (Cardwell 2002: 47-48). It also reveals Bluestone's crucial assumption of the superiority of words vis-à-vis images—the novel, 'less a norm than a point of departure' on the previous page (1957: x), now becomes 'a model', an original that the adaptation can at best only aspire to copy.

As Timothy Corrigan points out, and Bluestone himself recognised, 'the 1950s marked a major shift in the rapport between film and literature. Literature began ... to loose [sic] its hierarchical control over film' as film began to raise its cultural status from entertainment into art (Corrigan 1999: 48). In fact, the upward social mobility of film may be said to have its roots in the first decades of the sound era, the 1930s and 1940s, when the new medium clearly enlarged its audience to include the middle and upper-middle classes (Boyum 1985: 6-7). The 1950s, however, were a watershed in that they marked the emergence of an even younger medium, television, which brought about a revised perception of film—Joy Gould Boyum argues that 'in stealing away movies' great mass audience, [television] helped to make movies themselves more elite' (Boyum 1985: 11), eventually leading, over the 1960s and early 1970s, to the already-mentioned upsurge of film studies in the academy. Both Bluestone's holding on to the supposedly inherent superiority of literature and the French *nouvelle vague* polemic against adaptation make their fullest sense when placed in the context of the 1950s concern about the effects of mass culture on high culture and film's efforts over the same period to assert its uniqueness as art. François Truffaut's 'A Certain Tendency of the French Cinema', originally published in *Cahiers du Cinéma* in January 1954, inaugurated the polemic by attacking the 'tradition of quality' in French cinema (Truffaut 1976: 225), films—most of them adaptations of French classics—which Truffaut dismisses as literary, not truly cinematic, uncreative, the work of mere *metteurs-en-scène* (1976: 233). Instead, he praises the cinema of filmmakers such as Robert Bresson, Jean Cocteau, Jean Renoir or Jacques Tati—auteurs who, even when they are adapting literary material, bring something truly personal and original to it, thus turning their films into the expression of a personal vision (1976: 233). Behind Truffaut and, generally, the conception of the auteur that dominated *Cahiers* over the 1950s and early 1960s, there lay Alexandre Astruc's influential article 'The Birth of a New Avant Garde: *La Caméra-Stylo*', originally published in *L'Écran français* in March 1948. Even as it emphasised the specific artistic practices of film, Astruc's essay went on to compare it with literature—'cinema like literature is not so much a particular art as a language' (Astruc 1999: 159)—and the filmmaker with the literary Author expressing himself in his work. And it is precisely such comparisons that reveal the paradox at the heart of *nouvelle vague* auteurism, variously described by T. Jefferson Kline as the attempt to '[oedipically] usurp ... the role of literature' (1992: 3) and by Corrigan as the fluctuation 'between the deauthorization of literature and the reauthorization of themselves as authors' (1999: 53). Newly-established journals such as *La Revue du Cinéma* (1946) and, particularly, *Cahiers du Cinéma* (1951), which mirrored literary journals and reviews (Corrigan 1999: 50), published the group's self-conscious theorising, where the auteur was conceived as endowing his work with organic unity and meaning quite independently from industrial, technological, generic and other cultural factors—a conception not far removed from the literary Author-God. The *politique des auteurs*, in short, sought to supply film—a collective enterprise—with a unique creator in the person of the film director, and in the process greatly contributed towards a negative perception of adaptation (Boyum 1985: 13).[3]

---

[3] Although *Cahiers* was dominated by this perspective, other views, notably André Bazin's various interventions in the debate (e.g. Bazin 1981), were also given a voice

In the English-speaking context, the 1970s was the decade when film studies became fully institutionalised in the academy. In the field of adaptation, however, the assumption that literature was the superior medium was an enduring one. Geoffrey Wagner's *The Novel and the Cinema* (1975), for instance, is still trapped by an unspoken reliance on the fidelity criterion and a concomitant (formalist) focus on the literary source/filmed adaptation binary pair, to the exclusion of intertextual and contextual factors. As is well known, Wagner draws a distinction between three modes of adaptation, which he labels transposition, commentary and analogy. In transposition 'a novel is directly given on the screen, with the minimum of apparent interference' (1975: 222); commentary is 'where an original is taken and ... altered in some respect' (1975: 223), revealing 'a different intention on the part of the film-maker, rather than an infidelity or outright violation' (1975: 224); while an analogy takes 'a fiction as a point of departure' (1975: 223) and therefore 'cannot be indicted as a violation of a literary original since the director has not attempted (or has only minimally attempted) to reproduce the original' (1975: 227). Clearly, Wagner is obsessively concerned with 'defending' adaptations of any sort from the charge of 'infidelity', while his attempts at actually applying his tripartite classification to specific adaptations have the perverse effect of foregrounding the severely limited theoretical and practical validity of any model that relies on the centrality of the literary source or 'original'. Thus, classing the 1939 *Wuthering Heights* as a transposition does indeed seem problematic in the light of the fact that, as Sara Martín reminds us in this volume, the film leaves out a substantial part of novel, namely its second volume. Similarly, Wagner seems unable to determine whether Luis Buñuel's *Belle de jour* (1967) is a commentary or an analogy; he points out that the '[analogy] net could let in a very large number of fishes' (1975: 230); and his division of the James Bond films into the three categories leads him to acknowledge, in a footnote, that 'This is an admittedly over-schematic pigeon-holing' (1975: 231).

---

in the journal (Buscombe 1981: 23-6). Caughie (1981: 35-47) provides a sense of the variety of the writings published in *Cahiers* around the concept of the auteur, often overshadowed by the extreme, and extremely influential, version of the auteur popularised by Andrew Sarris, the American apologist of auteurism (Buscombe 1981: 25-9). As Andrew notes (1993: 78), Bazin's taste for impure, mixed cinema always stopped short of fetishising the auteur (see e.g. Bazin 1967a, 1967b and 2000). Bazin is referred to again below.

Published at the close of the 1970s, Maurice Beja's *Film and Literature* (1979) fascinatingly fluctuates between an apparent desire to challenge the primacy of literature and of the fidelity criterion— 'What relationship should a film have to the original source? Should it be "faithful"? Can it be? To what?', Beja famously asks (1979: 80)— and an inability to ultimately break away from it. Thus, while Beja dismisses 'betrayal' as 'a strong word ... needlessly or distractingly moralistic' (1979: 81) and denounces the use of the fidelity criterion to the detriment of judging adaptations as independent artistic achievements (1979: 88), he still invokes the foggy concept of the 'spirit of the original work' as that which an adaptation 'should be faithful to' (1979: 81), and (moralistically) wonders, 'What types of changes are proper or not, desirable or not?' (1979: 83). His formalist bias and implicit upholding of the superiority of (canonical) literature vis-à-vis film become obvious when he claims:

> The feeling is that truly first-rate works of written literature will be the most difficult to adapt, since they are the ones in which form and content have already been perfectly matched, so that any attempted disjunction between them is bound to produce problems [...] consequently filmmakers should avoid adaptations of major works of literature in favor of less imposing—or even mediocre—ones. (1979: 85)

A claim Beja seeks to substantiate by reference to Alfred Hitchcock's career, which 'provides evidence of what can be done with unexceptional material' (1979: 86)—a very different take on Hitchcock as adapter from that supplied by Thomas Leitch's approach in this volume, which reads Hitchock's deliberate selection of obscure literary sources and authors as part and parcel of his struggle 'to establish himself as an auteur [by] wrest[ing] authorship ... away from another plausible candidate: the author of the original property'. As a book designed for the courses on literature and film that had proliferated in American universities since the mid-1960s in the context of an increasingly audiovisual culture, Beja's *Film and Literature*, unlike Bluestone's and Wagner's monographs, no longer assumes confidently that it is addressing an audience of readers familiar with (canonical) literature. Thus, its stated aim is to turn its young university audience into 'book addicts' as well as 'movie fans'; in the process, as John Ellis pointed out in 1982 in his introduction to a symposium on adaptation published in *Screen*, its formalistic-cum-medium-specific approach 'elides the different historical moments into which novel and adaptation are produced and consumed' (1982: 5).

Ellis was writing at the start of the 1980s, a decade over which the fields of literary studies, film studies and their interface, adaptation studies, were to be utterly transformed. Writing, like Beja, at the close of the 1970s, Keith Cohen's *Film and Fiction: The Dynamics of Exchange* (1979) takes Bluestone's medium-specific approach to task on the basis of its leading to 'the regrettable conclusion that "the great innovators of the twentieth century, in film and novel both, have had ... little to do with each other, have gone their ways alone, always keeping a firm but respectful distance"' (Cohen 1979: 3; the quote is from Bluestone 1957: 63). Starting off from a semiotic perspective—with Christian Metz as a point of reference—Cohen assumes that 'visual and verbal elements are ... component parts of one global system of meaning' (1979: 3), and sets out to explore the 'exchange of energies from the movies, an art originally so thoroughly informed by a nineteenth-century sensibility, to the modern novel, whose major innovations will be seen as closely patterned after those of cinema' (1979: 2). The 'dynamics of exchange', in other words, work both ways between film and fiction—an argument which instantly undermines claims for the superiority of literature vis-à-vis cinema. As Cardwell claims, 'if we accept such examples of correlative characteristics in film and novel, then it becomes much harder to argue that textual characteristics within the end-products of different media arise from the unique properties of the media themselves' (2002: 49), and this in turn potentially liberates adaptation studies from the formalist, binary source/adaptation straitjacket.[4] Indeed, Dudley Andrew was quick to grasp this. Frequently reprinted, his 'The Well-Worn Muse: Adaptation in Film History and Theory', first published in 1980, broke new ground for adaptation studies by explicitly rejecting Bluestone's strong medium-specific stance, which 'ultimately condemn[s adaptation] to the realm of the impossible' (Andrew 1980: 12), and taking Cohen's arguments as a starting point:

---

[4] Both Cohen (1979: 3-4) and Cardwell (2002: 48-9) refer to Sergei Eisenstein's much earlier work in this connection, his 'Dickens, Griffith and the Film Today' (1944), where the Russian filmmaker argues that Charles Dickens's novels foreshadow D. W. Griffith's editing methods.

Cohen, like Metz before him, suggests that despite their very different material character ... verbal and cinematic signs share a common fate: that of being condemned to connotation [...] And since the implicative power of literary language and of cinematic signs is a function of use as well as of system, adaptation analysis ultimately leads to an investigation of film style and periods in relation to literary styles of different periods [...] This drops adaptation and all studies of film and literature out of the realm of eternal principle and airy generalization, and onto the uneven but solid ground of artistic history, practice, and disourse.

It is time for adaptation studies to take a sociological turn. (Andrew 1980: 14)

Adaptation, that is, is a cultural practice; specific adaptations need to be approached as acts of discourse partaking of a particular era's cultural and aesthetic needs and pressures, and such an approach requires both 'historical labor and critical acumen' (Andrew 1980: 16-17), as manifested in this collection in Manuel Barbeito Varela's reading of John Huston's *The Dead* (1987) as a film that challenges postmodern culture's effacement of the experience of death, or in Lindiwe Dovey's analysis of the politics of infidelity in relation to Ramadan Suleman's *Fools* (1997).

Writing in 1980, Andrew also pointed out that the discourse of fidelity was still 'the most frequent and most tiresome discussion of adaptation' (1980: 12). Four years later, Christopher Orr, reviewing four recently published books, similarly found the concern with fidelity to continue to dominate the field of adaptation studies (Orr 1984: 72).[5] Interestingly, Orr opens his review essay by providing a critique of the discourse of fidelity and by pointing to ways in which adaptation studies could seek to transcend it. Fidelity criticism, Orr argues, 'impoverishes the film's intertextuality' by reducing it to 'a single pre-text' (i.e. the literary source) while ignoring other pre-texts and codes (cinematic, cultural) that contribute to making 'the filmic text intelligible' (Orr 1984: 72-3). It also assumes that the literary source can only yield one single meaning, the 'message' of the Author-God, and that the aim of the adaptation process is to 'repro-

---

[5] The four books reviewed by Orr are: Gene D. Phillips (1980) *Hemingway and Film* (New York: Ungar), Michael Klein and Gillian Parker (eds.) (1981) *The English Novel and the Movies* (New York: Ungar), Andrew S. Horton and Joan Margretta (eds.) (1981) *Modern European Film-Makers and the Art of Adaptation* (New York: Ungar), and Syndy M. Conger and Janice Welsh (1981) *Narrative Strategies: Original Essays in Film and Fiction* (Macomb, Ill.: Western Illinois University Press).

duce' that meaning on the screen (Orr 1984: 73). Orr challenges the discourse of fidelity by reference to Roland Barthes's poststructuralist view of the text as 'a tissue of quotations drawn from the innumerable centres of culture' (Barthes 1988: 170). He also alludes to Ellis's 1982 piece, in particular his distinction between the marketing strategy commonly used for adaptations from literary classics—based on the idea that the adaptation aims to reproduce the source literary text on screen, and hence encouraging judgements based on fidelity—and 'the real aim of an adaptation', namely, to trade

> upon the memory of the novel, a memory that can derive from actual read-ing, or, as is more likely with a classic of literature, a generally circulated cultural memory. The adaptation consumes this memory, aiming to efface it with the presence of its own images. The successful adaptation is the one that is able to replace the memory of the novel. (1982: 3)

Ellis, in other words, does not assume that all viewers of an adaptation will have read the source text. The narrow, formalistic concept of fidelity is replaced by the much more productive, culturally-constructed notion of the 'successful adaptation', namely, the adapta-tion that fits in with the generally-held perception of the source text at a given time. In this light, fidelity remains of interest only in so far as 'lapses of fidelity—the changes that occur in the passage from literary to filmic text—... provide clues to the ideology embedded in the [filmic] text' (Orr 1984: 73). Orr's insight has been recently taken up by critics such as Erica Sheen (2000: 2-3) and Barbara Hodgdon (2002: v) when they claim that, while fidelity cannot be considered a valid yardstick with which to judge any adaptation, adaptation studies cannot afford to ignore the institutional and performative nature of the discourse of fidelity as found above all in reviews. The discourse of fidelity, as Sheen and Hodgdon point out, often involves a rhetoric of possession—the critic is convinced the s/he owns the Author's meaning as manifested in the work, and judges the success of an adaptation in terms of its perceived adherence to that meaning—and an articulation of loss—the critic denounces the adaptation if it is perceived to deviate from the literary work's Authorial meaning. Reviews are precisely the starting point for Deborah Cartmell's and Imelda Whelehan's discussion of the first Harry Potter film, *Harry Potter and the Sorcerer's Stone* (2001), as an adaptation which paradoxically undermines itself by aiming at a faithful replication of the source text. The paradoxes of fidelity are also the focus of Sara

Martín's essay, which sees Ralph Fiennes's successful performance as Heathcliff in Peter Kosminsky's *Wuthering Heights* (1992)— 'successful' in Ellis's sense of replacing the memory of the novel's character—as a by-product of the film's unsuccessful narrative fidelity to Emily Brontë's novel. Both chapters, as well as all others in this collection, also take good note of Ellis's warning against formalistic approaches to adaptation which elide the historical and institutional contexts in which the source text and the adaptation are produced and consumed (1982: 5), as well as of Orr's claim that an 'ideological perspective [focusing on] the adapted film's material and cultural conditions of production over its literary source guards against the reduction of intertextuality that often characterizes fidelity studies' as much as against the reinscription of the figures of the Author-God or the Auteur-God (Orr 1984: 73).

Andrew's, Ellis's and Orr's contributions to adaptation studies need to be placed in the context of the deep transformations affecting both film and literary studies in the 1980s. It is significant, in this respect, that Orr should seek to reconceptualise adaptation studies by reference to Barthes's seminal 1968 essay 'The Death of the Author', which 'killed' the Author-God and his finished, self-sufficient work, replacing it with the text as a 'multi-dimensional space in which a variety of writings, none of them original, blend and clash' (Barthes 1988: 170), and empowering the reader as the place 'where this multiplicity is focused' (Barthes 1988: 171). As Catherine Belsey recognised in 1980, in a book exploring the impact of (post)structuralist thought on literary theory and criticism, the death of the Author meant that the text was 'Released from the constraints of a single and univocal reading, [thus becoming] available for production, plural, contradictory, capable of change' (Belsey 1980: 134), rather than being enshrined as a sacrosanct work of art. This radical departure has had far-reaching consequences in the fields of both film and literary studies, leading to the proliferation of poststructuralist theories and critical practices, to an emphasis on intertextuality as a key to textual intelligibility, and to the interdisciplinary crosspollination of both film and literary studies with methods and concepts originating in linguistics, psychoanalysis, anthropology, history, semiotics, deconstruction, materialist theory, feminism and gender studies, or race and postcolonial theory. Needless to say, the notion that meaning is produced by an actively participating reader also had an impact on adaptation studies—the literary source need no longer be conceived as a work/original holding within itself a timeless essence which the adaptation/copy must faithfully reproduce, but as a text to be endlessly (re)read and appropriated in different contexts. In this respect, it is equally symptomatic that Andrew, Ellis and Orr should all see the future for adaptation studies to lie in the direction of cultural and film history—Andrew's 'sociological turn'; Ellis's and Orr's insistence on the need to pay attention to the contextual conditions of production and consumption—at a time when film studies, under the influence of the work emanating from the Centre for Contemporary Cultural Studies at the University of Birmingham and of French theorists such as Barthes himself, Michel Foucault or Louis Althusser, was experiencing the impact of the (relatively new) discipline of cultural studies (Turner 1993: 40-1; Hayward 1996: 15; Hodgdon 2002: vi).

Adaptation studies, then, were also substantially transformed over the 1980s in the light of both poststructuralism and cultural studies, as well as in the context of a firmly audiovisual culture—Ellis, as noted above, does not assume that viewers of adaptations will have read the literary sources they are based on (1982: 3). Joy Gould Boyum, whose *Double Exposure: Fiction into Film* appeared in 1985, provides revealing personal testimony as regards the changes adaptation studies underwent over the decade. As someone who came to film criticism from literature, Boyum had first-hand knowledge of the 'biases and preconceptions brought to bear on film by the literary establishment' (1985: ix), and these included 'a proprietary attitude toward books' and a view of adaptation 'as a suspect form' (1985: x). Significantly, it was reader-response theory which led her to revise her assumptions. Although deriving from a different intellectual tradition from Barthes's poststructuralism, reader-response theory also empowered the reader by emphasising the dialogical and 'eventful' character of literary texts. In the words of Hans Robert Jauss, the main proponent of the aesthetics of reception, literary works become events when newly appropriated by their readers:

> A literary work is not an object that stands by itself and that offers the same view to each reader in each period. It is not a monument that monologically reveals its timeless essence [...] A literary event can continue to have an effect only if those who come after it still or once again respond to it—if there are readers who again appropriate the past work or authors who want to imitate, outdo, or refute it. (Jauss 1982: 21-2)

A claim which, no doubt, is enormously relevant to adaptation studies, enabling as it does a view of adaptations as appropriating or re-creating past texts in/for different contexts. Moving into the 1990s, such an approach informs Jean I. Marsden's 1995 study of Restoration and eighteenth-century stage adaptations of Shakespeare's plays, *The Re-Imagined Text: Shakespeare, Adaptation, and Eighteenth-Century Literary Theory*. Written at a time before the sanctity of the Author as owner of his work had become firmly established, those adaptations, together with response to them, provide 'a dialogue between the literary play and its interpreters [whereby] the original work is perpetuated at the same time as it becomes itself almost irrelevant' (Marsden 1995: 2-3). Adaptation, that is, negotiates the past/present divide by re-creating the source text—as well as its author, historical context and, as emphasised below, a series of intertexts—an insight which studies of film adaptation have gradually come to terms with since the early 1990s.

The single most important monograph on adaptation to emerge in the 1990s was Brian McFarlane's *Novel to Film: An Introduction to the Theory of Adaptation* (1996). McFarlane's book was no doubt instrumental in unsettling the primacy of fidelity as a major criterion for judging film adaptations. He rightly points out that 'Fidelity criticism depends on a notion of the text as having and rendering up to the (intelligent) reader a single, correct 'meaning' which the film-maker has either adhered to or in some sense violated or tampered with' (1996: 8), a notion that had been thoroughly problematised by poststructuralist theory. Further, McFarlane claims that the focus on fidelity has obscured an awareness of issues that are fundamental to the study of adaptation, such as the need to distinguish between 'what may be transferred from novel to film', which he labels 'transfer', as distinct from 'what will require more complex processes of adaptation', which he names 'adaptation proper' (1996: 10 and 23). However, McFarlane's narratological approach, based on this ques-tionable distinction between transfer and adaptation proper as much as on the equally problematic treatment of films as texts subsumed under narrative, an 'overarching category derived from literature' (Elliott 2003: 28), is narrowly formalistic in its marginalisation of the bearing of cultural and industrial conditions on the process of adaptation—out of the five case-studies of adaptation included in McFarlane's book, only one, devoted to Martin Scorsese's *Cape Fear* (1991), features a

'Special Focus' section focusing on the effect of cultural conditions on the process of adaptation. Indeed, although McFarlane does seek to counter the pervasiveness of the fidelity criterion on the grounds that 'The fidelity critics ... inevitably premiss their reading and evaluation of the film on the implied primacy of the novel' (1996: 197) and that 'The stress on fidelity to the original undervalues other aspects of the film's intertextuality' (1996: 21), his proposed methodology for the study of adaptation privileges questions of narrativity—and hence, ultimately, both the source text and the film as text—because they can be formalised, to the detriment of other aspects—i.e. cultural and industrial conditions, intertextuality—for which 'it is difficult to set up a regular methodology' (1996: 22). While narratology remains an important tool for analysing certain formal aspects of film adaptations, an exclusively narratological approach simply leaves out crucial contextual and intertextual factors (Stam 2005: 41) and does not acknowledge the hybrid nature of adaptation as an art that bridges the verbal/visual or word/image divide (Elliott 2003: 12).

The crossfertilisation between adaptation studies and other disciplines proved very fruitful over the 1990s. Thus, Patrick Cattrysse (1992a and 1992b), whose contributions are referred to by Lindiwe Dovey and Pedro Javier Pardo in this collection, proposed the application of the polysystems theory of translation to the study of film adaptations, in his case by focusing on American *film noir*. Translation studies, much like adaptation studies, were traditionally source-oriented and normative—emphasising the faithful reconstruction of the source text—and narrowly formalistic—focusing on the linguistic comparison of pairs of individual texts, source (original) and target (translation), to the exclusion of wider (cultural, contextual, intertextual) mechanisms that may have determined the translation process (Cattrysse 1992b: 54). Polysystems theory focuses on the way the target (translated) text actually functions in its context, and on how and why shifts of emphasis take place during the translation process (Bassnett 2002: 7-8). When applied to the study of adaptation, such an approach opens up some interesting perspectives that go far beyond the concern with fidelity. Questions to be asked about the function of a film adaptation in its context include whether the adaptation presents itself as such and why; what is the adaptation's reception by the audience and critics, and how does it vary in time and space; and, above all, the study of the adaptation's intertextual universe, since 'Even film adaptations of famous literary texts generally do not limit themselves to adapting the literary source alone' (Cattrysse 1992b: 61). Ultimately, Cattrysse places adaptation studies in the framework of studies of intertextuality, whereby 'film adaptation had better be studied as a set of discursive (or communicational, or semiotic) practices, the production of which has been determined by various previous discursive practices and by its general historical context' (1992b: 62).

In an important collection published in 2000, *Film Adaptation*, editor James Naremore equally emphasises the need for adaptation studies to definitely move away from formalistic concerns and study adaptations in the light of contextual (economic, cultural, political, commercial, industrial, educational) and intertextual factors (Naremore 2000: 10 and 12). Robert Stam, in the same anthology, borrows M. M. Bakhtin's concept of dialogism to propose a highly productive view of adaptation as intertextual dialogism, where 'Film adaptations ... are caught up in the ongoing whirl of intertextual reference and transformation, of texts generating other texts in an endless process of recycling, transformation, and transmutation, with no clear point of origin' (2000: 66), an argument Stam pursues and expands on in his most recent contributions to the field of adaptation (Stam 2005a and 2005b). Inserting adaptation in the field of intertextuality has the effect of debunking the original/copy binary pair which lay at the basis of traditional adaptation studies. A poststructuralist move if there ever was one—Robert B. Ray reminds us of Jacques Derrida's deconstruction of the hierarchical opposition of original and copy, as meaning is always-already 'disseminated', both dispersed and dissipated, so that in every text and every word other texts and words inevitably resonate (Ray 2000: 45)—intertextuality, for one thing, leads adaptation studies in the direction of problematising so-called 'originals'—as Cattrysse succinctly puts it, 'how original are originals?' (1992b: 67). This may be done by highlighting the 'original' text's own intertextuality, as John Style does in this collection when he discusses Ralph Thomas's *A Tale of Two Cities* (1958), starring Dirk Bogarde, in the light of Thomas Carlyle's *The French Revolution* (1837), the single most important intertext for Charles Dickens's novel. Alternatively, it may be done by placing the source text in the intertextual network of criticism surrounding it and indeed of its adaptations, a possibility which is particularly relevant when it comes to the classics, whose process of adaptation is never a solitary encounter between a source text and an adapter but, as Imelda Whelehan has argued, 'is already burdened by the weight of interpretations which surround [the source text]' (1999: 7). This approach is exemplified in this volume by José Ángel García Landa's discussion of the two major film adaptations of Shakespeare's *Henry V*, Laurence Olivier's (1944) and Kenneth Branagh's (1989), from the perspective of the symbolic interactionist theory of meaning.

In this connection, in order to avoid even the appearance of a tendency to reinscribe the superiority of the literary source, it is important to stress, as Marsden does, that the relationship between the critical interpretations of an 'original' and the adaptation(s) of that source text is 'one of conjunction, not cause and effect [...] [the criticism] provides a part of the context rather than a cause' (Marsden 1995: 6-7). Thus, Hodgdon remarks on the conjunction between the lull in major English-language Shakespearean film adaptations over the 1970s and 1980s and the reshaping of the field of Shakespearean criticism over that period, both coming to a head with the release of Kenneth Branagh's *Henry V* in 1989, at a time when the study of both Shakespearean texts and Shakespearean films had moved from 'text-based concerns into more politicized relationships to both cultural history and film history' (Hodgdon 2002: vi). The field of Austenian adaptations reveals another significant conjunction, with an absolute pause from 1986 (when the last of the BBC classical, heritage adaptations, *Northanger Abbey*, was released) to 1995, when two BBC miniseries, *Persuasion* and *Pride and Prejudice*, and two feature films, *Clueless*—an updated reworking of *Emma*—and Ang Lee's *Sense and Sensibility*, were released, to be followed later in the decade by two adaptations of *Emma* (both 1996), Patricia Rozema's *Mansfield Park* (1999), the Bollywood feature *I Have Found It* (2000), which adapts *Sense and Sensibility*, and Gurinder Chadha's Bollywood-style *Bride and Prejudice* (2004), all of them to a greater or lesser extent belated, even post-heritage Austen adaptations inflected by, among other intertexts, critical rereadings of Austen's novels conducted over the 1980s and early 1990s. The chapter by Mireia Aragay and Gemma López in this volume examines the dialogic interactions between Jane Austen's *Pride and Prejudice* (1813), the BBC miniseries *Pride and Prejudice* (1995), Helen Fielding's *Bridget Jones's Diary* (1996) and *Bridget Jones: The Edge of Reason* (1999), and the two Bridget Jones films in the light of romance, female spectatorship and the trope of adaptation as intertextual inf(l)ection and cultural dialogue.

Performance theory in the 1990s, in challenging the 'ministerial' or 'derivative' relation of performance to the dramatic text (Worthen 1998: 1094), also contributed to undermining the formalistic, binary paradigm within adaptation studies. As W. B. Worthen persuasively argues, far from simply reiterating the dramatic text, performance 'reconstitutes' it (1998: 1097). In a formulation that chimes in with Marsden's arguments about Restoration and eighteenth-century stage adaptations of Shakespeare, Worthen sees performance as surrogation, that is, as

> An act of memory and an act of creation, [it] recalls and transforms the past in the form of the present [...] [it] involves not the replaying of an authorizing text, a grounding origin, but the potential to construct that origin as a rhetorically powerful effect of performance [...] performance reflects the transformative nature of the cultural transmission of meanings. (1998: 1101)

A view of performance, and of adaptation as a mode of performance, which permeates Baz Luhrmann's *William Shakespeare's Romeo + Juliet* (1996), a film that self-consciously engages with the dynamics of surrogation so as to reflect on

> The ways that contemporary modes of cultural production can and do constitute their authority through the surrogation of Shakespeare and the ways that Shakespearean drama, the Shakespearean text—which can be performed only in the citational regimes of contemporary performance behavior—emerges as the ghostly 'origin' of a contemporary process of surrogation. (Worthen 1998: 1104)

Adaptation, that is, problematises originality and authorship in a way which André Bazin, in one of his interventions in the French mid-century debate around auteurism and adaptation, his 1948 essay 'Adaptation, or the Cinema as Digest', clearly perceived. After pointing out that the 'individualistic conception of the "author" and of the "work"' is relatively recent and 'started to become legally defined only at the end of the eighteenth [century]' (2000: 23), Bazin, in what sounds uncannily like a poststructuralist battle cry, claimed that 'it is possible to imagine that we are moving toward a reign of the adaptation in which the notion of the unity of the work, if not the very notion of the author himself, will be destroyed' (2000: 26). Indeed, the

literary Author/owner, enthroned, as Marsden (1995: 4-5) and Court-
ney Lehmann (2001: 3) also remind us, at the end of the eighteenth
century, was 'destroyed' or 'killed' by poststructuralist critics in the
wake of Barthes's and Michel Foucault's seminal essays, 'The Death
of the Author' (1968) and 'What is an Author' (1969) respectively.
Poststructuralism also had an impact in film studies, where it shifted
the focus of attention from auteurs to the structural, ideological,
generic, institutional and cultural make-up of films as texts—a mode
of analysis where 'The vibrancy of the text, its fertility as a site for
productive reading, outlives the illusory vibrancy of some genius
behind or before the text' (Andrew 1993: 79). However, literary critics
have recently started to question the extent to which poststructuralism
succeeded in its aim to 'kill' the author, or whether it simply mytholo-
gised the text and anthropomorphically endowed it with 'a forceful
personality of its own', as Lehmann claims (2001: 4-8). This has led
to the argument that there is something in the text that exceeds the
text, inciting 'repeated inquiries into and identification with a body of
work' (Lehmann 2001: 2), a claim that signals not the return to/of the
tyrannical Author/owner, but rather a search for a redefined concept of
authorship.

Significantly, a parallel movement has taken place in film
studies since the early 1990s. 'Breathe easily. *Épuration* has ended.
After a dozen years of clandestine whispering we are permitted to
mention, even to discuss, the auteur again'—thus Dudley Andrew
opened his 1993 article on what he called the 'unauthorized auteur'.[6]
By reference to Edward Said's critical humanism as manifested in
Beginnings, published as early as 1975, Andrew points out that 'To
"begin" a project is not to originate a work, but rather to deflect a
flow, to branch off in a direction' (1993: 82), a view that challenges
any absolute notion of originality and autonomy and yet 'retains the
power of individual effort and critique' (Andrew 1993: 83)—a
concept of the auteur, in short, that seems particularly appropriate to
the field of adaptation, and that is explored in this collection by
Margaret McCarthy in her discussion of Doris Dörrie's auteurist
identity as a paradoxical blend of individual expression and adaptation
to pre-existing conventions and constraints. Indeed, such a redefined
notion of auteurism has become a central focus in recent writing on

---

[6] Three years earlier James Naremore had referred to 'the paradoxical "survival of the
author" in contemporary film criticism' (1990: 14).

adaptation. In her 2001 study of postmodern Shakespearean adaptations, Lehmann asks, 'Is there a way ... to eliminate the oppressive ideology of the Author while retaining a viable, responsible concept of agency that offers a foothold in the midst of this theoretical quicksand?' (2001: 10). Through an analysis of, in particular, Baz Luhrmann's *William Shakespeare's Romeo + Juliet* and Kenneth Branagh Shakespearean filmmaking career, she persuasively concludes that in postmodern culture authorship 'need not be conceived in terms of negation' (2001: 160)—a reference not only to the 'Death of the Author', but also to Frederic Jameson's influential theorisation of postmodernism as characterised by the empty, depthless, uncritical, commodified repetition of styles from the past (Jameson 1991). Instead, she claims, 'we might find that there's a place for ... *authors*—not a pedestal, but perhaps a pool—wherein, amidst the whirl of historical contingency and cultural expectation that attends any act of adaptation, they have the opportunity to sink *or* swim' (2001: 160 [emphasis in original]). It would indeed seem, as Erica Sheen has claimed, that 'the study of adaptation is, at its broadest level of significance, a study of authorship in a state of historical transformation' (2000: 4), a claim borne out by Sarah Cardwell's recently published study *Andrew Davies* (2005), which discusses the career of one of today's most prolific British television screenwriters and adapters in terms of exploring 'Davies's "authorship" of his work' (Cardwell 2005: 2). In this collection, Karen Diehl reads the traces of the authorial in four recent adaptations, Raoul Ruiz's *Le temps retrouvé* (1999), John Madden's *Shakespeare in Love* (1999), Stephen Daldry's *The Hours* (2002) and Spike Jonze's *Adaptation* (2002)—a film that fascinatingly thematises adaptation and is also briefly discussed in this volume by Celestino Deleyto and Margaret McCarthy—as revealing a return to/of the author for the purposes of critique and reconceptualisation. And Thomas Leitch addresses the 'commerce of auteurism' (Corrigan 1991: 104-36) in his discussion of Alfred Hitchcock's, Stanley Kubrick's and Walt Disney's construction of themselves as auteurs as not merely a function of their personal style as inscribed in their film texts, but of a series of strategies they deployed in order to defeat potential rivals (producers, directors, writers, stars), most crucially the adoption of a trademark public persona.

It seems apt to conclude by referring once again to recent translation theory. Since the early 1990s, translation historian and theorist Lawrence Venuti has insisted that concepts such as fidelity, equivalence or transparency need to be replaced by that of the translator's visibility or palpable presence in a translation, as a reminder that no act of interpretation—translation being, after all, interpretation— can be definitive (Venuti 1995: 1-42). The 'visible' translator 're-fracts' the source text—'inflects' is the term used in Mireia Aragay's and Gemma López's and in Belén Vidal's essays in this collection— rather than aiming to 'reflect' it, as André Lefevere has claimed (quoted in Bassnett 2002: 8)—a view of translation which no doubt chimes in with current debates within adaptation studies around notions of authorship, originality, fidelity and intertextuality, and with recent views of adaptation as recreation or rewriting rather than reproduction. Pressing further in this direction, Kamilla Elliott's recent *Rethinking the Novel/Film Debate* argues persuasively for a looking glass analogy for adaptation, 'a reciprocally transformative model of adaptation, in which the film ... metamorphoses the novel and is, in turn, metamorphosed by it. Adaptation under such a model ... is mutual and reciprocal inverse transformation' (2003: 229). In such a model, the metamorphic process of adaptation is not linear but cyclical, 'memory works both ways, forwards and backwards', and 'there can be no real return to origins' since 'film adaptation changes the books films adapt' (Elliott 2003: 230-1)—an insight variously explored in this collection in the chapters by Mireia Aragay and Gemma López, José Ángel García Landa, Sara Martín and Pedro Javier Pardo. Pursued in this way, over and beyond the institutional and pedagogical uses to which adaptation is still frequently put— where it is often taught in literature departments as a way of sugaring the pill of (canonical) literature for an increasingly cinema-oriented student population, in such as way as to reinscribe the 'superiority' of literature—adaptation studies may well turn out to be central to any history of culture—any discussion, that is, of the transformation and transmission of texts and meanings in and across cultures. Such is the overall thrust of this volume, one brought particularly to the fore in Pedro Javier Pardo's discussion of Kenneth Branagh's *Mary Shelley's Frankenstein* (1994) as a postmodern appropriation of the Franken-stein myth, where the author sees adaptation as a practice of cultural intertextuality; in Celestino Deleyto's analysis of the figure of the narrator in the film adaptations of two popular novels of the 1990s,

High Fidelity (1995) and *Bridget Jones's Diary* (1996), which, rather than comparing them to their respective literary sources, reads them in the light of the generic and ideological constraints of contemporary romantic comedy; and in Belén Vidal's exploration of Sandra Gold-bacher's *The Governess* (1997) and Patricia Rozema's *Mansfield Park* (1999), only the second of which adapts a literary source, as 'literary films' that rewrite the past in the 'minor' key of romance in terms of the self-conscious gestures of feminist revision.

Bibliography

Andrew, D. (1980) 'The Well-Worn Muse: Adaptation in Film History and Theory', in S. M. Conger and J. R. Welsch (eds.) *Narrative Strategies: Original Essays in Film and Prose Fiction*. Macomb, Ill.: Western Illinois University Press, 9-17. Repr. in D. Andrew (1984) *Concepts in Film Theory*. Oxford: Oxford University Press; in L. Braudy and M. Cohen (eds.) (1999 (1974)) *Film Theory and Criticism: Introductory Readings*. Oxford: Oxford University Press, 452-60; and in J. Naremore (ed.) (2000) *Film Adaptation*. London: Athlone, 28-37.

—— (1993) 'The Unauthorized Auteur Today', in J. Collins *et al.* (eds.) *Film Theory Goes to the Movies*. New York and London: Routledge, 77-85.

Astruc, A. (1999 (1948)) 'The Birth of a New Avant Garde: *La Caméra-Stylo*', in T. Corrigan, *Film and Literature: An Introduction and a Reader*. Upper Saddle River, N. J.: Prentice-Hall, 158-62.

Barthes, R. (1988 (1968)) 'The Death of the Author', in D. Lodge (ed.) *Modern Criticism and Theory: A Reader*. London and New York: Longman, 167-72.

Bassnett, S. (2002 (1980)) *Translation Studies*. London and New York: Routledge.

Bazin, A. (1967a (1958)) 'In Defense of Mixed Cinema', in H. Grady (ed. and trans.) *What is Cinema?*, vol. 1. Berkeley and Los Angeles: University of California Press, 53-75.

—— (1967b (1951)) 'Theater and Cinema', in H. Grady (ed. and
    trans.) *What is Cinema?*, vol. 1. Berkeley and Los Angeles:
    University of California Press, 76-124.
—— (1981 (1957)) 'La politique des auteurs' [extract], in J. Caughie
    (ed.) *Theories of Authorship*. London and New York:
    Routledge, 44-6.
—— (2000 (1948)) 'Adaptation, or the Cinema as Digest', in J.
    Naremore (ed.) *Film Adaptation*. London: Athlone, 19-27.
Beja, M. (1979) *Film and Literature*. New York and London: Long-
    man.
Belsey, C. (1980) *Critical Practice*. London and New York:
    Routledge.
Benjamin, W. (1968 (1936)) *Illuminations*. New York: Harcourt,
    Brace & World.
Bluestone, G. (1957) *Novels into Film: The Metamorphosis of Fiction
    into Cinema*. Baltimore: Johns Hopkins University Press.
Boyum, J. G. (1985) *Double Exposure: Fiction into Film*. New York:
    Universe Books.
Buscombe, E. (1981 (1973)) 'Ideas of Authorship', in J. Caughie (ed.)
    Theories of Authorship. London and New York: Routledge,
    22-34.
Cardwell, S. (2002) *Adaptation Revisited: Television and the Classic
    Novel*. Manchester: Manchester University Press.
Cartmell, D. (1999) 'Text to Screen: Introduction', in D. Cartmell and
    I. Whelehan (eds.) *Adaptations: From Text to Screen, Screen
    to Text*. London and New York: Routledge, 23-8.
Cattrysse, P. (1992a) *Pour une théorie de l'adaptation filmique: Le
    film noir américain*. Frankfurt am Main: Peter Lang.
—— (1992b) 'Film (Adaptation) as Translation: Some Methodologi-
    cal Proposals', *Target: International Journal of Translation
    Studies* 4 (1), 53-70.
Cohen, K. (1979) *Film and Fiction: The Dynamics of Exchange*. New
    Haven and London: Yale University Press.
Corrigan, T. (1991) *A Cinema Without Walls: Movies and Culture
    after Vietnam*. New Brunswick: Rutgers University Press.
—— (1999) *Film and Literature: An Introduction and a Reader*.
    Upper Saddle River, N. J.: Prentice-Hall.
Eisenstein, S. (1999 (1944)) 'Dickens, Griffith, and the Film Today',
    in T. Corrigan *Film and Literature: An Introduction and a
    Reader*. Upper Saddle River, N. J.: Prentice-Hall, 135-47.

Elliott, K. (2003) *Rethinking the Novel/Film Debate.* Cambridge: Cambridge University Press.

Ellis, J. (1982) 'The Literary Adaptation: An Introduction', *Screen* 23 (1), 3-5.

Foucault, M. (1986 (1969)) 'What is an Author', in P. Rabinow (ed.) *The Foucault Reader.* Harmondsworth: Penguin, 101-20.

Hodgdon, B. (2002) 'From the Editor', *Shakespeare Quarterly* 53 (2), iii-x.

Jauss, H. R. (1982) *Toward an Aesthetic of Reception.* Trans. T. Bahti. Intr. P. de Man. Brighton: Harvester.

Jameson, F. (1991 (1984)) 'The Cultural Logic of Late Capitalism', in F. Jameson *Postmodernism, or, the Cultuiral Logic of Late Capitalism.* London and New York: Verso, 1-54.

Lehmann, C. (2001) *Shakespeare Remains: Theater to Film, Early Modern to Postmodern.* Ithaca and London: Cornell University Press.

McFarlane, B. (1996) *Novel to Film: An Introduction to the Theory of Adaptation.* Oxford: Clarendon.

Marsden, J. I. (1995) *The Re-Imagined Text: Shakespeare, Adaptation, and Eighteenth-Century Literary Theory.* Lexington: The University Press of Kentucky.

Naremore, J. (1990) 'Authorship and the Cultural Politics of Film Criticism', *Film Quarterly* 44 (1), 14-22.

—— (2000) 'Introduction: Film and the Reign of Adaptation', in J. Naremore (ed.) *Film Adaptation.* London: Athlone, 1-16.

Orr, C. (1984) 'The Discourse on Adaptation: A Review', *Wide Angle* 6 (2), 72-6.

Ray, R. B. (2000) 'The Field of "Literature and Film"', in J. Naremore (ed.) *Film Adaptation.* London: Athlone, 38-53.

Rothwell, K. S. (2004 (1999)) *A History of Shakespeare on Screen.* Cambridge: Cambridge University Press.

Sheen, E. (2000) 'Introduction', in R. Giddings and E. Sheen (eds.) *The Classic Novel: From Page to Screen.* Manchester: Manchester University Press, 1-13.

Stam, R. (2000) 'Beyond Fidelity: The Dialogics of Adaptation', in J. Naremore (ed.) *Film Adaptation.* London: Athlone, 54-76.

—— (2005a) *Literature through Film: Realism, Magic, and the Art of Adaptation.* Oxford: Blackwell.

—— (2005b) 'Introduction: The Theory and Practice of Adaptation', in R. Stam and A. Raengo (eds.) *Literature and Film: A Guide to the Theory and Practice of Film Adaptation*. Oxford: Blackwell, 1-52.

Truffaut, F. (1976 (1954)) 'A Certain Tendency of the French Cinema', in B. Nichols (ed.) *Movies and Methods*. Berkeley and London: University of California Press, 224-37.

Turner, G. (1993 (1988)) *Film as Social Practice*. London and New York: Routledge.

Wagner, G. (1975) *The Novel and the Cinema*. Rutheford, Madison and Teaneck: Farleigh Dickinson University Press.

Whelehan, I. (1999) 'Adaptations: The Contemporary Dilemmas', in D. Cartmell and I. Whelehan (eds.) *Adaptations: From Text to Screen, Screen to Text*. London and New York: Routledge, 3-19.

Woolf, V. (1966 (1926)) 'The Cinema', in L. Woolf (ed.) *Collected Essays, vol. 2*. London: Chatto and Windus.

Worthen, W. B. (1998) 'Drama, Performativity and Performance', *PMLA* 113 (5), 1093-107.

PARADOXES OF FIDELITY

Harry Potter and the Fidelity Debate

Deborah Cartmell and Imelda Whelehan

This chapter takes as example the first Harry Potter book, *Harry Potter and the Philosopher's Stone* (1997), and its film adaptation, *Harry Potter and the Sorcerer's Stone* (2001), to show how a commitment to fidelity (in response to the perceived demands of readers/viewers) compromises the processes of adaptation. The intention to include 'everything' in the film adaptation of the book is analysed to show how this ultimately throws what is left 'out' into even sharper relief. Extraordinarily, what is left out is the cinematic dimensions of the novel—most essentially, the novel's appropriation of *Star Wars,* which has been argued to be the defining text of contemporary popular cinema. The impossibility of translating the narrative and literary traditions behind the Harry Potter novels onto screen is the focus of this chapter. Concentrating mainly on the most filmic episodes in the first Harry Potter novel, this chapter looks at Chris Columbus's missed opportunities, resulting in the virtually unanimous 'not as good as the book' reviews.

From Book to Film

Film reviewers today are largely unconcerned as to whether a film adaptation is 'faithful' to its literary source, in the sense of attention to detail and inclusiveness. Rather than what is left out, more attention is cast on what is added; it is the additions, not the deletions to the source that are largely responsible for an adaptation's box office and critical success. To take Shakespeare as an example, Kenneth Branagh's carrying of a dead child across the bloody battlefield of Agincourt in *Henry V* (1989), Baz Luhrmann's use of guns for swords in *William Shakespeare's Romeo + Juliet* (1996), the flashbacks in Branagh's adaptation of the complete 1623 text of *Hamlet* (1996), and the use of Blockbuster's video store in Michael Almereyda's *Hamlet* (2000) were applauded as defining moments in these films, moments which definitely do not come from Shakespeare. It was the liberties taken rather than faithfulness that was generally admired by reviewers. This was not the case in the Harry Potter films. Criticism was dominated by 'the not as good as the book' argument and the changes that were made were greeted with outrage. Through a close scrutiny of both J. K. Rowling's first Harry Potter novel, *Harry Potter and the Philosopher's Stone* (1997), and its film adaptation, *Harry Potter and the Sorcerer's Stone* (2001), this chapter tries to account for the seemingly anachronistic reviews of Chris Columbus's first Harry Potter film.

Undoubtedly, the announcement of the film, *Harry Potter and the Sorcerer's Stone*—controversially, 'Philosopher' was changed to 'Sorcerer' in order to accommodate the American audience—boosted sales of the book. The books became, and still are, best-sellers, indeed the best-selling children's books of all time, exceeding the sales figures of Roald Dahl (who, in turn, overtook Enid Blyton as the most popular children's writer). The trailer to the film took its inspiration from Disney, with the caption 'Let the magic begin' whetting expectations that the film would be even better than the book and reminding viewers that the magic the book asks them to imagine can be realised in realistic terms by the technological possibilities of film. Film adaptations of children's literature often begin with a picture of a book opening into a 'real' world, implying that the film of the book will be an infinitely superior experience to that of its literary source. Viewers reared on Disney will instantly recall the figure of Tinkerbell, who prefaces a movie by sprinkling fairy dust from her wand, dissolving the credits on the screen. The implicit message introducing the films is that the adaptation will be magical, vastly superior to its literary source which is, after all, only words. But the film did not transform the words into magic in the case of *Harry Potter and the Sorcerer's Stone* or, indeed, *Harry Potter and the Chamber of Secrets* (2002), which, due to the disappointment generated by the first film, had lesser expectations thrust upon it. What was originally a brilliant marketing strategy backfired. Albeit a commercially successful film, in no way was *Harry Potter and the Sorcerer's Stone* seen as coming close to the experience of the book, and the reasons for this are various. Rowling's involvement in the production (especially her insistence that the cast be British) and Columbus's attempt to keep as much of the book in as possible, extending the length of the film in order to ensure coverage of the text, ostracised audiences. Philip Nel reflects that 'watching *Harry Potter and the Sorcerer's Stone* is like watching a historical reenactment', and that constructed as it is as a 'faithful' copy, it cannot possibly provoke the passionate responses that the original inspired (Nel 2002). According to Adrian Hennigan, Columbus treated 'JK Rowling's debut novel with a reverence that wasn't even accorded to the Bible' but in spite of this attention to detail, fans of the book were bound to see it as merely a pale copy of the original (Hennigan 2001). The Internet Movie Database User's Page is dominated by this view. One fan speaks for many when he says:

> This movie was incredibly good in its own sense, but being a complete nerd about these books, I have to say that the movie is woefully inadequate. Daniel Radcliffe seems too wimpy for Harry Potter. He should be a little awkward but in this movie he's a complete pansy. All in all, it was a pretty good book to movie transition but it was not anywhere near as good as *The Fellowship of the Ring*.

In short, it was a film that tried too hard to *be* the book and one which was destined to suffer invidious comparisons with a much more successful book-to-film adaptation in the form of *The Fellowship of the Ring* (2001). If we look closely at the Harry Potter books and try to account for their extraordinary commercial success, it appears that they have been marketed and constructed as if *they* were the films. Inevitably, the books triumph and their adaptations suffer from this confusion of identity.

From Film to Book

The spin-offs, which John-the-Baptist-like come out prior to the film, were in the marketplace about six months before the release of *Harry Potter and the Sorcerer's Stone*, and they ranged from bookends, cuddly Norberts and Hedwigs, to copies of Bertie Bott's Every Flavour Beans. Although successful in marketing and generating income for the film, they also did the same for the book. In fact, it is easy to compare the marketing of the fourth instalment in the Harry Potter series, *Harry Potter and the Goblet of Fire*, released on 8 July 2000, to that of a film. The release of the fourth book was unashamedly promoted according to all the rules of Hollywood blockbusters, especially those which herald a series of films, like *Jaws*, *Star Wars*, or *The Lord of the Rings*.[1] The release-day was announced months before and was celebrated with queues of customers waiting through the night, hundreds of adults and children attending bookshop events in order to collect their pre-ordered volume. The point that the marketing of the book followed closely the practices of Hollywood is an obvious one; what is not so obvious is that, when examined in detail, the construction of the Harry Potter books themselves, even the very first one in the series, is revealed to adhere closely to the conventions of Hollywood. Perhaps this is the reason why the film adaptations disappointed so many viewers—that is, the films do not fulfil the cinematic potential of the books, on a number of levels. The Hollywood-factor of the books is perhaps the major objection to them raised by the 'serious' critics. Anthony Holden, for example, rages: 'Harry Potter is an activity marginally less testing than watching *Neighbours*. And that, at least is vaguely about real life. These are one-dimensional children's books, Disney cartoons written in words, no more' (Holden 2000).[2] Holden's assumption that if it is like Disney, then it must be of no cultural value, is left uninterrogated, and the underlying message here is that the novels are too much like films—popular films at that— to be of any literary merit. Like many, he expresses distaste at the way in which an already-successful series is marketed ever-more fiercely with the appearance of each new volume in ways designed to establish status of this unique phenomenon—where each volume practically becomes a popular classic on the day of its publication. The first Harry Potter novel and film were further downtrodden due to the release of *The Fellowship of the Ring* soon after that of *Harry Potter and the Sorcerer's Stone*. The later film eclipsed *Harry Potter and the*

---

[1] The first film in each series being, respectively, *Jaws* (1975), *Star Wars* (1977) and *The Fellowship of the Ring* (2001).
[2] On the whole, the books have been dismissed by a significant number of academic critics as derivative. Jack Zipes, for example, articulates the gap between popular taste and academic scholarship in the concluding chapter of *Sticks and Stones: The Troublesome Success of Children's Literature from Slovenly Peter to Harry Potter*: 'I am not certain whether one can talk about a split between a minority of professional critics, who have misgivings about the quality of the Harry Potter books and the great majority of readers, old and young, who are mesmerized by the young magician's adventures. But I am certain that the phenomenal aspect of the reception of the Harry Potter books has blurred the focus for anyone who wants to take literature for young people seriously and who may be concerned about standards and taste that adults create for youth culture in the West' (2001: 171).

Sorcerer's Stone, inspiring observations such as Brian M. Carney's editorial in the *Wall Street Journal* of 30 November 2001, entitled 'The Battle of the Books: No Contest. Tolkien Runs Rings around Potter' (quoted in Welsh 2002: 78). *The Lord of the Rings* was a better film because it adapted the novel to Hollywood conventions while, due to its huge band of young and loyal readers, Columbus felt the need to preserve Rowling's book as much as possible—despite the clear impossibility of this aim. It goes without saying that the Harry Potter series has revolutionised children's publishing and profoundly affected children's reading habits, so that these books are being consumed as videos commonly are—viewed over and over again and often with key sections committed to memory. With this in mind, the film had to cater to an audience who were against any free interpretation of the book, and therefore it had to preserve the much-loved episodes in the book, just as popular film novelisations aim to recapture the 'essence' of the film rather than produce a text with autonomous literary merit.

While the Harry Potter novels are full of references to books and reading, they also scrupulously adhere to the rules of classical Hollywood. Lists vary, but these rules generally consist of:

1. narrative prioritised over form—definite beginning, middle and end;
2. ending resolved—little moral or narrative ambiguity;
3. narratives are character-driven;
4. narratives organised through genre—science fiction, horror, gangster, Western, fantasy, epic (it is possible to combine genres in 'generic hybrids');
5. space and time are secure—film does not draw attention to itself;
6. camera is motivated by the needs of the character;
7. increasingly, films are directed to a global audience—plots need to be simple, predictable and dialogue not too complex;
8. expectation of action sequences—at least one big action sequence;
9. aimed at 16-24 year olds;
10. increasingly self-reflexive, ironic, full of quotations to other films.[3]

---

[3] This list is gathered from I. Q. Hunter (lecture at De Montfort University, February 2003) and Pam Cook and Mieke Bernick (1999: 39-42).

Harry Potter and the Philosopher's Stone is, for better or worse, close to Anthony Holden's condemnation of it as 'Disney cartoons written in words' insofar as it precisely conforms to our cinematic expectations, especially the blockbuster in its division into parts. Like a classical Hollywood film, the narrative is character-driven, it has little moral ambiguity, a definite beginning, middle and end, and it is organised around the genre of fantasy/detective. The narrative is visually drawn, with an emphasis on spectatorship throughout—for instance, Harry's passage to Platform 9 ¾ is quintessentially cinematic. This is a moment, like so many in the Harry Potter novels, that recalls the experience of watching a film. Like the movement from Kansas to Oz, one world instantaneously replaces another—Harry closes his eyes and opens them and we experience something like a dissolve in a film:

> ... leaning forward on his trolley he broke into a heavy run – the barrier was coming nearer and nearer – he wouldn't be able to stop – the trolley was out of control – he was a foot away – he closed his eyes ready for the crash –
> It didn't come ... he kept on running ... he opened his eyes.
> A scarlet steam engine was waiting next to a platform packed with people. A sign over head said *Hogwarts Express, 11 o'clock*. Harry looked behind him and saw a wrought iron archway where the ticket box had been, with the words *Platform Nine and Three Quarters* on it. He had done it. (Rowling 1997: 70-1)

The Sorting Hat sequence borrows from the technique of flash cutting. Harry sees students 'cramming to get a good look at him. Next second he was looking at the black inside of hat' (Rowling 1997: 91). After a minute or two, the hat is off, vision is blurred as Harry slowly comes to his senses where he finally 'could see the High Table properly now' (Rowling 1997: 90), and the sequence culminates in a long shot. Rowling repeatedly returns to the dissolve—a fade out becoming a fade in (famously utilised in Dorothy's departure from Oz and return to Kansas)—most prominently at the climactic moments of the novel. Harry's final moments of consciousness, during death-defying heroics, are followed by an awakening into another world, introduced through blurred focus and a close-up shot of Dumbledore's glasses:

> He felt Quirrell's arm wrenched from his grasp, knew all was lost, and fell into blackness, down ... down ... down ...

> Something gold was glinting just above him. The Snitch! He tried to catch
> it, but his arms were too heavy.
> He blinked. It wasn't the Snitch at all. It was a pair of glasses. How strange.
> 'Good afternoon, Harry,' said Dumbledore. (Rowling 1997: 214)

Action sequences, such as the roller-coaster-like ride through Gringotts, the defeat of the troll or the journey through the trapdoor,
punctuate the narrative in precisely the way they would be expected to
in a film. Throughout the book there is an emphasis on the eyes—
note, for example, the shifting points of view depending on who
controls the gaze in the Mirror of Erised scenes—and Rowling
constantly calls attention to Harry's glasses, which function like the
lens of a camera. Typical of Hollywood action movies, at the climactic moment of the book, the villain cannot resist explaining to his
victim how his criminality evolved, enabling the hero to be rescued
(curiously Quirrell's explanation is abbreviated in the film):

> It was Quirrell.
> '*You!*' gasped Harry.
> 'Me,' he said calmly. 'I wondered whether I'd be meeting you here, Potter.'
> 'But I thought – Snape –' (Rowling 1997: 209)

Five pages of explanation follow, providing us with time for the
rescue of Harry and Hollywood-style narrative closure.

At each level, the Harry Potter novels accord with classical
Hollywood norms that remained surprisingly fixed until the huge box
office successes of *Jaws* (1975) and *Star Wars* (1977), films that
revolutionised Hollywood (Krämer 2000). These new blockbusters
produced a dazzling array of spin-offs, including board games,
computer games, and a vast number of toys (King 1999: 103). Included in these spin-offs are movie tie-ins and novelisations, and due
to their explicit consumerism, they are largely dismissed by literary
critics as cheap and trivial, only really serving to redirect our attention
to the superiority of the film. It has been suggested that a common
feature of postmodern Hollywood cinema is its intertextuality, which
often takes the form of referencing other films, perhaps most frequently *Star Wars,* in homage to that film's enormous impact on the
film industry. In fact, Richard Keller Simon has gone so far to suggest
that *Star Wars* has replaced the Bible as the urtext of our civilisation

(1999: 30), and it undoubtedly provides a template for postmodern cinema.

In keeping with the current penchant for intertextuality in postmodern Hollywood, *Harry Potter and the Philosopher's Stone* combines influences of and echoes to numerous other children's texts—among them *Cinderella, Lord of the Rings, Alice in Wonderland*, the Narnia novels, the Famous Five series, *Just William*, the *Earthsea* sequence, *The Worst Witch, Matilda* and *The BFG*. Additionally, it recalls the experiences of films, such as *Superman* (with Harry as Clark Kent), and theme park rides—the ride through Gringotts draws on our experience of roller coasters, for example. The pleasure of reading the book depends upon the recollection of numerous experiences, ranging from the sublime to the ridiculous. In fact, the story of Harry Potter is based as much on *Star Wars* as it is on any other text. As the first film trilogy centres largely round Luke's enigmatic relationship to Darth Vader, so too Harry is incrementally associated with Voldemort, the 'dark father' of Rowling's series. Like Luke, Harry finds that he belongs to another world and that he possesses a force that makes him unique. Both texts feature two males and a female taking it upon themselves to fight against those who have gone over to the dark side. Voldemort betrays his teacher, Dumbledore, as Darth Vader did his master, Ben Obi-Wan Kenobi. Both Luke and Harry receive wands—Luke's originally belonged to his father, Darth Vader, whereas Harry's has sinister similarities to that belonging to Voldemort. Indeed, in both *Star Wars* and *Harry Potter*, the function of duelling (especially in matches between the dark father and the saviour/son) becomes increasingly important to the narrative—and whatever the superhuman properties of their weapons, the superior moral qualities of the hero are always emphasised in acts requiring real physical endurance and mental fortitude. It goes without saying that these duels take on phallic undertones as wands or light sabres are brandished: after all, these conflicts reinforce patriarchal order—whether good or bad—and this seemingly unquestioned acceptance of male hegemony has caused many to see Rowling's texts as essentially conservative.

Action sequences in *Star Wars* and *Harry Potter and the Philosopher's Stone* bear striking similarities—the passage through the trapdoor into the garbage compressor in *Star Wars* (where unexplained foul creatures threaten below the surface) is recalled in the journey through the trapdoor to the Devil's Snare in Rowling's book. In both a seemingly soft landing is transformed into a nightmare. Rowling's description of this instant reversal of fortune in undeniably cinematic:

> 'We must be miles under the school,' [Hermione] said.
> 'Lucky this plant thing's here, really,' said Ron.
> '*Lucky!*' shrieked Hermione. 'Look at you both!'
> She leapt up and struggled towards a damp wall. She had to struggle because the moment she had landed, the plant had started to twist snakelike tendrils around her ankles. As for Harry and Ron, their legs had already been bound tightly in long creepers without their noticing.
> Hermione had managed to free herself before the plant got a firm grip on her. Now she watched in horror as the two boys fought to pull the plant off them, but the more they strained against it, the tighter and faster the plant wound around them. (Rowling 1997: 201)

Quotations to *Star Wars* can be found in the entrance of Hagrid into the hut in the middle of nowhere, recalling the first appearance of the morally ambiguous Darth Vader:

> *SMASH!*
> The door was hit with such force that it swung clean off its hinges and with a deafening crash landed flat on the floor.
> A giant of a man was standing in the doorway. His face was almost completely hidden ... (Rowling 1997: 39)

And Harry's first visit to the Leaky Caldron (Rowling 1997: 54) prompts associations with the tavern in *Star Wars* where Ben Obi-Wan Kenobi and Luke Skywalker eventually find Han Solo.[4]

Fidelity and Nostalgia

The Harry Potter books are arguably at their best as popular cultural artefacts when they re-read the defining popular texts of a previous generation—the parents of the children who have contributed to the Harry Potter phenomenon—and produce something which appears new and groundbreaking to the next generation. There is no doubt that the generation of children growing up in the late 1990s will be as much defined by memories of the Harry Potter novel sequence

---

[4] Many thanks to Hester Bradley for drawing our attention to many of these parallels.

and all the debates it yielded about literacy and the return of reading, as they will by the key film texts of the period such as *Lord of the Rings*. The films based on the Harry Potter novels can only offer us a pale imitation of the fiction and merely serve as some of the more pleasurable merchandising products that such a phenomenon demands, not least because the books had seemingly appropriated every marketing ploy available before a single film was released. This is as much to do with the films' perceived subservience to the novels and their author—and how many directors could boast the notoriety or mystique of J. K. Rowling?—as with the inevitable effects of filming fantasy literature. As Suman Gupta observes in *Re-reading Harry Potter*, 'The precondition of the making and reception of the *Harry Potter* films was their ability to provide a convincing *illusion of reality* of the Magic World, and they were to be tested and judged accordingly' (2003: 143). To realise the magical effects of the books is to some extent to render them real and to necessarily conflate the worlds of wizards and muggles—particularly since the muggle world is a reflection on present-day middle Britain. Sophisticated film viewers would expect to be convinced by the special effects used to convey what are magical effects in the novels, and therefore to a large extent the film can only live up to their minimal expectations in this respect. Given that the Harry Potter books' existence as a phenomenon to be marvelled at, picked over, critiqued, but ultimately preserved underlines the importance of fidelity at the expense of the interpretive skills of the director, *Harry Potter and the Sorcerer's Stone* can only fail to dazzle or amaze, and must know its subordination to the written word. The Harry Potter audience is not ready for a radical critique of the novels, and their historical context is still too fresh for widescale cultural criticism, so that film adaptation as critical review is not an option—indeed, given that the characters and stories are trademarked in both media, it may never be.

It seems odd to enumerate the ways in which the Harry Potter sequence has prompted anxious debates about the possible return to primacy of the written word, but as Andrew Blake notes, Harry Potter is a '*retrolutionary,* a symbolic figure of the past-in-future England which is in desperate need of such symbols' (2002: 16). The Harry Potter novels nostalgically celebrate a reimagination of the past in the present by creating a fantasy world where quills and parchment are the key tools for getting on in the wizarding education system, but as fantasy these representations reside easily with the postmodern context in which readers absorb these texts. In the film versions, such artefacts live again in a conditional present, because the present tense is the key film tense, and their revival is portrayed without comment or awareness of the disharmony of such features. The books can provide all kinds of intertextual nostalgia for a readership whose access to the past may be mainly through fictional texts such as Blyton, Dahl or Barrie, but the films bring this to the present and produce something anachronistic and clumsy. The boarding school environment in the novels adds symbolic dimensions to Harry's lack of family support or emotional location; in the films, Hogwarts is an unpleasant reminder of the social entrapment of this generation of children, never likely to know the pleasures of playing in the local park without parental supervision, but having to accept that the 'forbidden forest' is forbidden for quite pragmatic reasons. At another level, the Hogwarts environment is infinitely seductive and in the film the boarding-school setting comes across as quintessentially English—the boarding-school story having been a staple of previous generations of children's fiction and made familiar to thousands of children never likely to experience such an education or its incumbent privileges through the works of Blyton and others. The imagery of the boarding school and the fantasy of being the orphaned child with as yet undiscovered magical powers speak to some of the most profound fantasies of children, who feel free to imagine a space without parental control, and with the superhuman strengths to repel the efforts of those who wish children harm. In the film version, magic needs to be portrayed with the same commitment to realism as the dull predictability of Privet Drive, and this has some perverse effects whereby Hogwarts seems the duller and Privet Drive occasionally bizarre. This conflation of the real and the fantastical must of necessity deny the possibility of retreat from the perceived dangers of being a child in the twenty-first century and ensure that children confront their demons as inevitably as they must recognise in the cinematic portrayal of Hogwarts the fact of their own control and surveillance in our contemporary world.

To return to the question of fidelity and the consensus view that *Harry Potter and the Sorcerer's Stone*, the film, is no match for *Harry Potter and the Philosopher's Stone*, the book, it could be argued that the film fails because it tries to be the book, or as close a

copy as a film can be of a book, without realising what the consequences of such fidelity are. Filmic conventions, a prominent feature
of the book, including postmodern intertextuality and cinematic
devices, are strangely ignored in the film. While the film fails to copy
the book, the book succeeds in copying a film and, in many ways, the
books usurped the role of the film even before the film was released.
The film disappointed viewers as it was a copy of the original which,
as a copy, could not live up to the experience of the book, a book
which is, arguably, more cinematic than its filmic adaptation and more
comfortable with its status as fantastic narrative, allowing numerous
symbolic outlets for contemporary childhood anxieties. Whether or
not *Harry Potter and the Philosopher's Stone*, the book, has any merit
as a 'film', or whether it merely panders to a tired old Hollywood
formula in order to achieve popular and commercial success, is
another question to be asked. What is clear in the context of the
fidelity debate is that any film which prioritises transposition over
interpretation is unlikely to recognise the pitfalls of aiming to bring
the novel 'to life' and will, moreover, spectacularly fail by freezing all
the action and events in an impossible simulacrum of the past made
present.

Bibliography

Blake, A. (2002) *The Irresistible Rise of Harry Potter*. London: Verso.
Cook, P. and M. Bernick (eds.) (1999 (1985)) *The Cinema Book*.
        London: British Film Institute.
Gupta, S. (2003) *Re-reading Harry Potter*. Basingstoke and London:
        Palgrave Macmillan.
Hennigan, A. (2001) '*Harry Potter and the Philosopher's Stone*'. On-
        line. Available HTTP: http://www.bbc.co.uk/films/2001/11/
        06/harry_potter_philosophers_stone_2001_review.shtml   (20
        January 2004).
Holden, A. (2000) 'Why Harry Potter doesn't cast a spell over me',
        The Observer (25 June). On-line. Available HTTP:
        http://observer.guardian.co.uk/review/story/0,6903,335923,00.
        html (20 January 2004)

Internet Movie Database User's Page. On-line. Available HTTP: http://www.imdb.com/title/tt0241527/usercomments (20 January 2004).

Keller Simon, R. (1999) *Trash Culture: Popular Culture and the Great Tradition*. Berkeley: University of California Press.

King, N. (1999 (1985)) 'New Hollywood', in P. Cook and M. Bernick (eds.) *The Cinema Book*. London: British Film Institute, 98-105.

Krämer, P. (2000) 'Post-Classical Hollywood', in J. Hollows *et al.* (eds.) *The Film Studies Reader*. London: Arnold, 174-80.

Nel, P. (2002) 'Bewitched, Bothered, and Bored: Harry Potter, the Movie'. On-line. Available HTTP: http://www.readingonline. org/newliteracies/jaal/10-02column/index.html (20 January 2004).

Rowling, J. K. (1997) *Harry Potter and the Philosopher's Stone*. London: Bloomsbury.

Zipes, J. (2001) *Sticks and Stones: The Troublesome Success of Children's Literature from Slovenly Peter to Harry Potter*. London and New York: Routledge.

Welsh, J. (2002) 'Editorial: Competing Wizards', *Literature/Film Quarterly*, 30 (2), 78-9.

Filmography

Columbus, C. dir. (2001) *Harry Potter and the Sorcerer's Stone*. Warner Bros.

—— dir. (2002) *Harry Potter and The Chamber of Secrets*. Warner Bros.

What does Heathcliff Look Like?
Performance in Peter Kosminsky's Version
of Emily Brontë's *Wuthering Heights*

Sara Martín

In the study of film adaptation, plot is often privileged over character. Studying character reveals that the adaptation of novels is dramatisation involving, as regards this particular factor, the transformation of a non-performative aspect of the source text into dramatic roles performed by particular actors. An adaptation can be said to succeed as far as character is concerned when the actor's performance usurps the reader's own mental performance and visualisation of character. Nonetheless, as Peter Kosminsky's adaptation of *Wuthering Heights* (1992)—and especially Ralph Fiennes's performance as Heathcliff in it—suggests, this process is not dependent on a single factor, be it the artistic quality of the adaptation, its narrative fidelity to the source or its adequacy for a particular historical period. Performance may even succeed in otherwise failed adaptations, as (arguably) happens in the case Kosminsky's film, which suggests that the reader's/viewer's particular response to adaptation deserves further attention.

Character in Adaptation: The Case of *Wuthering Heights*

Characters are substantially different in novels and films. As Robert Stam reminds us, 'although novels have only character, film adaptations have both character (actantial function) and performer, allowing for possibilities of interplay and contradiction denied a purely verbal medium' (2000: 60). This elementary fact, I would argue, holds one of the major keys to understanding what the process of adaptation is *really* about. The obsession for considering the analogies and differences between novels and films as *narrative texts* has obscured the basic fact that whenever a novel is adapted for the screen it is transformed into a *dramatic text*—the screen*play*—before it becomes a film proper, that is, drama performed before a camera.

Film adaptation of novels, in short, is always dramatisation, and character plays a major role in this process.

Film and theatre are not, of course, the same but rather, as Martin Esslin has insightfully claimed, branches of a common drama tree together with fiction for television and radio (1991: 9). The reliance on performance is, precisely, one of the main features shared by the different drama media, which can all be defined as text-based narrative performed by actors live in front of an audience, or recorded by a camera or microphone. The fetishism of the camera in film studies, however, has obstructed the realisation that cinema is closer to the stage than to the novel. The unique visual language of cinema was allegedly born when D. W. Griffith, inspired by the complex narrative editing of Charles Dickens's novels, discovered how to use the camera in order to break away from the static point of view spectators must assume in a theatre. The eye/I of the novelist became the inspiration for the eye/I of the film director. However, it must be noted, firstly, that novels contain plenty of dramatic action (Dickens himself always kept close ties with the Victorian stage); secondly, that directing for film and for the stage are not dissimilar activities (consider Sam Mendes, formerly prestige stage director, now famed film director); thirdly, that cinema depends on actors' performances as much as theatre; and, finally, that the novel and all drama media depend on both character and narrative.

The fidelity issue is invoked in discussions of adaptations mainly as regards narrative, and only secondarily as regards aspects such as characterisation. Robert Stam reluctantly grants that we might observe fidelity to character descriptions, but wonders rather naively, 'what if the actor who happens to fit the description ... also happens to be a mediocre actor?' (2000: 57). In order to avoid this pitfall, casting in screen adaptations usually relies on the actor's capacity to capture the personality of the original character rather than on finding a perfect physical match for it. In practice, screen roles, whether original or adapted, operate like stage roles, for which physical appearance is not fixed except along rough lines of age and gender. Indeed, an habitual side-effect of adaptations is that a skilled actor can erase from the mind of the novel's readers the original image sug-gested by the writer and replace it with his/her own in the film as, to all appearances, verbal descriptions pale before the impact a film image may have. This effect, quite annoying for readers who prefer keeping their visualisation of a particular novel unaffected by its screen adaptation, is, however, the mark of the actor's success. Intriguingly, this replacement can be caused by an otherwise unsatisfactory adaptation in the same way that we can appreciate an actor's performance in an otherwise mediocre stage production.

A case in point to study this phenomenon is the film version by Peter Kosminsky of Emily Brontë's *Wuthering Heights* (1992), so far the most recent in the series started by William Wyler (1939), also including Luis Buñuel's Mexican film *Abismos de pasión* (1954) and Robert Fuest's version (1971). The diverse adaptations offer readers and spectators the rare chance of choosing their favourite screen Heathcliff. Indirectly, they raise two important issues. Firstly, the character that Laurence Olivier, Jorge Mistral, Timothy Dalton and Ralph Fiennes play in the film versions by, respectively, Wyler, Buñuel, Fuest and Kosminsky, is *not* Emily Brontë's Heathcliff but a singular dramatic role created specifically for each screenplay and based more or less remotely on Brontë's villain, depending in the first instance on the avowed narrative fidelity of the film to the novel. Secondly, as Lin Haire-Sargent claims, each adaptation is conditioned by its degree of fidelity to Brontë as much as by how 'we can catch the shade of the male zeitgeist behind each screen Heathcliff' (1999: 190)—fated but noble for a pre-Second World War context in Wyler, primitive for post-war 1950s in Buñuel, wild and erotic in Fuest's 1970s film, and sadistic for the 1990s in Kosminsky's version. These two complementary approaches—narratological and cultural—still leave, however, an enormous theoretical gap, derived from the absence of a conceptual framework that would make it possible to theorise the way readers visualise as they read. In the end, personal factors (i.e. taste) also contribute to determining whether and why a particular performance usurps each reader's own view of Heathcliff.

Performance in Film Adaptation: Usurping the Reader's Vision

The criteria commonly used to judge the performance of a particular screen character adapted from a novel privilege the contrast between source and film above the adequacy of the actor's work to the screenplay. This amounts to judging an actor's performance of Romeo not by reference to Shakespeare's play, but to the sources from which he borrowed. Thus, even if we agree with U. C. Knoepflmacher that

Laurence Olivier's performance as Heathcliff in Wyler's film is 'mesmeric' and, so, crucial in the film's doing 'more to reinstate Emily Brontë's masterpiece than any sober revaluation by literary critics' in the twentieth century (1994: vii), this need not mean that Olivier's Heathcliff is faithful to the character in *Wuthering Heights*: rather, this is a performance that succeeds within the context of Wyler's romantic film, regardless of its literary source, from which it differs substantially. Unlike plays, however, which are the main focus of stage productions, screenplays are just one of the ingredients contributing to the film and hardly texts audiences read independently. Logically, audiences who know the original literary source judge performance by contrasting it with character in the book, forgetting that, unlike dramatists, novelists do not design character for performance. Audiences familiar with Brontë's novel consider, in short, the performances by Olivier, Mistral, Dalton and Fiennes in relation to whether they fit the way they mentally 'perform' Heathcliff as readers. If, however, the novel is read or re-read after seeing the film, the reader's visual representation of Heathcliff will be inevitably coloured to a greater or lesser degree—or even dominated—by the actor spectators feel best succeeds in the role.

Despite the subordination of drama to narrative in novels, performance *is* also part of reading. Students reading *Wuthering Heights* are often puzzled by *dramatic* aspects of characterisation: how loud is Heathcliff's voice when he damns Cathy in the famous death-bed scene? What does his face look like when he peers into the void to see Cathy's ghost in the last stages of the book? Students are confused but productively enticed by the discovery that depending on how Heathcliff's lines of dialogue and body language are read, a completely different character emerges, which is why they easily understand that each screen Heathcliff is an interpretation of the protean literary Heathcliff. Deconstruction has successfully argued that texts are actually conspicuous by their almost infinite potential for different readings that never exhaust them, as J. Hillis Miller proved in his analysis of precisely Emily Brontë's *Wuthering Heights* (1982). In this sense, we might say that film adaptations try to deny the multiplicity sanctioned by literary theory. Each new adaptation, I would argue, intends to erase the public memory of its predecessors rather than open a dialogue with them. While the reader mostly respects variety in interpretation, the adapter tries to validate a particular interpretation aided by the impact of the audio/visual medium s/he uses. The reader may reject an adapter's particular version but can hardly answer back by producing a new film in the way that, for instance, scholars write new papers to debate their readings of *Wuthering Heights*. In this respect, performance is film's main weapon in its capacity to seduce the spectator. What the many versions of *Wuthering Heights* suggest, however, is that, so far, readers prefer their own Heathcliff(s).

In the struggle between the verbal and the visual that arguably takes place in the reader's mind after seeing an adaptation of a novel previously read, film gains the upper hand when the reader can no longer return to his/her initial visualisation of the novel. It is, however, very hard to determine what exactly prompts this loss. An informal experiment I conducted along two academic years (2000-2002), consisting in exposing two different classes reading *Wuthering Heights* to the four film versions, produced mixed results. One class was entranced by Ralph Fiennes's Heathcliff—'it's *him*!', surprised students exclaimed—while the other dismissed all four Heathcliffs. Most students declared that fidelity to Brontë's physical description of Heathcliff was not relevant when judging performance, though they paid close attention to the actors' looks.[1] Students who did show a particular preference suddenly found themselves visualising Heathcliff as their chosen actor even in the scenes of the novel which do not appear in the corresponding film regardless of whether they had actually liked the adaptation. This coincided with my own experience as I afterwards told them, and would explain on a personal note why even though I rank Luis Buñuel's version quite above the others and Kosminsky's quite below, Ralph Fiennes's performance and not Jorge Mistral's has colonised my reading of Brontë's novel. The experiment also suggests that the factors that contribute to this usurpation effect are *dramatic* and not narrative: viewers open up to a particular actor's performance of a character they have met in a novel because the actor reflects the way they mentally 'perform' the character as they read the novel.

---

[1] This is hardly surprising considering that 90 per cent of the students in both classes were female. This is a point to bear in mind in relation to the Isabella complex, a concept I introduce below.

Misreading Heathcliff: The Isabella Complex and the Villain's Good Looks

Preceding more famed 1990s adaptations such as Francis Ford Coppola's *Bram Stoker's Dracula* (1992) and Branagh's *Mary Shelley's Frankenstein* (1994), Kosminsky's *Wuthering Heights*—which even features an Emily Brontë played by Sinead O'Connor, in an awkward attempt to legitimate the adaptation as 'faithful'—tries to replace former versions by encompassing, unlike them, the whole book and not just a segment.[2] Kosminsky and scriptwriter Anne Devlin imply that none of the other adaptations had the courage to reflect in full Heathcliff's villainy as Brontë displayed it in the second half of the novel. This is surely a valuable principle on which to base their adaptation, not because of its fidelity, but because of the attempt to break away from the partial, sentimental readings of the novel of the previous sixty years. Sadly, Kosminsky's film is *only* this, failing to simply *tell* the story with an adequate rhythm and enough clarity.

This failure, though, has the advantage of leaving spectators with nothing but performance to enjoy, which in turn forces them to reconsider characterisation, specifically Heathcliff's. Kosminsky's Heathcliff is the victimised lover of the other versions, but also a sadistic abuser, as he appears to be in the novel's second half. Paradoxically, the film's dutiful fidelity takes us back to 1848, when the novel was published, by recreating the strong dislike that original readers felt for the brutal Heathcliff, but it also belongs firmly in the 1990s, when the figure of the villain was given new depths quite beyond the habitual stereotypes—witness Hannibal Lecter. This new focus on the villain, together with the generalised interest in abuse within families, gave cinema for the first time in decades the critical

---

[2] Sinead O'Connor's appearance as Emily Brontë is 'awkward' for diverse reasons. Her distinct personality and the fact that she is not an actor but a singer colour her Emily Brontë so strongly that it is hard to give the role any credibility. O'Connor's singular beauty, besides, glamorises Brontë in a way that clashes badly with the habitual domestic portrait of the author of *Wuthering Heights*. Finally, the narrative framework created in the film by introducing Brontë is a poor substitute for the complex narrative frame of the novel and, what is more, contradicts the author's decision to erase herself from the text and use Nelly Dean and Mr Lockwood as (possibly unreliable) narrators. O'Connor's presence 'authorises' the film in a way the novel specifically avoids, offering as the truth what in the novel is possibly just a version of the events.

and cultural tools necessary to read Brontë's Heathcliff with absolute fidelity—perhaps clear-headedness is a better word— after a long spell of sentimentalised readings. This makes Kosminsky's Heathcliff both a product of the male zeitgeist of the time—the 1990s were the decade in which male abusers of all kinds were publicly exposed—and a singularly faithful rendition of Brontë's anti-hero. This might seem to endorse rather than question the fidelity criterion, at least in some particular cases.

Up to Kosminsky's version, adaptations of *Wuthering Heights* operated under what I would call, after Heathcliff's wife, the Isabella complex. By this I mean the delusion that Heathcliff is a heroic, positive character. As Lennard J. Davis explains, characters in novels must be not only solid 'simulacra' of real human beings, but also attractive illusions by virtue of their personality, physical appearance or both:

> In making a character attractive, the author can draw the reader towards that set of signs much as advertisers can draw consumers towards a product by associating it with a physically attractive model. In effect, it is not so much that we identify with a character, but that we desire that character in some non-specific but erotic way. In this sense, part of novel reading is the process of falling in love with characters or making friends with signs. (1987: 127)

This, I believe, is what generally happens to *female* readers when they meet Heathcliff.

In romantic fiction as articulated in novels, plays or films, lovers are conventionally beautiful, and *Wuthering Heights* is no exception in this respect. In the frustrated romance between the wilful, pretty Catherine Earnshaw and her foster brother, Heathcliff, physical attraction plays a minor role, if any at all, for theirs seems to be a spiritual affair only consummated after death. Yet Heathcliff's physical appearance is crucial in understanding both his enduring appeal for the female reader in the sense Davis comments on, as well as his troubled relationship with Cathy. His handsomeness is problematised by the fact that his colouring is quite different from that of those around him, but this physical otherness is what makes him attractive and mysterious. His dark skin, eyes and hair mark him as an outsider— perhaps a gypsy—but they are no obstacle for the child Cathy nor for her father, Mr Earnshaw, who picks up the starving boy from the streets of Liverpool to turn him into a beloved adoptive son. The naive childhood romance between her and Heathcliff, however, comes to a halt when, after her stay with their aristocratic neighbours the Lintons, subsequent to being bitten by their dog, Cathy returns to Wuthering Heights transformed from a rambling tomboy into a young lady, whereas Heathcliff remains the dirty, unkempt, surly servant that his jealous step-brother Hindley has turned him into after their father's death. Mocked by Cathy for his unbecoming appearance and bitterly jealous of Edgar Linton, Heathcliff only finds comfort in Wuthering Height's housekeeper, Nelly, also Brontë's main narrator:

> "A good heart will help you to a bonny face, my lad", I continued, "if you were a regular black; and a bad one will turn the bonniest into something worse than ugly. And now that we've done washing, and combing, and sulking—tell me whether you don't think yourself rather handsome? I'll tell you, I do. You're fit for a prince in disguise. Who knows but your father was Emperor of China, and your mother an Indian queen, each of them able to buy up, with one week's income, Wuthering Heights and Thrushcross Grange together? And you were kidnapped by wicked sailors and brought to England. Were I in your place, I would frame high notions of my birth; and the thoughts of what I was should give me courage and dignity to support the oppressions of a little farmer!" (E. Brontë 2000: 56)

Heathcliff's handsomeness is stressed again, much to Cathy's chagrin, after his return from a mysterious absence of three years provoked by her engagement to Edgar. When Heathcliff finds out that Cathy is already married, he retaliates by charming naive Isabella Linton, Edgar's sister, into eloping with him. Heathcliff's appalling treatment of the besotted, masochistic Isabella right after their wedding displays a side of his personality kept under wraps until then, presenting him unmistakably as a villain. As he himself tells Nelly, Isabella was wrong to fall in love with him:

> "picturing in me a hero of romance, and expecting unlimited indulgences from my chivalrous devotion. I can hardly regard her in the light of a rational creature, so obstinately has she persisted in forming a fabulous notion of my character and acting on the false impressions she cherished. But, at last, I think she begins to know me ..." (2000: 148)

With Heathcliff's sneering comment Brontë backstabs her own female readers, for most of us suddenly realise that we have been duped into liking him as much as Isabella and for exactly the same reasons: we fall for the stimulating combination of his good looks and what appears to be his victimisation by Hindley and Cathy, absurdly disregarding Cathy's warnings to Isabella about his brutality—and she should know, since she loves him. Like Isabella, most female readers resist the idea that the sympathetic wounded lover of the first half of the novel is the unrelenting villain of the second half, bent on destroying Cathy's daughter Catherine, his own son by Isabella Linton, and the late Hindley's son and heir Hareton. The Isabella complex, then, is ultimately the reason why most literary criticism and film adaptations tend to focus only on the romance with Cathy, which ends in the middle of the novel when she dies, aged only 18, after giving birth to her daughter.

The confusion created by Heathcliff's good looks derives ultimately from the conventions set by the Gothic novel, which cinema respects scrupulously even today and not just in the case of *Wuthering Heights*. This is so no doubt because of cinema's still insufficiently explored links with nineteenth-century Gothic-derived melodrama. As Elizabeth McAndrews observes, Gothic fiction derived its characterisation from the eighteenth-century belief in benevolism:

> Both good and evil are inner states of man's mind and, since beauty lies in God's order, the good and the beautiful are one, and evil is monstrous. These equations of goodness with beauty and wrongdoing with ugliness, which by mid-century were appearing in the writings of Adam Smith and others, were put to use by the authors of Sentimental and Gothic literature. They made their good characters physically lovely and gave the evil ones twisted bodies and ugly faces. (1979: 24)

The link between the classic Gothic villain and Heathcliff is the Byronic hero, perhaps most clearly presented as a mixture of attractive physical appearance and amoral behaviour not so much in Byron's own writings but in the story he inspired, John Polidori's 'The Vampire' (1819), the first of its genre published in Britain. Unlike Lord Ruthven, who might as well be called Lord Ruthless given the way he seduces and vampirises women, Heathcliff is as much sinner as sinned against, but, like Ruthven, he has an irresistible, sinister charm—at least for the likes of Isabella.

For all his charisma, though, Heathcliff often seems to be a blank. Q. D. Leavis called him 'merely a convenience' and complained that 'he is an enigmatic figure only by reason of his creator's indecision ... in being an unsatisfactory composite with empty places in his history and no continuity of character' (1986: 235). Without accusing Brontë of being an incompetent novelist, Heathcliff's characterisation does seem to depend too much on suspending our disbelief regarding the absence of three years during which he is magically transformed from lowly servant, aged 16, into rich gentleman, aged 19. It is hard to imagine how exactly he has gained his fortune. My students like to speculate that he has committed a crime, turned a master gambler as suggested by how he robs Hindley of Wuthering Heights, or even seduced a rich lady (or, indeed, gentleman), but no explanation seems really satisfactory.

Following a similar line of thought, Nina Auerbach notes that 'Heathcliff seems less a fully realised demon than a stricken Frankenstein monster, unable to live independently of the women who create him', among whom author and female readers should be included (1982: 102). Heathcliff, after all, possibly corresponds to women's need to fantasise about controlling unruly men through romance: 'Romance', Jane Miller explains, 'soothes women and mediates for them the painful ambivalence they internalise about men's power over them in the world by proposing to reduce men to their level, inducing dependence in a man on a woman, a dependence viewed by other men as grovelling and abject' (1986: 161). As most of my female students have confessed over the years I have taught the novel, Heathcliff is unforgettable because of his looks and his extreme dependence on Cathy's love. Male students, understandably, find Heathcliff weak and embarrassing, a character only women can believe in. Women tend, thus, to project onto Heathcliff idealised images of what a lover should be like because he is handsome and faithful to Cathy's memory, discounting his abuse of Isabella and the second-generation children on the grounds that he was himself victimised, and is therefore not fully responsible for his acts. Men reject him as a romantic female fantasy of male control.

Heathcliff on Screen: The Limits of Performance

Wuthering Heights only became the canonical novel it is now in the early twentieth century, thanks to the combined effect of Modernist women's admiration for Emily Brontë as a novelist (not so much for her hero and heroine) and, later, the film adaptation by William Wyler. Acceptance came by slowly precisely *because* of Heathcliff, considered a monster by most nineteenth-century readers, an opinion Charlotte Brontë may have helped spread. Except for his furtive love for Hareton and latent respect for Nelly, Charlotte Brontë writes, 'we should say [Heathcliff] was a child neither of Lascar nor gypsy, but a man's shape animated by demon life—a Ghoul—an Afreet' (2000: xlvi). A proof of the ambiguity of the Victorian reading public towards *Wuthering Heights* is the fact that there were no stage adaptations, a sure sign of a novel's acceptance then as much as film adaptations are now. Significantly, the first screen adaptation, a British film of 1920 now lost, insisted on Heathcliff's negative characterisation, presenting him following the conventions of melo-drama as an unheroic villain only redeemed by love (Stoneman 1996: 120).

The 1930s, however, inaugurated the tradition of reading Heathcliff exclusively as a victim of Cathy's manipulation in film and stage adaptations written and produced by *men*. As Patsy Stoneman explains, there was 'a movement from the melodramatic assumption that the story is motivated by 'the monster Heathcliff' to a more modern fear that the ambitious woman is the source of all its trouble' (1996: 124). This trend, present in John Davidson's stage adaptation (1937) and in Wyler's film, written by Ben Hecht and Charles McArthur, led to 'the "triangulation" of the plot' (Stoneman 1996: 155), a process by which *Wuthering Heights* has come to be read as the story of the adulterous triangle Edgar-Cathy-Heathcliff, thus obliterating the problematic second half of the novel in which Heath-cliff shows his villainous true colours. The adaptations of the 1930s are thus responsible for inventing a victimised Heathcliff who is quite different from Brontë's character but also far more popular, and who has certainly biased the canonisation of her novel in the twentieth century. No doubt, Laurence Olivier's good looks and subdued romantic performance are responsible for the frequent misreading of Brontë's Heathcliff as a victim, even more so because it suits the views of readers affected by the Isabella complex; perhaps also because it feeds on them.

On the whole, the existence of at least four film versions of *Wuthering Heights* suggests that all the film adaptations of Brontë's novel are globally unsatisfactory though they may succeed in part. As

John Ellis explains, 'the successful adaptation is one that is able to replace the memory of the novel with the process of a filmic or televisual representation' (1982: 3). It is hard to imagine, for instance, a Rhett Butler different from Clark Gable, and it is doubtful that a new version will ever be made of Margaret Mitchell's *Gone with the Wind* (1939). It is important to note, though, that if Gable's performance is still remembered today, it is because the whole film is memorable and not just his performance—which is not quite the case as regards the film versions of *Wuthering Heights*. The adaptations of *Wuthering Heights* have failed not because of their degree of narrative fidelity to their source, but because they have not managed to equal or surpass the possibilities offered by the narrative/dramatic material in the original novel and so produce a lasting impression on cinema audiences similar to the impression the novel produces on its readers. This is due, essentially, to the fact that while Brontë's saga covers about three decades, so that we meet the characters at different stages of their lives beginning with childhood, films can hardly do the same.

In Heathcliff's particular case, this means that no single actor can adequately cover all these stages, and this is where performance finds its limit. There are at least four Heathcliffs in the novel—the seven-year-old child Cathy accepts as a brother, the teenage boy she loves and rejects, the young adult who marries Isabella, and the man in his thirties who terrorises the second generation—yet the films do not reflect this variety satisfactorily. Buñuel partly solves the problem by focusing exclusively on the segment of the novel between Heathcliff's return and Cathy's death. Alejandro, closer to 30 than to 20, his age in this section of the novel, ends up being murdered by the Hindley character, Eduardo, in the crypt where Cathy has just been buried. This, obviously, quite limits the role in comparison to the novel's ever-developing Heathcliff. In the other cases, child actors are cast for the initial scenes but Olivier, Dalton and Fiennes are made to face the impossible task of playing teenage Heathcliff. This is easier for Dalton, aged just 24 when he played the role, but Olivier (32) and Fiennes (30) look plainly too old for the scenes covering Heathcliff's adolescence, and the same can be said of their leading actresses, Merle Oberon and Juliet Binoche respectively. The problems concerning this aspect of the adaptation depend thus on the inability to simultaneously maintain and ignore narrative fidelity. The decision to cover Heathcliff's boyhood as narrated in the novel is not accompanied by the casting of a different actor for this segment of the film, which makes actors look absurdly aged. This in its turn affects their performance so that none can fully succeed at playing the role.

The advantage Ralph Fiennes has over the other actors who have performed the role of Heathcliff is, precisely, that Kosminsky does try to transfer onto the screen the whole complex, multiple Heathcliff Brontë created. This is also a handicap in the sense that, at just under two hours, the film has hardly room for the actor to offer a nuanced performance at each point: every part of the plot flashes by too fast for spectators to really understand what is going on. However, Fiennes's performance at some of these scattered moments is striking enough to, at least, plant doubts in the spectators' minds and make them return to the text to check whether a particular scene does come from the novel. In the experiment mentioned above, I showed my students two scenes in the film that belong to the second half of the story: Heathcliff's abusing young Catherine when he imprisons her in his home to force the poor girl to marry his son Linton, and Heathcliff's sanctioning his foster son Hareton's love for the by then widowed Catherine. In the first case, Fiennes's passionate rendering of Heathcliff's hatred of the girl and his sheer violence against her called the students' attention to a scene that does appear in the novel pretty much as the film shows it, but that they had missed because of the effects of the Isabella complex. The other scene reflects the moment when, realising that his revenge against his dead enemy Hindley (Hareton's real father) is turning him into a worse abuser than Hindley was, Heathcliff surrenders and encourages Hareton to love Catherine. This is a crucial point in the novel since up to this moment and against all expectations, Hareton has loved Heathcliff, his abusive foster father, apparently more than he loves Catherine, and only Heathcliff's severing of the paterno-filial bond can help the couple move onto a happy end. Again, Fiennes's subtle performance in this scene—reported in the novel but dramatised in the film—forced me and my students to reconsider how this bond is dealt with in the novel, in which it does play a major role still neglected by criticism.

Peter Kosminsky and writer Anne Devlin made the decision to include these scenes, but if they stand out at all in an otherwise garbled film, it must be credited to Ralph Fiennes. Performance, on the other hand, is also conditioned by the intertextual contribution that casting makes to a particular role, that is, by the effect that the actor's looks, career and cast companions have beyond the adequacy or proficiency of the actual performance. Like the other three actors considered here, Fiennes is a handsome man with a large female following, a feature they all share with Brontë's character. Handsomeness, actually, appears to be the minimum common criterion of fidelity the four *Wuthering Heights* films obey while at the same time disregarding the exact nature of Heathcliff's appeal. By casting actors who are quite different from Brontë's dark, gypsy-looking Heathcliff, the films simultaneously expose their own racism and the very limits of fidelity, perhaps also conditioned by the reader's difficulties to visualise Heathcliff as Emily Brontë did: more like Antonio Banderas than like Olivier, Dalton or Fiennes. In Kosminsky's film, this implicit racism is accidentally emphasised by the decision to make Fiennes appear deeply tanned, with his light chestnut hair died black and, what is more worrying, always dirty and unkempt, even as a gentleman, in a way that recalls questionable acting practices of old times, exemplified, for instance, by Laurence Olivier's playing Othello in black make-up in Stuart Burge's film of 1965.[3] Mistral's Alejandro is no exception, since the film is set in Mexico, where his Spanish looks hardly stand out in the same way Heathcliff's do in the middle of Yorkshire. Given the importance of racial issues in our time, this might well turn out to be the main focus of a possible future adaptation of *Wuthering Heights*.

The *Wuthering Heights* films also show that actors contribute to each role the sum total of all the other roles in their careers, and that the contrasts brought about by interaction between members of the cast carrying their own intertextual 'baggage' also affect the inner dynamics of adaptation. Inevitably, many spectators will associate Fiennes's Heathcliff with his later role as Nazi fiend Amos Goeth in Steven Spielberg's *Schindler's List* (1993), but also with his role as the desperate lover in *The English Patient* (1996). Accounts differ as to why Spielberg chose Fiennes to play Goeth, the role that made him world famous, some claiming that Spielberg saw him play T. E. Lawrence in a TV series, others claiming he discovered Fiennes in *Wuthering Heights*. Whatever the case may be, the role of Heathcliff requires an actor capable of playing heroes and villains, a very limited

---

[3] The film was based on an Old Vic production directed by John Dexter in 1964, also with Olivier in the main role.

category singularly dominated by British actors such as Fiennes himself, Jeremy Irons, Alan Rickman, Anthony Hopkins, Jeremy Northam (Hindley in Kosminsky's film) and, more recently, Jude Law or Dougray Scott. As the failure of the embarrassing Cinderella film, *Maid in Manhattan* (2002) shows, Fiennes is not cut for romantic comedy, but his roles in *Red Dragon* (2002)—the third Hannibal Lecter film—and in David Cronenberg's *Spider* (2002) suggest that his *forte* is playing tortured souls, exactly what Heathcliff is.

Besides this, Heathcliff's characterisation is certainly conditioned on the screen by the leading actress playing Cathy and the supporting actors playing Edgar and Hindley. In Kosminsky's film, Juliet Binoche's double casting as both Catherines—only distinguished by their hair colour—is intriguing but misses, like all the other adaptations, an enigmatic point in the novel: it is Hareton, her nephew, who looks like the late Cathy, and not her daughter Catherine. Binoche is a fine actress and plays both Catherines quite creditably, yet by having her play the daughter Kosminsky raises an issue he fails to address: why Heathcliff feels no attraction for her, as should be expected since she is her mother's double. In this sense, Fiennes's performance is also undermined, whereas Olivier's subdued Heathcliff is much more convincingly paired off with Merle Oberon's ice-queen Cathy and Mistral's vampiric Alejandro with Irasema Dilián's fierce Catalina. On the other hand, all four adaptations coincide in exaggerating Edgar's cowardice and poor qualities as a husband so as to emphasise Heathcliff's appeal, casting less handsome actors who play Edgar as an effeminate man. In Kosminsky's version Hindley (Northam) is given so little screen time and Edgar (Simon Shepherd) is played so ineffectively that they hardly impress the spectator as Heathcliff's rivals. Yet in Wyler's version, David Niven contradicts this rule by bringing to the role of Edgar a dignity and maturity that make this character soar above the childishness of his wife and her lover.

Conclusion: The Paradoxes of Narrative Fidelity

To conclude, character and performance in film versions of novels are crucial factors, as important as the issues surrounding the transfer of narrative from page to screen. This is so not only because film *is* drama and, hence, is dependent on performance, but also because novels include plenty of dramatic elements and because reading itself is a performative activity, especially as regards character. This means that characters in film adaptations may certainly affect subsequent readings of the original novel, not simply because the actors' performance may be faithful to the dramatic elements in the novel, but also because it captures the way a certain character is imagined ('performed') by most readers at a given time. The case of Fiennes's Heathcliff is problematic because the obsession for narrative fidelity in Kosminsky's film has negatively affected the actor's performance, which had all the potential for being *the* Heathcliff for the 1990s.

The failure of the film has thus given this performance a limited projection, but Fiennes has nonetheless given some readers new insights into Brontë's text and, thus, usurped their visualisation of the original novel. This is a peculiar side-effect of Kosminsky's narrative fidelity to the text—complete on the film screen for the first time— and of the male zeitgeist, which encourages the public exposure of male abusers like Brontë's sadistic lover-villain. Fiennes's Heathcliff is, in short, faithfully Victorian *and* radically postmodern, but the film depends too much on an academic, old-fashioned view of fidelity that hampers the performance. This, however, survives in the minds of the readers, especially those interested in overcoming the Isabella complex that has so absurdly obscured the reading and adaptation of this classic. Narrative fidelity, thus, turns out to be paradoxically productive as regards the adaptation of character.

Bibliography

Auerbach, N. (1982) *Woman and the Demon*. Cambridge, Mass. and London: Harvard University Press.

Brontë, C. (2000 (1850)) 'Editor's Preface to the New Edition of *Wuthering Heights*', in E. Bronte. *Wuthering Heights*. Ed. P. Nestor. Harmondsworth: Penguin, xliii-xlvii.

Brontë, E. (2000) *Wuthering Heights*. Ed. P. Nestor. Harmondsworth: Penguin.

Davis, L. J. (1987) *Resisting Novels: Ideology & Fiction*. London and New York: Methuen.

Ellis, J. (1982) 'The Literary Adaptation: An Introduction', *Screen* 23 (1), 3-5.

Esslin, M. (1991) *The Field of Drama: How the Signs of Drama Create Meaning on Stage and Screen.* London: Methuen.

Haire-Sergeant, L. (1999) 'Sympathy for the Devil: The Problem of Heathcliff in Film Versions of *Wuthering Heights*, in B. T. Lupack (ed.) *Nineteenth-Century Women at the Movies.* Bowling Green: Popular Press, 167-91.

Hillis Miller, J. (1982) '*Wuthering Heights*: Repetition and the "Uncanny"', in J. Hillis Miller. *Fiction and Repetition.* Cambridge, Mass.: Harvard University Press, 42-72.

Knoepflmacher, U. C. (1994) *Wuthering Heights: A Study.* Athens, Ga.: Ohio University Press.

Leavis, Q. D. (1986 (1966)) 'A Fresh Approach to *Wuthering Heights*', in G. Singh (ed.) *Q.D. Leavis: Collected Essays, Vol 1. The Englishness of the English Novel.* Cambridge: Cambridge University Press, 228-74.

MacAndrew, E. (1979) *The Gothic Tradition in Fiction.* New York and Guilford, Surrey: Columbia University Press.

Miller, J. (1986) *Women Writing about Men.* London: Virago.

Stam, R. (2000) 'Beyond Fidelity: The Dialogics of Adaptation', in J. Naremore (ed.) *Film Adaptation.* London: Athlone, 54-76.

Stoneman, P. (1996) *Brontë Transformations: The Cultural Dissemination of Jane Eyre and Wuthering Heights.* London: Harvester Wheatsheaf/Prentice Hall.

Filmography

Buñuel, L. dir. (1954) *Abismos de pasión.* Tepeyac.

Wyler, W. dir. (1939) *Wuthering Heights.* Samuel Goldwyn.

Fuest, R. dir. (1971) *Wuthering Heights.* AIP.

Kosminsky, P. dir. (1992) *Wuthering Heights.* UIP/Paramount.

Dirk Bogarde's Sidney Carton
More Faithful to the Character than Dickens Himself?

John Style

Measured by the standards of a simple binary model, the 1958 film adaptation of Charles Dickens's *A Tale of Two Cities* (1859), starring Dirk Bogarde, could be considered faithful. However, by considering the origins of Dickens's novel in his personal life, in the literary influence of Thomas Carlyle's *The French Revolution* (1837), and in the political climate of England during and after the Indian Mutiny, judging the fidelity of the transfer becomes much more complex. The delimitation implied by the word 'original' is challenged when the 'original novel' is contextualised. The film portrait of Sidney Carton acquires a new complexity in Bogarde's queer performance, which opens up questions about the original novel that the novel itself does not dare to fully address. It is suggested that Homi Bhabha's model for 'cultural difference', where the adaptation 'adds to' rather than 'adds up', describes the relationship between 'original novel' and 'film adaptation' better than the binary model. In raising radical questions about Carton's identity in particular and the performative quality of identity in general, the film is arguably being more faithful to the spirit of Dickens's 'original'—Carlyle—than the original novel itself.

Who is Being Faithful to Whom, or What?

This chapter discusses Charles Dickens's historical novel, *A Tale of Two Cities* (1859), and its 1958 film adaptation starring Dirk Bogarde, and considers questions of fidelity and adaptation arising from that discussion.[1] It begins by addressing the question of the

---

[1] Page references to Dickens's novel are to the 1970 Penguin edition, edited by George Woodcock.

fidelity of the film adaptation in fairly conventional terms, by commenting briefly on the extent to which key elements of the book survive the transformation from a written into a visual medium. This type of discussion presupposes a rather simplistic binary model, in which transference is assumed to be unidirectional, always from the original novel to the film adaptation. This model relies on the understanding that there is such a thing as an 'original novel' in the adaptation process, which implies, along the lines of New Criticism, that the original has an autonomous existence of its own, in the sense that it manages to contain among other things a certain number of plot and character elements whose transference in the adaptation process can be traced. The answer to the question of fidelity depends, from this perspective, on how many of these elements are seen to be transferred successfully.

The excessively simplistic nature of this fidelity model becomes clear as soon as both Dickens's novel and the film adaptation are historicised, and attention is paid to how traces of the two distinct historical periods and their dominant ideologies persist in the novel and film respectively. Within these broadened contexts, the question of the fidelity of the adaptation as answered in the strictly formalistic terms modelled in the initial analysis appears at best very narrow and limited. By also bringing into consideration the function of Thomas Carlyle's *The French Revolution* (1837) as the most significant single intertext for the original novel, it is suggested that the film adaptation's treatment of the protagonist subtly alludes to some fundamental issues raised in that source text, which arguably Dickens's novel fails to face, and that the novel can be seen to participate in the very strategies of 'avoidance and dread' embodied in Dr Manette that it so vigorously denounces. The more intertextuality is acknowledged, the larger the extent to which any text may be called 'original' becomes a moot point. And once the idea of the novel as a self-contained, discrete original is questioned, the starting point of the binary model outlined above disappears, and with it the simplistic fidelity criterion itself. The issue of who is being faithful to whom or what becomes fascinatingly complex if one appreciates that the 'original' contains meanings that are derived from its cultural context. Perhaps the term 'original' should be expanded to include not only the material elements of the story—plot, characters, atmosphere and so on—but also the constellation of ideas from which they are generated, bearing in mind that these ideas, though contained in the novel, may have their origin outside it, within the contemporary cultural context. When assessing the fidelity of an adaptation in terms of the extent to which these ideas survive the transformation into film, we may find that the adaptation reveals ways of expressing them in (visual) ways that are paradoxically more faithful to the 'original' than the 'original novel' itself.

A Faithful Adaptation

When Dirk Bogarde and his director, Ralph Thomas, first began filming *A Tale of Two Cities*, Thomas had already directed Bogarde in the first of the four 'Doctor' comedies they were to make together, *Doctor in the House* (1954), the film which according to the second volume of Bogarde's autobiography, *Snakes and Ladders*, 'was the absolute turning point' (Bogarde 1988: 140) in that it secured him in his profession. The fact that Thomas could switch from contemporary light comedy to costume drama and back suggests, as does the range of genres covered in his 30-year career as film director, that he was a professional all-rounder, rather than someone aspiring to the status of an auteur, who might be inclined to leave a more obviously personal imprint upon their work. Not surprisingly, then, his 1958 film adaptation of Dickens's novel is clearly intended as a competent, faithful adaptation, and as such has not attracted a lot of critical acclaim among film historians.

In line with Brian McFarlane's discussion of such enterprises, the film clearly 'seek[s] to preserve the major cardinal functions' (1994: 14) of the novel, following the plot structure and the interaction of the characters closely. The novel's 'indices'—which McFarlane defines as 'the means by which character information, atmosphere and location are presented' (1994: 14)—are adapted effectively to the visual medium in conventional ways. For example, the film uses a standard flashback as an equivalent to the episode in the novel where Dr Manette's confession is read out at Darnay's French trial (Dickens 1970: 348-62), thereby revealing the background of his relationship to the Evrémonde family, and thus the source of Mme Defarge's unremitting hate. As for establishing atmosphere and location, the film's sets and costumes evoke the 1790s in a way which still looks convincing to a modern eye used to the marvels of computer-generated backdrops.

Thomas's film provides memorable large-scale filmic events by using large sets packed with extras for the big set-pieces, such as the storming of the Bastille, or the final scene when Carton goes to the guillotine. These are events which in Robert Giddings's words 'provide narratives which somehow fill the "gaps"' in the original (Giddings *et al.* 1990: xv), in the sense that they show events which the novel covers in a more indirect way. At the same time, the director finds a visual equivalent to Dickens's use of the metaphor of the sea to describe the powerful movement of the *sans-culotte* crowd, by choosing high camera angles to show the complex movement of the mass, or low angles to capture running legs going in a variety of directions in order to suggest the mayhem and unpredictability of the mob. The excellent supporting cast shows the traditionally acknowledged strength of British acting, with actors embodying their characters in ways which complement the original text. The women in particular are outstanding: Dorothy Tutin manages to make the rather pallid, static and excessively angelic Lucie into a believable female lead, supported by the redoubtable Athene Seyler in the role of Miss Pross, while Rosalie Crutchley shines, as she transforms the sinister Mme Defarge into an even more forceful character, worthy of Dickens's damning comment that 'there was absolutely no pity in her' (391). Even the rather wooden performance and slightly pedantic delivery of Paul Guers as Charles Darnay is arguably an example of fidelity to the original, if we accept George Woodcock's observation on Darnay that 'he is the most unconvincing character in *A Tale of Two Cities*, as shallow as a mirror' (Dickens 1970: 24). In this regard, the transfer of the novel's main 'indices' into film is handled very well.

Rather than making any major structural changes, scriptwriter D. E. B. Clarke cut the original plot and some characters out or down in the interests of economy and rhythm. Thus, the two Lucies' visit to La Force to wave hopefully to the imprisoned Charles and their conversations with the Sawyer are lost, as are Carton's hard work on law cases for Stryver, Stryver's frustrated attempt to propose marriage to Lucie, and the discovery that Barsad/Solomon is Miss Pross's long-lost brother. Carton's final walk through the night streets of Paris as he broods on transfiguration and the apotheosis of the sunrise and the death of Charles's and Lucie's son are also excised. Individually, none of these elements are what McFarlane might categorise as 'cardinal' features, and as such their loss does not threaten the film's aspirations to fidelity in a significant way.

'Avoidance and Dread'

Critics have found various origins for Dickens's story. As Woodcock demonstrates (Dickens 1970: 9-11 and 13), the central Carton-Darnay-Lucie triangle, and its notion of two men in love with the same woman leading to one of those men sacrificing his life for the other, repeats the plot of Wilkie Collins's play, *The Frozen Deep*, adapted from a short story first published in *Household Words* in the Christmas number of 1855. Dickens had performed the lead—in the role equivalent to Carton, the frustrated lover—in 1857, opposite the young Ellen Ternan, towards whom he certainly felt deep affection at the time, and whose presence in Dickens's life was influential in the subsequent break-up of his marriage in 1858, the year in which he published *A Tale of Two Cities*. The connections between Dickens's private life and the story he wrote were presented in public in veiled form. In the author's Preface, Dickens acknowledges, albeit in very general terms, his close identification with his work: 'Throughout [the book's] execution, it has had complete possession of me; I have so far verified what is done and suffered in these pages, as that I have certainly done and suffered it all myself' (29). His close identification with the two protagonists, the dutiful husband and the doomed lover, is also encoded in the alphabet game he plays with the characters' names, where the 'C-D' of Charles Darnay is mirrored in the Carton-Darnay doubling, suggesting that they represent different sides of Dickens's personality (Marcus 1965, cited by Woodcock in Dickens 1970: 24). The propriety required of a public figure and perhaps the complexity of his feelings at the time of the collapse of his marriage meant that Dickens was understandably not inclined to address the deeper emotional significance of the story and the way it paralleled his own life directly in his public writing. What is certain, however, is that one of the recurrent themes in the novel is the power that memories and the emotions attached to them have over the person in the present, and how that power grows in relation to the extent to which those memories are denied attention. The character who most clearly suffers the consequences of this process of denial is Dr Manette.

In Dickens's novel, after being released from the Bastille and leaving Revolutionary France for England, Dr Manette and his daughter, Lucie, establish themselves in London, where Lucie plays the triple role of dutiful daughter, fiancée and eventually wife to Charles Darnay and unobtainable ideal for the unfortunate Sidney Carton. In the middle of the book, soon after their marriage, Charles and Lucie go off on a honeymoon trip to the West Country and leave her father in the care of Miss Pross, Lucie's nurse, and the lawyer and family friend, Jarvis Lorry. It is during Lucie's absence that the doctor suffers a relapse into the mental torment associated with his time as a prisoner, and begins making shoes again; but he eventually overcomes this state of distraction thanks to the subtle ministrations of his companions. While the recovery is sound, his friend still detects the traces of the doctor's tragic past lurking within his character: 'In the composure of his manner he was unaltered, except that to the shrewd glance of Mr Lorry it disclosed some shadowy indication that the old air of *avoidance and dread* had lately passed over him, like a cold wind' (223 [my emphasis]). This 'old air of avoidance and dread' is a key diagnosis, which the narrator reinforces by his comment about Lorry's—rather uncharacteristic—shrewdness. 'Avoidance and dread' of the past contributes directly to its powerful resurgence. According to George Woodcock, resurgence, here as elsewhere in the novel in the form of past events coming back to haunt the present, is also linked 'with the theme of resurrection that permeates every level of *A Tale of Two Cities* and assumes an almost grotesque variety of forms' (Dickens 1970: 22). It ranges in its expression from Jerry Cruncher's body-snatching activities, through various instances of past events coming back to haunt the present, such as the reappearance of the doctor's damning written testimony of the Evrémonde family or the discovery of Miss Pross's long-lost brother Solomon as the despicable spy Barsad, to Carton's repetition of the Anglican funeral liturgy as he walks the streets of Paris on the night before he sacrifices his own life to save Darnay's. The destructive power of the past over the present, embodied most powerfully in Mme Defarge's obsessive determination to eliminate all present and future members of the Evrémonde family in particular and the French aristocracy in general, thrives in the climate of 'avoidance and dread', and can only be overcome when it is faced fearlessly and embraced. In choosing to avoid the past out of deep fear instilled during his imprisonment, Dr Manette unwittingly becomes a helpless agent of its destructiveness, when his testimony is used against his own son-in-law.

Woodcock also discusses the theme of resurgence in terms of 'moral resurgence', pointing to those moments in the story when characters act fearlessly and selflessly to change the apparently preordained course of events. To some extent, Darnay's immediate return to France in response to Gabelle's letter from prison calling for help exemplifies this, in the sense that he does not hesitate to put himself in danger in an attempt to act as one who has left behind his aristocratic origins and the injustice associated with them in order to obtain freedom for his ex-servant. The supreme example of moral resurgence, however, is Carton's overcoming dread to face his own death willingly. As he faces the guillotine, he knows what his sacrifice will mean for Lucie, his beloved; but he is also able to envision a future in which justice is done to him. For not only is Darnay virtually eliminated from the imagined picture of the happy family that Carton's sacrifice is ensuring, being referred to only in passing, but Little Lucie will have a son named after him, Sidney, and this son will become a judge, as will Little Lucie's grandson. Not only will this bring Carton's legal talents to final fruition, in a triumph of his genes over Darnay's, but together son and grandson will visit Paris where the story of Sidney's sacrifice will be handed down from one generation to the next (404).

The idea of moral resurgence is also present in Dickens's choice of setting, the French Revolution, as it was in his single most important source, Thomas Carlyle's *The French Revolution*, a book Dickens claimed to have read 500 times (Sanders 1996: 404). Dickens had first met Carlyle in 1840 and was attracted by the sage's powerful writing and bizarre personality. Almost twenty years before *A Tale of Two Cities*, *Chartism* (1840) and *The French Revolution* had already influenced Dickens's portrayal of mob violence during the Gordon Riots in *Barnaby Rudge* (1840-1). But as well as being of value as a thoroughly researched history, Carlyle's *The French Revolution* attracted Dickens for its rhetorical power and for being 'midway between a prophetic essay and a novel', showing how 'when basic human needs are denied they burst through the flimsy structure of social shams to create anarchy and then a new order' (Holloway 1953:

60). Not only did Carlyle's book record events which were still within living memory for posterity, but it also acted prophetically as a warning to Victorian England of what would ensue if pressing social issues such as Chartism and economic reform were not undertaken. This warning to the Establishment finds its echo in the famous opening of Dickens's novel:

> There were a king with a large jaw and a queen with a plain face, on the throne of England; there were a king with a large jaw and a queen with a fair face, on the throne of France. In both countries it was clearer than crystal to the lords of the State preserves of loaves and fishes, that things in general were settled for ever. (35)

By equating the English and French monarchies in their persons, and their respective 'lords' in their complacency, Dickens implies that the setting of the revolution his book describes is also interchangeable.

Carlyle's use of French history to criticise and warn his English contemporaries of the dangers of social injustice is taken up by Dickens. The sense of moral outrage at the bloodshed and torture perpetrated by both sides during the 1857 Indian Mutiny, which was finally quelled in the summer of 1858, and at the incompetent administration perceived as its cause, was one in which Dickens fully participated. Stories of massacres of British women and children by frenzied 'foreign' crowds—which also make their terrifying presence felt in the scenes of revolutionary Paris in *A Tale of Two Cities*—led Dickens, adding his voice to what William Oddie describes as 'an almost universal demand for bloody revenge on the mutineers' (1972: 3), to suggest in a letter to *The Times* that the natives involved be 'exterminated'. This vehement expression is echoed within *A Tale of Two Cities* on four separate occasions, always in the mouths of Mr and Mme Defarge, as when they discuss how far the revolution and its killing should go: '"Well, well", reasoned Defarge, "but one must stop somewhere. After all, the question is still where?" "At extermination", said madame' (369).[2] It might seem surprising and deeply ironic to find the author of *A Tale of Two Cities* using the same vocabulary in connection with the Indian mutineers as the most evil character in his

---

[2] The word is chillingly echoed in Joseph Conrad's *Heart of Darkness* (1899), in Kurtz's post-script/summary of the advice contained in his report on 'The Suppression of Savage Customs': 'Exterminate the brutes!' (Conrad 1973: 103).

novel uses against the French aristocracy. But Dickens's ability to criticise the behaviour of the complacent ruling classes did not imply any sympathy with the perpetrators of the violence such behaviour gave rise to, as evidenced in both *A Tale of Two Cities* and a later Christmas story with an overtly colonial theme, *The Perils of Certain English Prisoners*.[3] In both the novel and the short story, Dickens chooses socially marginalised protagonists, Sidney Carton and Gill Davis respectively, who occupy an indeterminate position between the opposing forces outlined in each text. As such, they can be seen as attempts to find an imaginative position in which Dickens can come to terms with his own tendency to 'avoidance and dread': dread of the destructive power of the social masses once their anger is aroused and yet avoidance of, in the sense of distancing oneself from, identification with cruel power-wielding social structures. I want to argue that the 1958 film version of *A Tale of Two Cities* manages to adopt a challenging, interstitial position, largely due to Bogarde's central performance, and it is to the film version that I now return.

Fidelities beyond the Text

If the Ralph Thomas film of Dickens's novel meets the formal criteria of fidelity, when looked at more closely the cinematic portrayal of Sidney Carton raises some interesting issues beyond the requirements of a superficial fidelity. Gabriel Miller claims of the adaptation process that 'the novels' characters undergo a simplification process when transferred to the screen, for film is not very

---

[3] In *The Perils of Certain English Prisoners*, co-authored with Wilkie Collins and published in *Christmas Stories* (1871), Dickens addresses the theme of colonial disorder directly, although rather than an Indian setting, the story is displaced to Belize in Central America. Dickens's protagonist, the pragmatic soldier Gill Davis, whose prompt action re-establishes peace and order in the colony, is at odds with both the world of officialdom and Christian George King, the leader of the unruly natives. Through identification with Davis, the reader is invited to occupy a position in which both the Establishment above and the natives below can be duly criticised. Laura Peters concludes that the story ends with a paradox, which requires Gill's reconciliation with imperial officialdom and distancing from 'British internal social systems ... [because] Dickens needs to validate the colonial power structure as proper and civilised in response to the Cawnpore mutiny, while maintaining his long held criticism of English society' (1998: 181). For further reflections on the Dickens section of *The Perils*, see Stewart (1999).

successful in dealing either with complex psychological states or with dreams or memory, nor can it render thought' (1980: xiii). In this light, it is perhaps not surprising that Book 2 Chapter 5 of *A Tale of Two Cities*, 'The Jackal', in which Stryver refers to Carton by his strange nickname, 'Memory', is one interesting chapter the script does not deal with at all. It is an important one for establishing the psychological complexity of Carton, as it makes clear that the drinking and self-disgust that characterises him existed before he conceived of his love for Lucie. It also makes clear that despite his existential *ennui*, whose origin is never really satisfactorily explained, and his reproachable habits, he still gets a lot of good work done for Stryver, whose success in the profession very much depends on Carton's ability to work through the night preparing the cases for court. The virtues Carton shows, such as self-discipline, a capacity to work long hours despite the alcohol, and perspicacity, add to the sense of loss at his apparent degeneracy.[4]

As one might predict from Miller's observation, the film also fails to account in any way for Carton's final dream on the scaffold, his 'vision' of Lucie's future family's affinities with him rather than Darnay, referred to earlier. The final chapter is represented in a 35-second scene, in which we hear Carton's voice saying:

> [in VO] Suddenly, I want to weep but I must hold my tears in check, lest they think it is myself I weep for, and who would weep for Sidney Carton? A little time ago, none in all the world. But somebody will weep for me now, and that knowledge redeems a worthless life. Worthless but for this final moment, which makes it all worthwhile. It is a far, far better thing that I do, than I have ever done. It is a far, far better rest that I go to than I have ever known.

Apart from the last two sentences, which are the famous last lines of Dickens's book, this monologue is the creation of the scriptwriter. The

---

[4] In this chapter and in Book 2 Chapter 11, 'A Companion Picture', Dickens interestingly characterises Carton's degeneracy in a way which has striking connotations given the author's reactions to the Indian Mutiny. In both cases, Carton wraps his aching, hungover head in wet towels which look like a turban. Clearly, the association of the wet towel wrapped around Carton's head with the turban worn by certain Sikh regiments which participated in the Indian Mutiny is so strong for the author that his racist feelings about the events in India irrupt into his account of late eighteenth-century London.

film makes no attempt to account for Carton's thoughts during his final prophetic vision, which amounts to the last page of the novel, in which he sees the revolutionaries and Jarvis Lorry each receiving their just deserts at their deaths, as well as the future of Lucie's family and its remembrance of him. In the film script, the sentiments expressed, limited as they are to the sense that Lucie's love gives his life and sacrifice meaning, are appropriate in the sense that in the process of simplification of Carton's character his portrayal is basically reduced to that of the thwarted lover. During the above monologue, Bogarde's face stares resolutely into the middle distance as he is bound, before we see the falling blade and a fortissimo discord from the orchestral soundtrack tells us that the deed is done. Dickens's casting of Carton as an eighteenth-century Christ figure, as a harbinger of moral resurgence and a prophetic visionary both in the novel's last scene and in his last night walking the streets of Paris before dawn heralds his acceptance of his chosen path—an analogy of Christ's experience in the Garden of Gethsemane—is reduced to a character of more modest pretensions, appropriate to the spiritual scepticism of the late 1950s.

What seems crucial is that while the film simplifies the novel's portrait of Carton by focussing on his interaction with Lucie and the love triangle involving Darnay, it also introduces a new aspect to the Carton character which gives rise to a complexity of its own. The novel's doubling of Darnay and Carton takes on a new dimension when one notices how 'feminine' Bogarde's performance is, especially in the early scenes. Opposite the bland, impassive features and wooden gestures of Paul Guers as Darnay—possibly more the result of excellent casting of a rather limited actor, rather than intentional acting in itself—Bogarde's performance has all the queenish gestures of a diva. The scene where this contrast is most striking is the one in which Darnay and Carton as shown drinking in a pub after the court victory, where Carton obliges Darnay to come clean about his love and drink a toast to Miss Manette. In contrast to Guers's plain, marble-like features, Bogarde's face is made-up heavily and obviously, emphasising high cheekbones, pouting lips and heavy-lidded eyes, which blink in Garbo-like slow-motion to suggest splendid disdain. His hair, combed forward in the way we have come to accept as 'eighteenth century', is also curled very prettily along the fringe. The appearance is perfectly complemented by the excessive theatrical gestures and the mobility of the head and shoulders, always in contrast to the immobility and inexpressiveness of Guers's performance, to suggest a masculine-feminine duality.[5] Is the film suggesting that perhaps Carton's real secret love was for Charles, rather than Lucie? Should this be the case, this would surely be a case of outrageous 'infidelity' to Dickens's novel. Certainly, there is a very heavy ambiguity to the words which the script salvages and reorders from Dickens. Once Darnay leaves Carton in the inn, the latter gets up and goes over to look at himself in the mirror:

> When he was left alone, this strange being took up a candle, went to a glass that hung against the wall, and surveyed himself minutely in it.
> 'Do you particularly like the man?' he muttered, at his own image; 'why should you particularly like a man who resembles you? There is nothing in you to like; you know that. Ah, confound you! What a change you have made in yourself! A good reason for taking to a man, that he shows you what you have fallen away from, and what you might have been! Change places with him, and would you have been looked at by those blue eyes as he was, and commiserated by that agitated face as he was? Come on, and have it out in plain words! You hate the fellow'.
> He resorted to his pint of wine for consolation, drank it all in a few minutes and fell asleep on his arms, with his hair straggling over the table, and a long winding-sheet in the candle dripping down upon him. (116)

Darnay serves to show Carton what might have been, and the scene to introduce the idea of substitution. In the film version, Bogarde stares at his own face, and says:

> Why should I like a man because he resembles me? There's nothing in me to like. I'm a disappointed drudge, Sir. I care for no man on Earth, and no man on Earth cares for me.

---

[5] In the preceding court scene, Bogarde's performance already has plenty of diva-ish disdainful languidity, in the way he sits sideways brooding for the early part of the scene, the way he nonchalantly tosses the note to Stryver to suggest he be compared to Darnay, the casually pushed-back wig to reveal the curly fringe (unlike all the other court officials, who wear their wigs 'properly'), the splendidly arched single eyebrow as he looks at Barsad in disdain, the languid parting of the lips before he speaks, not to mention the extremely tight trousers, which nevertheless show none of the signs which held Britain in its thrall during the showing of the BBC's 1995 tabloid-headlining 'sex-romp' production of *Pride and Prejudice*. His performance does not of course stay fixed in this mode. When Lucie faints, he becomes a man of action, ordering the court officials to look to her. And by his death scene, he is reduced to a manfully open necked shirt, and his hair has lost its crimped look.

The first two sentences are a rewriting of the novel's text, of course; the last two are a direct quotation from earlier in the same scene in the novel. The script's rewriting, replacing the 'you' (addressed to the mirror image) for 'me', has the effect of increasing the narcissistic effect of the scene. By emphasising 'liking a man', 'caring for a man' and 'being cared for by a man' or not as the case may be, and by cutting out the reference to Lucie's blue eyes in the novel, the film seems to be at least allowing for a queer reading of the scene. The film only opens up the possibility of justifying such a reading in one other scene, where Carton substitutes himself for Darnay. As Bogarde dictates his last testimony and letter of love to the seated Guers, he approaches him from behind and puts his two hands on his shoulders, upon which Darnay jumps in a way that suggests that the physical contact, expressed in a gesture which could be interpreted as affectionate, is both surprising and meaningful. It is a fleeting moment, which may or may not be significant, just as Carton's words in the mirror may or may not have an underlying queer significance.

Rereading Dickens's text in search of more evidence to support a queer reading proves fairly fruitless. The extent to which we entertain the possibility of this reading will depend on meanings which have their origin outside the text, in the contemporary cultural context of the film adaptation itself. Of course, our later knowledge of Bogarde's life and the fact that he eventually publicly acknowledged the homosexual dimension of his relationship with his companion and manager implies that the actor might have had some interest in expressing a truth about himself through indirect means such as a performance as another. The famous mirror scene in *Death in Venice* (1971), in which Bogarde starred, and its overt treatment of the theme of homosexual love undoubtedly contribute, in a retrospective way, to what we read into his performance in *A Tale of Two Cities*. Yet in *Snakes and Ladders*, the volume of his autobiography which deals with this period of his life, Bogarde has nothing to say on any aspect of his performance in *A Tale of Two Cities*, other than recording the fact that he made the film and that 'it was later to be advertised in America as "Two men and a Girl in Turbulent Paris"' (Bogarde 1988: 169). This jokey aside not only subtly reaffirms European disdain for American cultural ignorance, but also highlights the way the film focuses closely on the love story alone, and was to be sold and seen as a heterosexual romance.

Beyond the possible nuances which Bogarde's own life and career give to the film, the screen adaptation also reflects aspects of its own cultural moment. At the end of the 1950s, homosexual activity was the object of hostile persecution by certain members of the police and the judiciary. Describing the atmosphere of the time, Sheridan Morley's biography of John Gielgud sets the scene for that actor's arrest for soliciting in late 1953 by recalling a series of high-profile arrests that had occurred recently, making it clear how ill-advised it would be for an actor to make known their homosexuality (Morley 2001: 231-63), and how brave Bogarde's decision was to act in the 1961 film *Victim*, which dealt with a lawyer being blackmailed by a threat to reveal his homosexual inclinations.[6] By suggesting there is a queer dimension to the film's reading of Dickens's *A Tale of Two Cities*, I do not wish to imply anything as oversimplified as that Sidney Carton's existential problems are explained by the fact that, under it all, he is in fact in love with Charles Darnay and yet cannot admit this. That would simply substitute one polarity, the male-female, with another, male-male. I would argue instead that the very nebulous trace of queerness in Bogarde's performance—so nebulous indeed that it may be invisible to some viewers—opens up the story in challenging ways, as it suggests that Sidney Carton occupies a mid-position between the standardised masculine-feminine binary repre-sented by Charles Darnay at one end of the scale and Lucie Manette at the other. According to Harry M. Benshoff's description of Queer Theory, it aims to 'overturn those binaries and the labels which go with them to acknowledge a fuzzy interstitial area where most of us really belong' (Benshoff 2003)—an apt description of the area in which Bogarde's Carton can be located, especially as, by not referring to the novel's closing vision of the future generations of his and Lucie's (albeit symbolic) descendants, Carton's sacrifice is not incorporated into a heterosexual framework, where fertility produces future generations to prolong class and system. In the film, Carton, like all the other main characters with the exception of the Manettes and Charles, is no perpetuator of the system.

By queering Sidney Carton, the film adaptation is doing some-thing other than simply producing a faithful cinematic version of the

---

[6] See also Sinfield (1989: 60-85) for an illuminating discussion of homosexuality in the postwar period, including the Wolfenden Report of 1957.

novel. And yet as this queering is a nuance, rather than anything fully stated, it resists any attempt at achieving a sense of closure in our reading, such as providing a specific explanation of Carton's character. The layer of unstated meanings—articulated mostly through visual images and symbols: Bogarde's make-up, gestures, the mirror, etc.— that film adds to the original novel suggests that the relationship between film adaptation and original novel might best be seen as not dissimilar to the fruitful tension that Homi Bhabha describes in 'DissemiNation' (1990: 291-322). Analogising from Bhabha's discussion of cultural difference, the potential of film adaptation may be seen as 'adding to' rather than 'adding up' the meanings of Dickens's novel, which 'serves to disturb the calculation of power and knowledge, producing other spaces of subaltern signification' (1990: 312). The disturbance engendered 'is the enemy of the *implicit* generalization of knowledge or the implicit homogenization of experience' (Bhabha 1990: 313 [emphasis in original]), and is represented in the film and book by Carton's non-conformist behaviour in general and his radical final action in particular. In these two respects, his loving sacrifice represents a challenge—especially in the film, deprived of the novel's final happy heterosexual vision of the future— to the homogeneity of 'France', where revenge and hate dominate the land, and of 'England', where the establishment is complacent, allowing bullies like Stryver to accede to positions of power, or fossilised, as in the ancient customs of Tellson's bank. Carton's action, if it is to be seen as powerful and capable of changing others, must have its origins outside the homogenous systems of France and England, for if it did not, it would simply reaffirm either. The film's presentation of Carton as coming from a fuzzy interstitial area between the masculine-feminine poles is a brilliant metaphor for his outsider quality, and his ability to disturb norms. So, rather than representing a radical departure from the original novel, I would argue that the 1958 film's subtle queering of Sidney Carton gives brilliant expression to his radically marginal position in relation to the rest of society already implicit in the novel, but which is there subsumed in the homogenising effect of his final vision.

It might be objected that taking ideas from Queer and Postcolonial Theory to elucidate a film which predates that theory is to blithely disregard historical chronology. However, the seminal ideas behind Benshoff's and Bhabha's formulations predate both the film and the novel in question. If we suspend the simplistic original novel/film adaptation binary for a moment, and allow the notion of the 'original' ideology that pre-exists the 'original novel', then Bogarde's 'interstitial' performance as Carton and the theoretical ideas that have been used here will be found to be present in Dickens's key source, Carlyle. In *Sartor Resartus*, first published in 1834, three years before *The French Revolution*, Carlyle had written: 'He who first shortened the labor of Copyists by the device of *Movable Types* was disbanding hired Armies and cashiering most Kings and Senates and creating a whole new Democratic world: he had invented the Art of printing' (1973: 29). According to Isobel Armstrong, Carlyle's awareness that the art of printing and the concept of 'moveable types' had radical implications as regards the overthrow of existing power structures can be seen as leading to his disruption of essentialist thinking and the conviction that oppositional dualities are illusory—the France of the Revolution could be read as his England of the 1830s (1993: 4-5 and 10). It also led to his awareness that the process of signification is a political matter, entailing ambiguities which have interested poststructuralists in the twentieth century. Furthermore, 'moveable type' as a metaphor for the complexity of the politics of signification is embodied in Carlyle's portrait of King Louis, especially in the chapter 'Place de la Revolution' in *The French Revolution*, which draws the distinction between the physical man and the royal persona, and shows how the royal identity is constructed from the performance of a mere man acting as a king—a performative identity whose meaning is constructed from the many ways it is interpreted by the witnesses who are present during the King's last hours before his execution. And the idea that identity is performative, an idea which has been worked out more thoroughly in postmodern texts such as Judith Butler's *Gender Trouble* (1990), a seminal text for Queer Theory, would seem to be anticipated by Bogarde's splendid performance—as histrionic and excessive as it is sexually ambiguous.

Returning to the initial question of the fidelity of the film adaptation of an original novel, and the terms in which such a question can be meaningfully asked, this chapter has attempted to show that while the question, 'is the film a "faithful" adaptation of the original novel?', can certainly be answered, it presupposes acceptance of a very limited binary model. Consideration of the extent to which the film adaptation transfers the original novel's founding ideology forces the critic beyond the simple book-film model, to acknowledge the possibility of a significant fidelity to important factors that lie beyond the strict limits of the source text. Bogarde's queer performance as Carton, while adding something not overtly stated in the novel, nevertheless expresses something implicit in the original character's indeterminacy, an indeterminacy which is more fully grasped in Dickens's main source, Carlyle's account of the French Revolution, than it is in the novel itself. In giving such subtle expression to the radical indeterminacy to be found at the 'origin' of Dickens's setting, arguably the 1958 film of *A Tale of Two Cities* is more faithful to the original ideology underlying *A Tale of Two Cities* than Dickens's book itself.

Bibliography

Armstrong, I. (1993) *Victorian Poetry: Poetry, Poetics and Politics.* London and New York: Routledge.

Benshoff, H. M. (2003) 'Notes on Gay History/Queer Theory/Queer Film'. On-line. Available HTTP: http://www.unt.edu/ally/queerfilm.html (15 October 2003).

Bhabha, H. (1990) 'DissemiNation', in H. Bhabha (ed.) *Nation and Narration.* London and New York: Routledge, 291-322.

Bogarde, D. (1988) *Snakes and Ladders.* Harmondsworth: Penguin.

Butler, J. (1990) *Gender Trouble: Feminism and the Subversion of Identity.* London and New York: Routledge.

Carlyle, T. (1973) *Sartor Resartus: On Heroes and Hero Worship.* London: Dent.

—— (2002) *Chartism: Past and Present.* Boston: Elibron Classics.

—— (2002) *The French Revolution.* New York: Random House.

Conrad, J. (1973) *Heart of Darkness.* Harmondsworth: Penguin.

Dickens, C. (1970) *A Tale of Two Cities.* Ed. G. Woodcock. Harmondsworth: Penguin.

Giddings, R. *et al.* (1990) *Screening the Novel: The Theory and Practice of Literary Dramatization.* Basingstoke and London: Macmillan.

Holloway, J. (1953) *The Victorian Sage: Studies in Argument.* London: Macmillan.

Marcus, S. (1965) *Dickens from Pickwick to Dombey*. New York: Basic Books.

McFarlane, B. (1996) *Novel to Film: An Introduction to the Theory of Adaptation*. Oxford: Clarendon.

Miller, G. (1980) *Screening the Novel: Rediscovered American Fiction in Film*. New York: Frederick Ungar.

Morley, S. (2001) *The Authorised Biography of John Gielgud*. London: Hodder & Stoughton.

Oddie, W. (1972) 'Dickens and the Indian Mutiny' *The Dickensian* 68, 3-15.

Peters, L. (1998) 'Dickens and Popular Orphan Adventure Narratives', *The Dickensian* 94, 172-83.

Sanders, A. (1996 (1994)) *The Short Oxford History of English Literature*. Oxford: Clarendon.

Sinfield, A. (1989) *Literature, Politics and Culture in Postwar Britain*. Oxford: Blackwell.

Stewart, N. (1999) '"The Perils of Certain English Prisoners": Dickens' Defensive Fantasy of Imperial Stability'. On-line. Available HTTP: http://www.qub.ac.uk/english/imperial/india/perils.htm (13 October 2003).

Filmography

Dearden, B. dir. (1961) *Victim*. Allied Filmmakers/Parkway/ Rank.

Thomas, R. dir. (1958) *A Tale of Two Cities*. Rank.

Visconti, L. dir. (1971) *Death in Venice*. Warner/Alfa.

AUTHORS, AUTEURS, ADAPTATION

Once Upon an Adaptation:
Traces of the Authorial on Film

Karen Diehl

In several recent adaptations, one can note the addition of author characters to a literary narrative. This chapter analyses the meanings of these authorial appearances, be they of the adapted author or of additional characters, in *Le temps retrouvé* (1999), *Shakespeare in Love* (1999), *The Hours* (2002) and *Adaptation* (2002). Formerly, the author of the literary text appeared in adaptations mostly indirectly, by means of narrative techniques such as voice-over, titles or narrator figures. Those narrative techniques are still being used to create an authorial narrative, but now in conjunction with characters claiming author status. Through the different ways narrative techniques are employed to shape the authorial character and his/her position within the narrative, recent adaptations propose different concepts of authorship. The relationship between literary texts and their adaptations to film is thus defined beyond an exchange of narratives. Instead, adaptation potentially becomes an instrument of cultural critique of the concept of the author.

To Tell a Tale of an Author

Uses made of the author upon whose texts a film is based date back to the beginnings of film. The realisation soon dawned that the middle-class could be won as an audience of the new medium by linking film to literature (as well as to well-known historical figures and to the Biblical stories; see Uricchio and Pearson 1993), and more specifically to the classics of a given national literature (Albersmeier 1992). From early on, the appeal of the book found its entry into the marketing materials and the films themselves in word and image: at the time of its release in the teens, the name of Thomas Dixon as well as the title of his book *The Clansman* (1905) was prominently displayed on different posters of *The Birth of a Nation* (1915); on the poster of the 1944 adaptation of *Pride and Prejudice*, the book by Austen was iconically inserted between images of Greer Garson and Laurence Olivier. Using the book as a visual prompter that metonymically indicated the presence of the author was not restrained to subsidiary material, but appeared in the narrative of films itself. In 1941, the adaptation of *Jane Eyre* (1847) not only represented the opening book at the beginning of the film, it furthermore replaced Brontë's original text with one written by the studio (Sconce 1995).[1] The connection between the literary source text and the narrative of the film purporting to be based on that text, like the phrase 'Once upon a time', is one that posits itself through narrative convention rather than through adherence to the text. The literary text is a trace marked on the film by textual and visual prompters.

Film and literature were regarded as narrative arts, and thus narrativity was established as the definitive shared feature. This tied film more closely to literature than to its earlier twin art, the theatre.[2] Directly or indirectly, narrative studies of film have already given authorial narrative techniques extensive attention (Branigan 1984, Chatman 1990, Gaudréault and Jost 1990). In this chapter, the authorial is understood as instances where the film gives specific indicators of a narrative authority, as in voice-over, frame narratives, or the look at the camera. These techniques were and are employed in both original scriptwriting and adaptations of literary material. Having become more or less the stock-in-trade of the conventions by which narrative film tells a story, they are not necessarily to be interpreted as instances where the authorial (let alone the author of the literary material) leaves its mark on a film. Rather, they seem to have had two effects. First, film appeared to have effaced the 'hand of the literary author', not least by replacing him/her with the subsequent authorial figures of scriptwriter, producer, star, and most notably the director as *auteur*. Secondly, in theoretical approaches to narrative film, it was of little import whether or not the film had a literary author present

---

[1] By making the text appear on the first page of a book titled *Jane Eyre* which is opened at the beginning of the film, it was suggested that the text seen on screen was a verbatim quote from the novel.

[2] Apart from the affinities created through mode and sphere of consumption, the earliest adaptations of literary texts were films based on plays. However, these films were more often than not merely filmed theatre productions.

behind the subsequent authorial figures of scriptwriter, director, producer, and even actors (Géloin 1988, Green 1988, Cattryse 1992).

Thirty years after the author's theoretically proclaimed dissolution as entity and origin (Barthes 1967, Foucault 1969), the figure of the literary author has made a return in several recent adaptations. In very different films such as *Shakespeare in Love* (1999), *The Hours* (2002), *Le temps retrouvé* (1999) and *Adaptation* (2002), the uses made of the authorial have been developed into a meta-commentary that explicitly refers to the figure of the author of the literary source text on the basis of different conceptualisations of authorship. The purpose of telling a literary tale in film adaptation thus becomes the enterprise of narrating an idea of the author itself. The traces of the authorial on film (as written text, as opening books, as voice-over, as quotation) construct the figure of the author as a point of narrative origin, the 'Once upon a time' of adaptation. In this chapter, instances where the film suggests a narrative authority and thus reconnects it to what is posed as a literary author (or as originating with an author) shall be termed the 'authorial' in the strict sense. The interesting question to be asked is whether the continued use of the authorial in its meta-manifestations has to be interpreted as an affirmation of an author-principle after the theoretical demise of the author, or whether these new films are an ironic commentary on authorial power. In either case, this chapter argues, access to the authorial is negotiated through narrative.

In previous studies of adaptation, narrative was approached as a means of testing fidelity (Andrew 1980, Seitz 1981). As literature and film seemed to share the feature of narrativity above all, narrative became a focal point in the study of adaptation. From a semiotic perspective, film as an art was compared to literature in terms of what, as a distinct sign system, it could not narrate and vice versa. Films based on literature were measured against literature by studying how they transposed the narrative. If the transposition had been achieved satisfactorily, the film would be labelled as being faithful to the novel. While this is not the place to map out the fallacies operative in such a view, especially as fidelity as a term of analysis has become the object of criticism, it is worth pointing out that to disclaim an approach to adaptation rooted in fidelity does not automatically entail a transcending of its implications.[3]

Whereas fidelity previously stipulated that ideally nothing be added or omitted from the literary narrative except for 'valid' reasons (e.g. shortening to fit the feature-length format, or to efficiently motivate characters), recently narrative additions to the literary text in the act of adaptation have explicitly been legitimised as a form of fidelity to the text by postulating them as inherent in the text itself (Sheen 2000) or as a defining feature of the relationship between literary text and its filmic adaptation with the different exigencies of their respective medial formats and circulation modalities (Gelder 2000). While terming such narrative additions faithful remains a problematic issue, the change of attitude as regards liberties taken with the literary narrative in its adaptation to film seems expressive of a more emancipated understanding of the practice of adaptation. The adaptation is regarded as a new narrative in its own right, one that creates a new reference system and new narratives—a development not least supported or influenced by the commodification, commercial exploitation and genre-codification of various types of adaptation.[4]

Several recent adaptations, then, have played upon the theme of the authorial without explicitly introducing an author as a character independent of the adapted narrative. Some of these films took their cue from the book they adapted. Thus, the doubling of the central characters in the film *The French Lieutenant's Woman* (1981) has been read as a way of if not reproducing, then at least filmically representing the novel's play of the authorial commentator that inhabits the literary text next to its (here John Fowles's) characters (Chatman 1990). In the film *Orlando* (1991), the adaptation took it upon itself to write the novel's narrative into the film's present. In that added narrative, the central character became not only a mother but also a writer in Thatcher's Britain. While the author does not inevita-

---

[3] Studies such as Joyce Gould Boyum's (1985) or MacFarlane's (1996) argue against fidelity as an appropriate approach to adaptation, yet their case studies, which measure the narrative of the film against the original narrative of the literary text, thereby still devise the relationship as hierarchical.

[4] The recent successive adaptations of best-seller author John Grisham or of heritage favourite E. M. Forster serve as prime examples where a string of adaptations of the same author results in instant generic recognisability.

bly take anthropomorphic shape, the author in these adaptations becomes a theme that is added to the literary narrative.

Will/Shakespeare

In *Shakespeare in Love*, the character Will suffers from crippling authorial self-doubt. His ability to write increases as his sex life with and emotional attachment to the character Viola gets underway. Over the course of the film, this author manages to produce writing only if prompted either by colleagues or by his lover. He is, thus, the antithesis to the received image of the author William Shakespeare of world fame. The film has half of its narrative ready-made by using the plays of Shakespeare. While the film leaves open the question as to how Will manages to write the remaining Shakespeare plays after the departure of his muse, it firmly establishes the character Will as author of greatness by making the Queen concede 'that a play can show the very truth and nature of love'. Whereas the narrative constantly embroils Will in doubts about his writing and the production of the play on stage, the film further underscores the transcendent qualities of literature by repeatedly narrating the difference between a reality and a play. In the transition, for example, from the love story between Viola and Will to the play *Romeo and Juliet*, the owl and the rooster are ennobled as the nightingale and the lark, respectively.

Given that the film presents itself as a romantic comedy to its potential audience, there is no friction between the figure of the author and his literary production. Out of the troubled life of Will grows the play *Romeo and Juliet* as written by Shakespeare, just as, in the film *The Hours*, out of the troubled life of Virginia comes the novel *Mrs Dalloway*. This, added to the conventional use of repetitive quotation (visual and verbal), of titles, voice-over and sound-over in scene transitions, for interrelating various subplots, for indicating a historical context, and for explaining character motivation, reveals that in both *Shakespeare in Love* and, as the following will show, in *The Hours*, the idealist concept of authorship as an arduous but elevated creative process goes unquestioned.

Virginia/Woolf

The narrative expansion of a literary classic has been explored
in different ways in contemporary rewritings, and then even further in
films based on either such postmodern literature or on so-called
literary classics. The novel *Wide Sargasso Sea* (1966) by Jean Rhys
rewrote the story of *Jane Eyre* from the point of view of Rochester's
first Creole, allegedly insane wife. Tom Stoppard's play *Rosencrantz
and Guildenstern Are Dead* (1967) did the same for the two hapless
characters from *Hamlet* (c. 1600). The narrative of a well-known piece
of literature was supplemented with other narratives. Michael Cunningham's *The Hours* (1999) also takes this step prior to its adaptation
to film. The novel uses the story of *Mrs Dalloway* (1925), the story of
Virginia Woolf writing *Mrs Dalloway*, and the story of *Mrs Dalloway*
being read, to create a new tripartite narrative.

In the film *The Hours*, the different story strands are connected in various ways. First, there are a number of motifs that recur
in each of them separately: flowers (yellow roses in particular); eggs
being cracked for cooking; food thrown away or disregarded; two
women kissing each other (in two cases there is a small child watching); parties (in all three stories). In addition, the characters in various
instances repeat dialogue lines—'What does it mean to regret, if you
have no choice?'(Virginia to Leonard and Laura to Clarissa); 'I don't
think two people could have been happier than we have been' (Virginia to Leonard and Richard to Clarissa); speaking of 'the hours'
(Virginia to Leonard and Richard to Clarissa). The lines that are
repeated always originate with the character Virginia, either in her
writing or her dialogue. In this way, the literary author from whose
life and literary production the three stories take their cue is staged as
a narrative origin.

The three stories are rendered distinguishable from each other
implicitly by period mise-en-scène and different cast, and over the
first scenes of the film by being explicitly separated by titles—another
fairly conventional mode of establishing setting in narrative cinema.
The titles give first the location and then the year in which the stories
take place ('Sussex, England 1941'; 'Los Angeles 1951'; 'Richmond,
England 1923'; 'New York City 2001'). It is after the indication 'Los
Angeles 1951' that the opening credits also start appearing and

continue through the morning rituals of the three women. They close with the director's name just prior to the first scene where two characters (Virginia and Leonard) engage in dialogue for the first time. The dialogue closes with Virginia remarking to Leonard at his desk that she may have found her first sentence,[5] which is then promptly repeated as quote by Clarissa saying she will buy the flowers herself, and as anti-quote by Laura, reprimanding her husband for buying her flowers on his birthday, when she should be doing things for him. It is thus the dialogue spoken by the character Virginia that triggers off the narrative.

As the character Virginia is shown pondering upon and writing her novel and discussing it with her sister, her niece, and her husband, the narratives of the other two stories model themselves on both Virginia and on *Mrs Dalloway*. Laura thinks about the simplicity of suicide, knowing Virginia Woolf committed suicide just ten years earlier. In the film's story of Clarissa, Laura speaks of the (autobiographical) novel her son Richard wrote. In that book, she was made to die. Within the reality of the filmic narrative, it is this son Richard that dies. The story of Richard and Laura thus follows the progression of Virginia planning her novel. Explaining her thoughts to her niece, she says: 'I was going to kill my heroine, but I changed my mind. [...] I'm going to kill someone else instead'. In the ellipsis of the preceding dialogue quote, the film cuts from Virginia in the 1923 story to Laura in the hotel room jumping up from her fantasy of drowning (Virginia Woolf's chosen mode of suicide), and deciding against death. The film then cuts back to Virginia, who has changed her mind. In a later scene with Leonard, Virginia says, 'Someone has to die, so the rest of us value life more ... The poet will die, the visionary'. The character Virginia is thus represented as endowed with the authorial power not only to write Woolf's novel, but also to prevent the character Laura from committing suicide. This suggests that the story strands set in Los Angeles and New York are subsidiary narratives, mere variations of the chronologically earlier story strand of the author writing her novel. In the film *The Hours*, narrative techniques are employed to reinforce the authorial power of Virginia and Virginia Woolf.

---

[5] The mise-en-scène closely resembles the portrait of Leonard Woolf by Vanessa Bell, done in 1940.

Marcel/Proust

In the films *Adaptation* and *Le temps retrouvé*, the relationship between the author(s) and the texts they produce is more complex. Where *Adaptation* mobilises the credits, titles, voice-overs and
storyline to establish its semi-invented twin authors (Charlie/Donald)
as real and its real author (Susan Orlean) as a fiction (Susan), the film
Le temps retrouvé engages its author, Marcel Proust, to provide a
loose frame narrative and to undo the mythical autobiography behind
the literary production.

The film *Le temps retrouvé* provides the narrative of the novel
with a frame narrative of Marcel Proust writing the novel. One of the
reasons for this clearly resides in the perception of *A la recherche du
temps perdu* as an autobiographical fiction.[6] Unlike *Mrs Dalloway*,
The Orchid Thief, and *Romeo and Juliet*, the life of the central
character of the novel *Le temps retrouvé* has striking parallels to the
life of its author. The film, however, both affirms and contradicts the
biographical narrative in its usage of several actors for the character
Marcel. All in all, four actors (plus another one doing Marcel's voice-
overs) represent the character at different ages: as a child, as a youth,
as an adult, and as an old man. The biographical dimension is most
obviously ascertained in the casting of Marcello Mazzarella as the
adult Marcel. Not only was he picked for his physiognomic resemblance to Proust, he also imitates gestures of Proust's taken from
photos of the author. The biographical dimension is further underscored in the frame narrative, where the central character is defined as
the old Marcel Proust. The character is lying in his bed, being served
by a character named Céleste. Thus, the scene is set in Marcel Proust's
life, rather than in the life of the novel's *je*, as the name of the faithful
servant in *A la recherche du temps perdu* is Françoise, whereas
Céleste Albaret was the real-life servant of the author. In the stage
directions that appear in the script, the location is furthermore given as
'rue Hamelin', where Marcel Proust lived during the last years of his
life. The film, however, contradicts the biographical affinity by

---

[6] What is referred to as *A la recherche du temps perdu* consists of several parts
published between 1913 and 1927. *Le temps retrouvé* is the seventh and last part of *A
la recherche du temps perdu*, and like the sixth part was published in 1922, after the
death of the author.

making the character Marcel appear at the wrong age in several scenes that relate to specific biographical episodes. Thus, the child appears in a surreal sequence of scenes at the matinée in 1919 (when the historical Marcel Proust was 47) as well as in the scenes set in Venice in the company of the Grandmother. The journey to Venice historically took place in 1900, when Marcel Proust was in his late twenties, and it was undertaken in the company of his mother. The film achieves a de-familiarisation of its central protagonist, that is, a non-identification incompatible with classical narrative film, predominantly through editing and the way it stages the character within scenes: it repeats segments of the film but embeds them in different diegeses; it has a seated Marcel float through the projection space of a bar-cinema, or freeze as the background changes from Paris to Venice.

Finally, the author comes face to face with his subject: there is a scene when the child Marcel looks into the mirror and is looked at by his old self. As they talk about the book the old Marcel is writing, the child asks him if he can read it, oblivious to the fact that the old man is writing the child's own story. The child does not recognise himself in that mirror, nor is he informed of his later literary identity. This moment of non-recognition serves as an admonition reminding the spectator that Marcel Proust himself was fabricated as an author *a posteriori*: not only were his first publications initially not considered serious writing let alone masterpieces, but his writing was radically re-evaluated by literary criticism in the 1970s. Together with the de-familiarising strategies deployed in the film, this undoes a conceptualisation of the author as immutable origin and unifying principle.

Susan/Orlean and Their Adaptors

In the film *Adaptation*, the scriptwriting Kaufman twins are an addition made to Susan Orlean's novel *The Orchid Thief* (1998) directed by Spike Jonze—one a 'real' addition, the other a 'fictional' one. In the film, the real writer Charlie Kaufman becomes the character Charlie (Nicholas Cage), a professional scriptwriter who is commissioned to write an adaptation of Orlean's acclaimed *The Orchid Thief*. Orlean appears in the film as the semi-fictional character Susan. Donald Kaufman (also played by Nicholas Cage), Charlie's fictional twin brother, starts out on a scriptwriting career by attending a seminar given by Robert McKee (Brian Cox) and goes on to produce an original script.[7] It is 'original' in several respects: a wild mix of genres with a highly improbable plotline and nearly impossible to imagine on screen, it is also an 'original' script because it is not an adaptation. The character Donald—unlike Charlie, who is shown struggling to adapt Susan's/Orlean's virtually plotless *The Orchid Thief*—has to be faithful only to the principles of his scriptwriter-mentor. As the films progresses, the stories of *The Orchid Thief*, of Susan, and of the twins begin to intertwine. *Adaptation* expands the novel's narrative through the story of Charlie adapting the novel, Donald becoming a screenwriter, and through the twins' joint investigative approach to adaptation.

The film also dwells on the authorial function of the twins. Not only do they appear as the adaptors of *The Orchid Thief* in a storyline of their own, but the character Charlie is also represented as the scriptwriter on the set of *Being John Malkovich* (1999), Spike Jonze's previous film, whose script the real Charlie Kaufman also wrote. Furthermore, in the film's opening and end credits both of the twins, i.e. Charlie *and* Donald, are listed as the authors of the screenplay. By giving both twins writing credits, the film endows them with a claim to authorship on another level of reality: they can lay claim to having jointly written a screenplay just as the writer Susan Orlean can claim to have written a book. In *Adaptation*, Susan Orlean becomes the semi-fiction of Susan and Charlie Kaufman plus his twin become a semi-reality.

Adaptation stretches the narrative possibilities of titles and voice-over much further than *The Hours*. First of all, there are no absolute dates given in the titles but they are relative to the first title, 'On the Set of "Being John Malkovich" Summer 1998'. After having shown Charlie having lunch with a film producer in order to discuss what the adaptation of the book should be like, the first introduction of *The Orchid Thief* as narrative is indicated by a subtitle, 'New Yorker Magazine, Three Years Earlier'. The film leads the explanatory function of titles ad absurdum when giving a title like 'Hollywood, CA, Four Billion and Forty Years Earlier'. From the very outset, the film also destroys the illusion of a narrative unfolding within a

---

[7] The character McKee, too, is based on a real person: the writer Robert McKee, a successful screenwriting guru who teaches his 30-hour, three-day 'Story Seminar' all over the world.

beginning-middle-end structure. It does so first of all by introducing several non-beginnings. For one, the (then still unseen and unknown) character Charlie speaks in voice-over over a black screen about his failings as a writer and as a human being, establishing himself as anti-hero and the act of writing as impossible. The opening credits appear in Roman typeset in one line and in the same size throughout on the bottom of that black screen—very much like subtitles and in the font used for writing screenplays. Thus, in contradiction to Charlie's voice-over, the script is established as having been written by Charlie Kaufman and the film as having been made by those credited.

In several episodes thematising the process of scriptwriting, the film, while obviously poking fun at various approaches to the profession, also explains them. It does so by using the twins as antithetical writerly positions in the studio machinery. The opposition between the brothers is technologically demonstrated by having Charlie type on an old typewriter (as fetishised by some scriptwriters), whereas Donald produces his new writing on a laptop.[8] *Adaptation* tells the story of the character Charlie with all his doubts and scruples as to how to do justice to a book that does not have a story, but also shows him diligently marking the text for usable phrases or what he considers important, and working with a tape recorder and typing. The film also demonstrates a possible solution to the problem of the non-existent story. As Charlie's agent tells him to make up a story if there is none, so *Adaptation* itself makes up a story and adds it to *The Orchid Thief*—the story of the Kaufman twins with its action-cinema showdown in the swamp, complete with shootout and predatory alligator. When the film shows how would-be scriptwriter Donald blithely ignores all realist considerations and the limits of cinematic representation (with his schizophrenic multi-personality serial mur-derer protagonist), the film *Adaptation* provides rules of scriptwriting for narrative film. Charlie's criticism that Donald's multiple-personality protagonist cannot be realistically represented resurfaces in *Adaptation* itself when the twins played by the same actor repeat-edly appear in the same frame.

The theme of what writing means in terms of authorial power interlinks the story of *The Orchid Thief* and of its adaptation in several

---

[8] The authorial also features prominently in the film *The Hours* through repeated close-ups of Virginia Woolf's pen scratching across paper.

ways. On the one hand, the character Charlie is unable to adapt the book, because he is too much in awe of it: it is too beautiful and too complex to be reduced to a feature film, and he himself feels too inadequate as a writer to face Susan, even though he flies to New York in order to meet her. He interprets the fact that he has written himself into the screenplay as an expression of his fear of the author. In the event, it is his twin who has to go and confront the author Susan, thereby taking control of the narrative. There is, however, a dialogue exchange between Charlie and Susan prior to the narrative conjunction of the twin story and the Susan story. Like the mirror scene in *Le temps retrouvé*, the confrontation between two figures representing author(s) undermines the concept of the author as a unifying origin and legitimation: as Charlie struggles to choose the right segments of *The Orchid Thief* lying on his bed at home, looking at the back flap photo of Susan, he says he likes to look at her, to which Susan 'replies' that she likes looking at him too. Charlie then engages in full-fledged fantasy. He not only imagines himself having a prep-talk conversation with the photo of Susan, he also fantasises about having sex with her. Voice-over is used to convey his fantasy: as he speaks to the back flap photo of Susan, the film has her speak back to him in voice-over. The choice of words, 'I like looking at you too, Charlie', may be illuminatingly read in the light of cinema theory, where the gaze is the mode of address for illusionist cinema, which absorbs the spectator into its narrative and ideology (Mulvey 1975, Staiger 2001: 11-27). In this scene, the film not only uses voice-over to let Charlie engage in a fantasy of his to-be-adapted-author's goodwill towards him and from there to sexual satisfaction, it also reveals the element of fantasy operative in the soliciting of any authorial figure in the process of adaptation: just as Susan's photo cannot realistically be speaking to Charlie, film adaptation provides the *illusion* of a dialogue with a literary author in the imagination of its makers and spectators (or reviewers).

As Charlie and Donald follow Susan from New York to Florida, the title accordingly inverts the diegetic relationship. Where previous titles of the type 'X years earlier' indicated that an earlier narrative was about to be retold, one subordinated to the main diegesis of the two twins, here the two twins arrive in Florida as part of the narrative they were supposed to re-tell. The scene's title indicates not a regression in time but a progression: 'Three years later'. From now on, the narrative moves forward chronologically with the twins as the unwitting heroes in a suspense plot, as part of the narrative and not as creators of narrative.

In fact, the chronology of narrating and representing is subverted over the entire film: several scenes are first shown and later retold as the character Charlie discusses how he will adapt the book— e.g. the sequence of (pre)historic Los Angeles is retold much later by having Charlie dictate it into a handheld recorder. Not only does the scene when shown at the beginning of the film pose as an enigmatic non-sequitur opening for the narrative, but by having it re-represented the film undoes the chronology of the filmmaking process itself, where the dictating of a scene comes before its writing, let alone its shooting, editing and screening. In *Adaptation*, the story of the adaptation and the story of *The Orchid Thief* undo the process of adaptation by having the adapting author Charlie devise a scene of his film post factum, that is, after it has been shown in the film already. Furthermore, by expanding the story of *The Orchid Thief* and inserting the twins into it as homodiegetic characters rather than as heterodiegetic narrators, it relocates the question of authorial power—of who controls whom in the process of adaptation—into the dynamics of a thriller-suspense plot where Charlie survives as 'the hero'. While the last scene of the film, with the character Charlie driving along the road and saying, in interior monologue, that he will end his script with this scene (i.e. with him driving along the road), seems to subvert the conventions of illusionist narrative cinema in the doubling, it is also the moment when, for the first time, the film's adapting narrative does exactly what it says it is doing with a sense of resolution: there is no more deferment, either through already having represented the scene described as in other instances, or through immediately retracting it as unfeasible or banal writing. It is also the moment when the number of author-characters is reduced from three to one. With Donald dead, and Susan probably detained by law enforcement, Charlie is the sole authorial character left. As intention, ability, and image of Charlie coincide with Charlie Kaufman as author, the film ends with an equal degree of narrative harmony as any Hollywood movie—underscored by the previous scene in which Charlie, for the first time, manages to successfully communicate to Amelia his (amorous) feelings. However, while the ending of the film suggests resolution, what goes before remains a disjunctive enterprise. At the end of this film, ascertaining an authorial origin is rendered impossible due to its multiple beginnings, multiple author characters, and narrative additions.

Happily Ever After?

The narrative additions to the novels in these four films enable the appearance of the literary author on the screen and thus represent a return of the author. At first sight, then, such 'adaptations' appear to propagate an idea of the author as origin of and master of his/her writing. But just as the return of the author in metafiction has been read as a deconstruction of authorial power, the return of the literary source's author on screen in fact can signify a disempowerment of the author. As Luigi Cazzato formulates it, the reading of what he terms 'hard' metafiction demands not a suspension of disbelief on the part of the reader but the suspension of belief (1995: 35). Reader and spectator alike are thus persuaded not to believe in what they read or see, but to accept it as fictitious. In a certain sense, the appearance of the author on the screen does insert the writer's biography in the film, but at the same time it subverts the idea of rendering a truthful account by virtue of being a narrative construction. As historiography has redefined itself as a discipline fundamentally linked to narrative (White 1973), in filmic representation too the historical author is not necessarily obtainable through cinema's realism as objective reality, but rather appears as an additional fiction to underscore the process at work, that is, adaptation.

The added narrative in the film *Adaptation*, especially in the role-play between the able amateur writer-twin and the disabled professional writer-twin, functions as a cautionary tale on what Cazzato terms 'the possibility of cultural manipulation' inherent in the figure of an author (1995: 35). Making the author return within the fiction can dismantle him/her as an ideological figure imagined as master of his/her literary production. In the film *Le temps retrouvé*, the biographising of the central character as Marcel Proust does confirm the cultural power the author Marcel Proust has been invested with over the course of his reception, but the ways in which the figure Marcel Proust is represented (or rather his figures) undermine the concept of an omnipotent literary author. In adaptation this is a decisive move for, in particular regarding films that are based on so-called classics or modern classics, to be faithful to the text is implicitly understood as fidelity to its famous author.

What the four films all illustrate in various ways by their expansion of narrative and the return of the author as part of the narrative, is that the author him/herself becomes a narrative over the process of literary and/or filmic reproduction and over the process of reception. *Adaptation* tries to endow its writer-characters Charlie and Donald with an identity based in fiction and reality by showing them on the set of a previous film really made, where both the real Charlie Kaufman and his invented twin appear as Charlie and Donald played by one actor, and by crediting Donald among the other makers of the film. The films *The Hours* and *Le temps retrouvé* provide the spectator with an affirmative narrative of how Virginia Woolf lived and worked, and with a visualisation of Marcel Proust deconstructive in its casting multiplicities, respectively.

All of these films add narratives to that of their source literary text that relocate film and literature as cultural practices determined and shaped by a specific context. These added narratives variously include the narrativisation of the process of writing, the process of reading and the process of adapting to the screen itself. Rather than representing adaptation as an exchange of narratives between media, they thus explore the socio-cultural practice of literature and the uses made of literature by readers and by film. The various (re)appearing authors represent rather different narratives on the theme of authorship. While the overall practice of adaptation may have a vested interest in highlighting its literary origins, a mythical 'Once upon a time' of well-known literature through marketing and publicity, the author characters that appear on screen are also ideated as historical persons that were/are members of the writing profession. And unlike fairy tales, which are in most cases guaranteed a 'happily ever after', the stories of reappeared authors are open as to how and where they will end up as authorial figures in adaptation.

The final problematic legacy of defining film as a narrative art, then, is that in the cultural practice of adaptation, film is more often than not tied to certain types of literature. Film adaptation has turned to many of the nineteenth-century realist novels or literary classics from the theatre for its narrative raw material. The choice of material to be adapted thus often already produces an exclusion of certain types of literature, such as poetry. The resulting films, then, done as narrative films, enable the perpetuation of an already established literary canon, most evidently in the domain of teaching. The pedagogical usefulness of being able to supplement the reading of a realist novel by watching a film made of it renders such literature more attractive to teachers and students alike. It does not stringently exclude other types of literature from the curriculum, but it limits the possible forms in which they can be offered and made palatable to generations of students living in a culture of television, VCR and DVD, not to mention the World Wide Web. Furthermore, with the decline of reading, more often than not the only medial version of literature that reaches a wider public are its film adaptations. Adaptation can thus affirm the canonisation of authors by affirmatively representing them on film. As shown, adaptation can also, however, undo that process of cultural affirmation of a canon through narrative itself. While not all of the four films looked at in this chapter do so, adaptation can employ the narrative techniques of film conventionally used to convey the authorial in ways that work against a replicative fidelity to both the adapted text and the author. While narrativity remains a defining feature of both film and literature, it is precisely authorial narrative techniques at the disposal of film which enable both the affirmation of the idea of the author as origin and justification, as well as a critique of that idea in the process of adaptation. Depending on how voice-over, titles, and other devices are used, adaptation as an interpretative process, rather than as a transposing process aiming at fidelity, enables not only a new engagement with a literary author and his/her writing, but with the very idea of the author as such.

Bibliography

Albersmeier, F.-J. (1992) *Theater, Literatur und Film in Frankreich: Medienwechsel und Intermedialität.* Darmstadt: Wissenschaftliche Buchgesellschaft.

Andrew, D. (1980) 'The Well-Worn Muse: Adaptation in Film History and Theory', in S. Conger and J. R. Welsch (eds.) *Narrative Strategies: Original Essays in Film and Prose Fiction.* Macomb: Western Illinois University Press, 9-17.

Barthes, R. (1981 (1967)) 'The Death of the Author', in J. Caughie (ed.) *Theories of Authorship*. London: Routledge, 208-13.

Boyum, J. G. (1985) *Double Exposure: Fiction into Film*. New York: Universe Books.

Branigan, E. (1984) *Point of View in the Cinema*. Sulzburg and Berlin: Sulzburg Druck GmbH and Bauer Buchgewerbe.

Cattrysse, P. (1992) *Pour une théorie de l'adaptation filmique: le film noir américain*. Berne and Paris: Peter Lang.

Cazzato, L. (1995) 'Hard Metafiction and the Return of the Author-Subject: The Decline of Postmodernism', in J. Dowson and S. Earnshaw (eds.) *Postmodern Subjects/Postmodern Texts*. Amsterdam and Atlanta: Rodopi, 25-41.

Chatman, S. (1990) *Coming to Terms: The Rhetoric of Narrative in Fiction and Film*. Ithaca: Cornell University Press.

Cunningham, M. (1999) *The Hours*. London: Fourth Estate.

Foucault, M. (1984 (1969)) 'What is an Author?', in P. Rabinow (ed.) *The Foucault Reader*. Harmondsworth: Penguin, 101-20.

Gaudréault, A. and F. Jost (1990) *Le récit cinématographique*. Paris: Nathan.

Gelder, K. (1999) 'Jane Campion and the Limits of Literary Cinema', in D. Cartmell and I. Whelehan (eds.) *Adaptation: From Text to Screen, Screen to Text*. London and New York: Routledge, 157-71.

Géloin, G. (1988) 'The Plight of Film Adaptation in France: Toward a Dialogic Process in the *auteur* Film', in W. Aycock and M. Schoenecke (eds.) *Film and Literature. A Comparative Approach to Adaptation*. Lubbock: Texas Tech University Press, 135-48.

Green, G. L. (1988) 'The Author behind the Author: George Cukor and the Adaptation of "The Philadelphia Story"', in W. Aycock and M. Schoenecke (eds.) *Film and Literature: A Comparative Approach to Adaptation*. Lubbock: Texas Tech University Press, 69-79.

McFarlane, B. (1996) *Novel to Film: An Introduction to the Theory of Adaptation*. Oxford: Clarendon.

Mulvey, L. (1975) 'Visual Pleasure and Narrative Cinema', *Screen* 16 (3), 6-18.

Orlean, S. (1998) *The Orchid Thief*. New York: Random House.

Sconce, J. (1995) 'Narrative Authority and Social Narrativity: The Cinematic Reconstitution of Brontë's *Jane Eyre*', in J. Staiger (ed.) *The Studio System*. New Brunswick: Rutgers University Press, 140-62.

Seitz, G. (1981) *Film als Rezeptionsform von Literatur*. Munich: Tuduv Verlagsgesellschaft.

Sheen, E. (2000) 'Where the Garment Gapes: Faithfulness and Promiscuity in the 1995 BBC *Pride and Prejudice*', in R. Giddings and E. Sheen (eds.) *The Classic Novel: From Text to Screen*. Manchester: Manchester University Press, 14-30.

Staiger, J. (2000) *Perverse Spectator: The Practices of Film Reception*. New York and London: New York University Press.

Uricchio, W. and R. E. Pearson (1993) *Reframing Culture: The Case of the Vitagraph Quality Films*. Princeton: Princeton University Press.

White, H. (1973) *Metahistory: The Historical Imagination in Nineteenth-Century Europe*. Baltimore: Johns Hopkins University Press.

Filmography

Daldry, S. dir. (2002) *The Hours*. Paramount/Miramax.

Jonze, S. dir. (2002) *Adaptation*. Columbia/Intermedia Films.

Madden, J. dir. (1999) *Shakespeare in Love*. Miramax/Universal.

Ruiz, R. dir. (1999) *Le temps retrouvé*. Gemini Films/France 2 Cinéma/Les Films du Lendemain/Blu Cinématografica.

The Adapter as Auteur: Hitchcock, Kubrick, Disney

Thomas Leitch

The careers of Alfred Hitchcock, Stanley Kubrick, and Walt Disney show the ways in which certain filmmakers whose body of work consists almost exclusively of films based on material adapted from another medium have risen from the ranks of metteurs-en-scène to become auteurs. Their success in establishing themselves as auteurs depends less in each case on any artistic aspirations of the filmmaker or textual features of the films, than on the filmmaker's success in establishing control over a diverse series of projects, defeating the claims of potentially competing auteurs (producers, directors, writers, stars), and projecting a public persona capable of being turned into an appealing and recognisable trademark.

Auteurs, Metteurs-en-scène, Adapters

It is ironic that François Truffaut's seminal essay 'A Certain Tendency of French Cinema' bequeathed the term *auteur* to critical discourse, since the central subject of Truffaut's withering survey was the *metteur-en-scène,* the mere scene-setter who functioned as the auteur's opposite. Unlike Jean Renoir and Robert Bresson, who create their own cinematic worlds, metteurs-en-scène merely furnish and photograph what Truffaut calls the literary worlds of their screenplays. 'Scenarists' films', Truffaut sniffs of the work of Jean Aurenche and Pierre Bost: 'When they hand in their scenario, the film is done; the *metteur-en-scène* is the gentleman who adds the pictures to it' (Truffaut 1976: 1, 233). Since Truffaut, the term has largely fallen into disuse, replaced by the term *adapter,* even though adapters ought logically to be screenwriters rather than directors. The term metteur-en-scène could profitably be resurrected, for example, to describe at least two sorts of filmmakers: the anonymous directors at Granta and the BBC who toil over often highly-regarded adaptations of literary classics from *The Golden Bowl* (1972) to *Pride and Prejudice* (1995), and the more visible partnership of Ismail Merchant and James Ivory, whose devotion to the literary values of their sources has made them, if the formula is not too contradictory, the leading auteurs among contemporary metteurs-en-scène, filmmakers who have become famous precisely for placing their craft first and foremost at the service of their great originals.

Although it might seem that metteurs-en-scène and auteurs represent polar opposites defined in absolute contradistinction to one another, many directors whose films are based largely on literary adaptations have nonetheless established a reputation as auteurs. Several of Ernst Lubitsch's greatest films, from *Trouble in Paradise* (1932) to *The Shop Around the Corner* (1940), are adaptations of a series of forgotten Hungarian plays. Orson Welles, who wrote or co-wrote all his screenplays, rarely tackled an original subject after *Citizen Kane* (1940). Even most of Bresson's key films are adaptations of novels. Why do some adapters remain metteurs-en-scène while others avoid or outgrow the label? The careers of three unquestioned auteurs whose body of work consisted almost entirely of adaptations—Alfred Hitchcock, Stanley Kubrick, and Walt Disney—suggest that the auteur status of filmmakers depends at least as much on their temperament and working habits, their triumphs in conflicts with other aspiring authors, and their success at turning themselves into brand names, as on their artistic aspirations or any textual features of their films.

The Genre Trademark as Auteur

Audiences long accustomed to Hitchcock's signature traits— his close identification with a single genre, his cameo appearances, his cherubically corpulent figure tricked out in a series of outrageous costumes for the prologues and epilogues to the long-running television series *Alfred Hitchcock Presents*—may well have forgotten that most of Hitchcock's films were adaptations. Among his fourteen films before his breakout thriller *The Man Who Knew Too Much* (1934), only two, *The Ring* (1927) and *Champagne* (1928), were based on original screenplays, and many of his early credits cast him as the metteur-en-scène of such properties as *Easy Virtue* (1927), *The Manxman* (1929), *Juno and the Paycock* (1930), and *The Skin Game*

(1931), whose credits describe it as 'a talking picture by John Galsworthy'. Despite the prophetic freedom with which *Sabotage* (1937) adapted its great original, Joseph Conrad's *The Secret Agent* (1907), David O. Selznick, after luring England's star director to America, consistently treated Hitchcock as a metteur-en-scène rather than an auteur.

The resulting conflict over Hitchcock's notorious first treatment for *Rebecca* (1940), which began with a farcical scene in which a cigar-smoking Maxim de Winter made his shipboard guests seasick, seems inevitable only because we think of Hitchcock as an auteur. But the freedom Hitchcock had taken with Daphne du Maurier's best-selling novel left Selznick 'shocked and disappointed beyond words'. In a stinging memo to Hitchcock, Selznick, who would assure du Maurier of 'my intention to do the book and not some botched-up semioriginal [like] ... *Jamaica Inn* [1939]', laid down the formula that distinguishes auteurs from metteurs-en-scène: 'We bought *Rebecca*, and we intend to make *Rebecca*' (Selznick 1972: 266-72, 266). Years later, Hitchcock summarised his own auteurist attitude toward adaptation equally trenchantly in his interview with Truffaut: 'There's been a lot of talk about the way Hollywood directors distort literary masterpieces. I'll have no part of that! What I do is to read a story only once, and if I like the basic idea, I just forget all about the book and start to create cinema' (Truffaut 1984: 71).

Hitchcock's graduation from the metteur-en-scène of *Juno and the Paycock* to the auteur of *Strangers on a Train* (1951), *Rear Window* (1954), and even *Dial M for Murder* (1953), whose screenplay by Frederick Knott follows Knott's play almost line for line, was gradual and laborious. The process begins in Hitchcock's films of the 1940s, especially his loanouts from the literary-minded Selznick, which include both more free adaptations like *Foreign Correspondent* (1940) and *Suspicion* (1941) and more original screenplays like *Saboteur* (1942), *Shadow of a Doubt* (1943), *Lifeboat* (1944), and *Notorious* (1946). Surprisingly, Hitchcock's two films as an independent producer for Transatlantic Pictures, *Rope* (1948) and *Under Capricorn* (1949), are not notable for any striking departures from their sources; indeed, the long takes that are the principal innovation of both films might be described as an attempt to be as faithful as possible to the claustrophobia of Patrick Hamilton's stagebound play and the romantic period detail of Helen Simpson's novel respectively.

By the time Transatlantic folded in 1950, however, Hitchcock, bound
for a series of new studio contracts that gave him far greater freedom
than he had enjoyed under Selznick, who had always treated him as a
metteur-en-scène, was evidently determined to make and market his
films as Hitchcock originals.

In order to establish himself as an auteur, however, Hitchcock
had to wrest authorship of his films away from another plausible
candidate: the author of the original property. Here he was helped by
his close identification with a powerful Hollywood genre and the
obscurity of his literary sources, an obscurity he deliberately cultivated by his refusal to make films based on classic novels like *Crime
and Punishment* whose authorship would leave no room for his own.
Avoiding brand-name authors like Dostoevsky, Hitchcock created his
own brand-name franchise by steamrolling authors whose work he
coveted. By bidding through intermediaries who kept his name secret,
he was able to purchase the rights to *Strangers on a Train, The
Trouble with Harry* (1955), and *Psycho* (1960) cheaply, to the consid-
erable chagrin of all three novelists. Once he had purchased their
properties, he banished the authors; only Frederick Knott and Leon
Uris, the best-selling author of *Topaz* (1967), were invited to work on
the screenplays based on their books. Instead the films were retooled
as Hitchcock originals that promised not the literary values of their
properties but the reliable generic thrills, set-pieces, and ironic yet
reassuringly familiar markers of the Hitchcock universe: mysterious
doubles, icy blondes, sinister staircases, brandy snifters, and the
explosion of self-references in *Frenzy* (1972).

Even though Hitchcock continued to rely on literary sources—
among all his films after *Rope,* only *North by Northwest* (1959) and
Torn Curtain (1966) are based on original screenplays—he deliberately avoided literary cachet as an area in which he could not successfully compete and instead embraced a generic identification that he
was able to promote through his carefully crafted public image as well
as his films. His success in turning his own corporeal presence into a
trademark in his cameo appearances, his witty endpapers to *Alfred
Hitchcock Presents* and *The Alfred Hitchcock Hour* beginning in
1955, the coeval monthly mystery magazine and the later board game
to which he lent his name and image, and even the signature eight-
stroke silhouette with which he often signed autographs established
him as the quintessential directorial brand name, an auteur capable of

eclipsing authors whose claim to authority was simply less powerful. And the mark of this success was the fact that early champions of Hitchcock's work like Andrew Sarris and Robin Wood did not dismiss the claims of traditional literary aesthetics in assessing Hitchcock's films, but retained those terms as a basis on which to pronounce Hitchcock superior to the forgettable authors whose work his films adapted—a stance that until recently remained uncontested by Hitchcock scholars, who by and large ignored his literary sources (Barr 1999: 8-12).

The Craftsperson as Auteur

Hitchcock, so averse to conflict that he once left Ingrid Bergman's tirade on the set of *Under Capricorn* twenty minutes before Bergman noticed his absence, preferred to finesse around the authors he eventually eclipsed beneath the success of his generic branding. Stanley Kubrick, by contrast, earned his auteur status the old-fashioned way: by taking on authors directly in open warfare. Just as the crucial period in the rise of Hitchcock the auteur was the 1940s and 1950s, the much shorter pivotal period for Kubrick was the 1960s, the very period that film studies were first entering the academy under the banner of auteurism. At the beginning of the decade, he was a moderately successful genre director associated with war and crime films; by decade's end, the release of *2001: A Space Odyssey* (1968) and *Clockwork Orange* (1971) confirmed his status as one of the most strikingly individualistic auteurs in or out of Hollywood. Kubrick transformed himself from metteur-en-scène to auteur mostly by his work, and his increasingly skilled infighting, on three films: *Spartacus* (1960), *Lolita* (1962), and *Dr. Strangelove; or, How I Learned to Stop Worrying and Love the Bomb* (1964).

Weeks before arriving on *Spartacus* at the request of its executive producer and star, Kirk Douglas, Kubrick had parted ways with another powerful star, Marlon Brando, who, having hired him to direct *One-Eyed Jacks* (1961), clashed with him over the story's shape and casting and ended up directing the film himself. Douglas, watching Anthony Mann lose control of the sprawling Roman epic after only three weeks of shooting, was eager to hand the project over to Kubrick, who had directed him in *Paths of Glory* (1957) as the first of a projected multi-picture deal. But the atmosphere on the set of

Spartacus was just as combustible. Male prima donnas like Laurence Olivier, Charles Laughton, and Peter Ustinov—'guys who are bigger than any director', Kubrick's friend Norman Lloyd recalled (LoBrutto 1997: 178)—jousted with the famously volatile Douglas and with each other over blockings and line readings.

Remarkably, the screenwriters managed to be equally quarrelsome. Because principal screenwriter Dalton Trumbo was still blacklisted and scorned by Howard Fast, author of the novel the film was adapting, his authorship was hidden by the front writer Edward Lewis and the fictitious 'Sam Jackson', the two names credited on the shooting script. When Lewis indicated his unwillingness to accept either that credit or sole credit for the screenplay, there seemed no solution but to credit the screenplay under a pseudonym—a tactic Douglas deplored—until Kubrick, who had taken screen credit for writing each of his earlier features, suddenly suggested, 'Use my name'. When Douglas asked, 'Stanley, wouldn't you feel embarrassed to put your name on a script that someone else wrote?', Kubrick, looking puzzled, said that he wouldn't (Douglas 1988: 323). Although a 'revolted' Douglas resolved the problem by crediting Trumbo under his own name, Kubrick had made his point: the brains behind the film were, or ought to be, his. Yet editor Robert Lawrence reported that Kubrick 'never really would agree to the concept that this was his movie' (LoBrutto 1997: 184), and Kubrick described his status to Joseph Gelmis as 'just a hired hand' (Gelmis 1970: 294). The lesson he drew from this experience was to avoid projects on which a strong producer or star could withhold the control he craved.

It might seem paradoxical, then, that his next film, *Lolita*, perhaps 'the biggest creative watershed in Kubrick's career' (Kagan 2000: 104), was based on a well-known novel by an author who received sole screen credit for the screenplay—the only time in his career Kubrick voluntarily relinquished such a credit. But the withdrawal was merely a strategy by Kubrick and his partner, producer James B. Harris, who had amused Kirk Douglas throughout *Paths of Glory* by posting 'HARRIS-KUBRICK' signs wherever they could (Douglas 1988: 275). Having sold their rights to Kubrick's caper film *The Killing* (1956) in order to raise the $75,000 Vladimir Nabokov asked for the screen rights to his censor-baiting novel, Kubrick and Harris had every intention of capitalising on the author's name as a cardinal selling point in marketing *Lolita*. When Nabokov resisted their invitation to write the screenplay himself, they pressed him further after several months until he finally agreed, turning out an adaptation that ran to 400 typescript pages. Enjoined to cut his work to filmable length, Nabokov obliged with a highly original 200-page version whose general outline Kubrick followed even though he proceeded to revise Nabokov's dialogue virtually line by line, often restoring material from the novel Nabokov had carefully deleted or transformed in his own screenplay and swearing the actors to secrecy. Kubrick's concern lest the author discover what was happening to his screenplay was abundantly justified. When the completed film was screened privately for Nabokov, he realised that 'only ragged odds and ends of my script had been used' and complained in the Foreword to his own screenplay, published with still further revisions in 1973, that 'most of the [newly invented] sequences were not really better than those I had so carefully composed for Kubrick, and I keenly regretted the waste of my time while admiring Kubrick's fortitude in enduring for six months the evolution and infliction of a useless product' (Nabokov 1996: 675-76).

Kubrick's experience on both *Spartacus* and *Lolita* illustrates a revealing split among the different functions of authorship. In *Spartacus,* Kubrick grasped at the most obvious mark of the cinematic auteur, the credit as writer/director which would stamp the film as a Kubrick property rather than the property of Kirk Douglas, Dalton Trumbo, or Howard Fast, without being able to assume the primary task of shaping the dramatic material into a distinctive world. *Lolita,* by contrast, shows him attempting to appropriate the opposite func-tions of authorship—the right to invent new scenes, revise dialogue, and approve or reject Peter Sellers's on-set improvisations as Clare Quilty—while just as deliberately farming out its most visible sign of public attribution to an author who could contribute prestige value and head off the censors' most high-handed objections to the whole nature of the story of a middle-aged man with an irresistible lust for his prepubescent stepdaughter. Whether the press thought Nabokov's novel was a literary classic or a pornographic fantasy, it would be far better to have Nabokov's name on the screenplay, even if Kubrick had essentially rewritten it, even to the point of removing the cameo appearance Nabokov wrote himself as a butterfly collector (Nabokov 1996: 769-70) and substituting his own authorial signature, a pair of framing references in which Quilty is first seen pretending to be

Spartacus, waiting for someone to 'come to free the slaves or something', and is last described as 'on his way to Hollywood to write one of those spectaculars'.

In the middle of shooting the film, Kubrick took pains to establish his own claims to the film's authorship when he contended that directing was nothing 'more or less than a continuation of the writing' and observed that a psychological novel like *Lolita* was 'the perfect novel from which to make a movie' because it gave the adapter 'an absolute compass bearing ... on what a character is thinking or feeling at any given moment in the story' which allowed him, as the adaptation's author, to 'invent action which will be an objective correlative of the book's psychological content'. Asked how anyone could possibly adapt *Lolita* to the screen, he replied: 'To take the prose style as any more than just a part of a great book is simply to misunderstand what a great book is ... Style is what an artist uses to fascinate the beholder in order to convey to him his feelings and emotions and thoughts. These are what have to be dramatised, not the style. The dramatising has to find a style of its own' (Kubrick 1977: 306-8). Twenty-five years after Nabokov's screenplay earned the film's only Oscar nomination, however, Kubrick acknowledged his failure to find a cinematic equivalent for Nabokov's voice when he told an interviewer: 'If it had been written by a lesser author, it might have been a better film' (LoBrutto 1997: 225). Kubrick's search for greater control led him to produce as well as direct all his subsequent films; his search for a lesser author took him first to Peter George, whose 1958 novel *Red Alert* provided a textbook illustration of what Kubrick called 'people's virtually listless acquiescence in the possibility—in fact, the increasing probability—of nuclear war' (Walker *et al.* 1999: 114).

Originally cast in the form of straightforward antiwar melodrama like *On the Beach* (1959) or *Fail-Safe* (1964), or indeed like *Paths of Glory*, *Dr. Strangelove*, which he had begun 'with every intention of making [it] a serious treatment of the problem of accidental nuclear war', took on a life of its own: 'As I kept trying to imagine the way in which things would really happen, ideas kept coming to me which I would discard because they were so ludicrous. I kept saying to myself, "I can't do this. People will laugh". But after a month or so I began to realise that all the things I was throwing out were the things that were most truthful'. So Kubrick resolved that 'the only way to tell the story was as a black comedy or, better, a nightmare comedy where the things you laugh at most are really the heart of the paradoxical postures that make a nuclear war possible' (Gelmis 1970: 309).

Once he had reached the decision to turn *Dr. Strangelove* into a nightmare comedy, Kubrick brought satirist Terry Southern in to pump up the sex jokes and outrageous proper names (Jack D. Ripper, Lionel Mandrake, Buck Turgidson, Merkin Muffley, Dmitri Kissoff, Bat Guano) that increasingly displaced George's emphasis on serious ideological opposition to the Red Menace and fear of death as the engine of the film's race to destruction. The Doomsday Machine, designed to counter any nuclear attack with retaliatory world-wide destruction beyond the possibility of human intervention, General Ripper's reflexive ascription of his temporary impotence to a communist plot to fluoridate drinking water, and Dr. Strangelove, whose artificial arm keeps rising reflectively in a Nazi salute, all became metaphors for the characters' attempts to purge themselves of all humanity in order to embrace a system of lockstep beliefs and actions they foolishly believed would save them from the mortal frailties that made them human.

The catastrophic embrace of dehumanisation, once Kubrick uncovered it, became the formative theme of all his later films from *2001* to *Eyes Wide Shut* (1999), the one that most firmly enshrined him as an auteur in critics' eyes. Yet Kubrick's auteur status depended at least equally on the work habits these three films showcased: his obsessive attention to detail, his domination of every aspect of production from screenwriting to special effects editing, his need to stamp every one of his films as his regardless of the competing claims of writers, producers, and stars. Although Kubrick was every bit as dictatorial as Hitchcock in his temperament, his auteurist persona was different in crucial ways. Unlike Hitchcock, who turned his public persona into a voluble trademark for a transmedia genre franchise, Kubrick, retreating to England to produce a series of non-genre films marked by thematic affinities and ever-lengthening intervals in between, became identified with individual craftsmanship. The image of the last solitary romantic artist who embraced the technology of cinema only to recoil from its chilling institutional implications—an image dovetailing equally well with his films' fear of technology and technologising and with the heroically individualistic auteurs canon-

ised by the emerging academic field of film studies—was promoted
equally by the films and the filmmaker's reclusive public persona.

The Paterfamilias as Auteur

If Hitchcock represented the adapter/auteur as generic trademark and Kubrick the adapter/auteur as solitary artist, Walt Disney
managed to combine both figures. It might seem odd to consider
Disney as either adapter or auteur, since he neither wrote nor directed
any of the features for which he is best remembered. And yet Disney
is clearly both adapter and auteur, since all the Disney features before
The Lion King (1994) were based on earlier stories or novels, and they
were all marketed as products of Disney and no one else.

The rise of the Disney trademark is marked by two pivotal
reversals in Disney's ascent. The first is his loss of control in 1928 of
Oswald the Lucky Rabbit, the animated hero Disney had brainstormed
and Ub Iwerks animated, to Universal Studios and distributor Charles
Mintz, who had hired most of Oswald's animators away from Disney's studio. Furiously refusing to accept Universal's offer to finance
the Oswald shorts in return for half the profits and recognition of their
copyright to the character, Disney, who had forthrightly renamed the
Disney Brothers Studio the Walt Disney Studio as early as 1925,
broke with Mintz, renounced all rights to Oswald, and worked with
Iwerks to create Mickey Mouse, whose third short, *Steamboat Willie*
(1928), used innovative synch-sound techniques to make him a star.
Still stung by the memory of his failure to share any of the royalties
from Oswald's reproduction on badges or candy boxes and by the
distributors who had written to the studio asking for Oswald's auto-
graph instead of his creator's (Mosley 1985: 93-94), Disney vowed
that he would never again create a character or a film whose name
could be separated from his own.

This stance may seem paradoxical in view of the fact that
Disney's shorts had depended from the beginning—*Little Red Riding
Hood* (1922), *The Four Musicians of Bremen* (1922), and *Jack and the
Beanstalk* (1922)—on adapting familiar stories. Even Disney's best-
known pre-Oswald franchise, the 57 'Alice Comedies' (1923-27),
took off from a short, *Alice's Wonderland* (1923), whose heroine's
live-action/animated visit to an animation studio and Cartoonland
traded on the title and premise of Lewis Carroll's children's classic.

Not until Mickey Mouse's coattails had made Walt Disney a house-hold name did the studio attempt such original shorts as *Flowers and Trees* (1932) and *The Old Mill* (1937), now trading on Disney's name instead of Mickey's. The studio's first feature, *Snow White and the Seven Dwarfs* (1937), remained within the genre of the fairy tale less because of its literary cachet than because of its familiar genre.

Disney's one early flirtation with frankly upscale cultural values marked a second pivotal reversal in his career. Following the success of *Snow White and the Seven Dwarfs,* the studio embarked on a project called *The Concert Feature* whose premise, the attempt to provide animated visuals for such classical musical selections as Bach's *Toccata and Fugue in D Minor* and Beethoven's *Pastoral Symphony,* marked the only time in his career when Disney would act as a metteur-en-scène. The result, released as *Fantasia* (1940), was a financial flop that belied Disney's prediction that the film 'makes our other pictures look immature, and suggests for the first time what the future of the medium may well turn out to be', and stopped his plans 'to make a new version of *Fantasia* every year', or at least to update the film by constantly shuffling different sequences into and out of its loose continuity (Solomon 1995: 126, 121). Instead, the studio returned to free narrative adaptations of fairy-tale properties whose authors, unlike Beethoven and Leopold Stokowski, could not compete with Disney because they were indeterminate (*Snow White* and *Cinderella,* 1950), defunct (*Alice in Wonderland,* 1951; *Peter Pan,* 1953), or as obscure as the novelists Hitchcock's expanding trademark effaced (*Pinocchio,* 1940; *Dumbo,* 1941; *Bambi,* 1942).

Although he did not write or direct any of these features, or indeed more than a handful of his animated shorts after 1930, Disney maintained his status as their auteur by the simple expedient of claiming their most prominent credits. When his employees at the Walt Disney Studios, whose numbers had grown from 150 to 750 during the production of *Snow White,* demanded fuller credits on the completed film, Disney, who had suppressed all but Iwerks's name on the credits of his silent shorts, added so many names in such tiny type that his own name was the only one that stood out. Nor did the seventy-two contributors credited include either Jacob or Wilhelm Grimm, whose version of the story served as the film's basis, or any of the performers who supplied the characters' voices or whose rotoscoped bodies served as the models for their animated images.

Adriana Caselotti, the young Italian soprano who voiced Snow White, was not only uncredited but forbidden, according to persistent rumours, to accept an invitation from Jack Benny's radio program when Disney ruled that by contract her voice belonged to him, not her.[1]

What may seem like Disney's dictatorial control over his productions' marketing should be seen in the light of two mitigating factors. One is the general invisibility of children's authors, whether or not their work was adapted by Disney, between the death of L. Frank Baum, the self-styled 'Royal Historian of Oz', in 1919 and the fame Theodore Geisel won as Dr. Seuss not with his first picture book, *And to Think That I Saw It on Mulberry Street* (1937), but with his innovative primer for new readers, *The Cat in the Hat* (1957). Throughout the period of Disney's early animated features, the by-lines of the best-known children's franchises were either subordinated to those of their publishers (e.g. Golden Books, the early-childhood picture books whose gold bindings were their most distinctive feature) or actually created by the publishers (most notably the Stratemeyer Syndicate, whose anonymous and interchangeable authors produced among many other series Nancy Drew and the Hardy Boys). The other is Disney's paternalism toward his employees, whose unionising efforts he staunchly resisted because he saw their enterprise as a utopian 'community of artists ... where work and leisure—perhaps even family life—could be totally integrated to the benefit of all' (Schickel 1997: 191). In subsuming the work of hundreds of creators and craftsmen under an individual signature as imperious as the writing credit Kubrick offered to take on *Spartacus* and as graphically recognisable as Hitchcock's drawn or photographed silhouette, Disney presented himself as an artisan or craftsman in the Kubrick mould who could recount homespun tales of his youth drafting cartoons in a Kansas City garage (in an eerie prefiguration of the story told by the founders of Hewlett-Packard), while still following the general tendency of children's mass-produced entertainment to emphasise the centralised, paternalistic creation of a utopian imaginative world whose trademark had the widest possible application.

---

[1]   See, for example, <http://us.imdb.com/name/nm0143314/bio>, <http://web. ukonline.co.uk/m.gratton/Ladies%201st%20-%20A.htm>, and <http://www.findad-eath.com/Decesed/ c/Adriana%20Caselotti/adriana_caselotti.htm>.

Disney's emergence as a transmedia brand name, which coincided with Hitchcock's in the mid-1950s, was sparked by three successive developments. First was the extension of the Disney franchise to two kinds of live-action films, a nature series beginning with *Seal Island* (1948), inspired by the frequent need of the studios' animators for live footage of animals who could serve as models for characters they were developing, and a series of fictional narratives beginning with *Treasure Island* (1950), both series billed under Disney's name although they were linked to the studio's animated films neither by agency nor by any visual resemblance. Second was the opening of Disneyland, a theme-park utopia whose visitors could briefly live the Disney dream, in 1954. Third was the premiere of *The Mickey Mouse Club* in 1955, giving Walt Disney an in-person television venue that made him quite as visible, and ultimately more influential, than Hitchcock's. *The Mickey Mouse Club* had many more features—a relatively constant cast of Mouseketeers, ongoing stories like *Spin and Marty,* themed days of the week like 'Exploring Day', 'Circus Day', and 'Anything Can Happen Day'—that unified the series than *Alfred Hitchcock Presents,* which depended on Hitchcock as its main continuing feature. But Disney's smiling face and avuncular manner were the sole features that linked *The Mickey Mouse Club,* whose afternoon airtime aimed at an audience of children, to *Disneyland* (1954; later redubbed *Disney's Sunday Movie, Walt Disney Presents, Walt Disney's Wonderful World of Colour,* and, after Disney's death, *The Wonderful World of Disney*), the prime-time hour aimed more generally at family audiences.

By this time, the maintenance of the brand name had become routine and its power imperialistic. The studio, which had always had a sharp ear for the distinctive voices of character actors from Billy Gilbert to Sterling Holloway, buried the identities of the performers who supplied its cartoon characters' voices in interminable lists of newsprint credits unless their fame could promote the films rather than the other way around. Disney's reach would soon extend to a truly distinguished list of authors whose work the studio had adapted, including J. M. Barrie, Jules Verne, Rudyard Kipling, and T. H. White. New authors would be considered for adaptation only if they agreed to make their characters available to the company's merchandising arm and agree to forgo any future claims concerning the results, and Disney attorneys became legendary for their vigilance in detecting possible infringements of the company's valuable copyright of material it had more often adapted than created. When Cynthia Lindsay described Disney in 1960 as 'the well-known author of *Alice in Wonderland,* the *Complete Works* of William Shakespeare, and the *Encyclopaedia Britannica*' (Schickel 1997: 113), she was only confirming popular belief in his status not only as the author of the films he neither wrote nor directed, but, in an unparalleled back-formation of marketing, of their original properties, now frequently reissued in children's versions as *Walt Disney's 20,000 Leagues Under the Sea* or *Walt Disney's The Jungle Book.*

The opening of Walt Disney World in 1971 and EPCOT Center, a true merchandising utopia, in 1982, marked a triumphant demonstration of the franchise's ability to survive the demise of its namesake in 1966. As Disney's direct involvement in his properties had diminished, the imperialistic power of his status as auteur had steadily increased, even though he functioned less as creator than as co-ordinator, impresario, merchandiser, enforcer, and ultimately, though his still-recognisable signature, corporate logo. The widely-remarked renascence of the studio's animation unit with *The Little Mermaid* (1989), *Beauty and the Beast* (1991), and *Aladdin* (1992) marked still another triumph of transmedia corporate hegemony, flooding the marketplace with *Aladdin* storybooks, costumes, lunchboxes, action figures, video games, and Happy Meals under the guise of individual craftsmanship implied by the promise of returning to Walt Disney's values and vision.

Yet it would be a mistake to think of the corporate model of Disney's continuing success as an exception to the general rules of authorship whereby adapters can aspire to the condition of auteurs. No less than Disney do Hitchcock and Kubrick imply corporate models of authorship that seek to hide any signs of corporate production beneath the apparently creative hand of a single author whose work—that is, whose intentions, whose consistency, whose paternal individual care for the franchise, even if that franchise is as suspenseful as Hitch-cock's, as prickly as Kubrick's, or as horrific as Stephen King's—can be trusted. Auteurs of this sort are made, not born; they emerge victorious in battle with competing auteurs, whether writers, produc-ers, or stars; and their authorial stamp is less closely connected with original creation than with brand-name consistency and reliability, from Hitchcock's suavely amusing scares to Disney's wholesome family entertainment. Rising from the ranks of metteur-en-scène to the status of auteur depends on an alignment of several marketable factors: thematic consistency, association with a popular genre, an appetite for the co-ordination and control of outsized projects, sensitivity to the possibility of broad appeal in such disparate media as movies, television, books, magazines, and T-shirts. Perhaps the most indispensable of these factors is a public persona—Hitchcock's archly ghoulish gravity, Kubrick's fiercely romantic quest for control, Disney's mild paternalism—that can be converted to a trademark more powerful than any of the other authorial trademarks with which it will inevitably compete. Such an account of the rise of cinematic auteurs, if pursued to its logical conclusion, would raise pointed questions about the provenance and construction of literary authorship itself.

Bibliography

'Adriana Caselotti'. On-Line. Available HTTP: http://www.findadeath.com/Decesed/c/Adriana%20Caselotti/adriana_caselotti.htm (30 October 2003).

Barr, C. (1999) *English Hitchcock.* Moffat: Cameron & Hollis.

'Biography for Adriana Caselotti'. On-line. Available HTTP: http://us.imdb.com/name/nm0143314/bio (30 October 2003).

Douglas, K. (1988) *The Ragman's Son: An Autobiography.* New York: Simon and Schuster.

Gelmis, J. (1970) *The Film Director as Superstar.* Garden City: Doubleday.

'Her Name Is A—'. On-line. Available HTTP: http://web.uk-online.co.uk/m.gratton/Ladies%201st%20-%20A.htm (30 October 2003).

Kagan, N. (2000 (1972)) *The Cinema of Stanley Kubrick.* New York: Continuum.

Kubrick, S. (1977 (1960-61)) 'Words and Movies', in R. Koszarski. *Hollywood Directors: 1941-1976.* New York: Oxford University Press, 306-9.

LoBrutto, V. (1997) *Stanley Kubrick: A Biography.* New York: Donald I. Fine.

Mosley, L. (1985) *The Real Walt Disney: A Biography*. London: Grafton.

Nabokov, V. (1996 (1973)) *Lolita: A Screenplay*, in V. Nabokov. *Novels 1955-1962*. New York: Library of America.

Schickel, R. (1997 (1968)) *The Disney Version: The Life, Times, Art and Commerce of Walt Disney*. Chicago: Ivan R. Dee.

Selznick, D. O. (1972) *Memo from David O. Selznick*. Ed. Rudy Behlmer. New York: Viking.

Solomon, C. (1995) *The Disney That Never Was: The Stories and Art from Five Decades of Unproduced Animation*. New York: Hyperion.

Truffaut, F. (1976 (1954)) 'A Certain Tendency of the French Cinema', in B. Nichols (ed.) *Movies and Methods*. Vol. I. Berkeley: University of California Press, 224-37.

——— (1984 (1967)) *Hitchcock*. New York: Simon and Schuster.

Walker, A. *et al*. (1999) *Stanley Kubrick, Director*. New York: Norton.

Filmography

Algar, J. dir. (1948) *Seal Island*. Disney.

Allers, R. and R. Minkoff. dir. (1994) *The Lion King*. Disney.

Brando, M. dir. (1961) *One-Eyed Jacks*. Paramount.

Cellan Jones, J. dir. (1972) *The Golden Bowl*. BBC.

Clements, R. and J. Musker. dir. (1992) *Aladdin*. Disney.

Disney, W. dir. (1922a) *Little Red Riding Hood*. Laugh-O-gram.

——— (1922b) *The Four Musicians of Bremen*. Laugh-O-gram.

——— (1922c) *Jack and the Beanstalk*. Laugh-O-gram.

——— (1923) *Alice's Wonderland*. Laugh-O-gram.

——— and U. Iwerks. dir. (1928) *Steamboat Willie*. Disney.

Geronimi, C. and W. Jackson. dir. (1950) *Cinderella*. Disney.

——— (1951) *Alice in Wonderland*. Disney.

Gillett, B. dir. (1932) *Flowers and Trees*. Disney.

Hand, D. supervising dir. (1937) *Snow White and the Seven Dwarfs*. Disney.

——— dir. (1942) *Bambi*. Disney.

Haskin, B. dir. (1950) *Treasure Island*. RKO/Disney.

Hitchcock, A. dir. (1927a) *Easy Virtue*. Gainsborough.

——— (1927b) *The Ring*. British International.

—— (1928) *Champagne*. British International.
—— (1929) *The Manxman*. British International.
—— (1930) *Juno and the Paycock*. British International.
—— (1931) *The Skin Game*. British International.
—— (1934) *The Man Who Knew Too Much*. Gaumont-British.
—— (1937) *Sabotage*. Gaumont-British.
—— (1939) *Jamaica Inn*. Mayflower.
—— (1940a) *Foreign Correspondent*. Walter Wanger Productions.
—— (1940b) *Rebecca*. Selznick International.
—— (1941) *Suspicion*. RKO.
—— (1942) *Saboteur*. Universal.
—— (1943) *Shadow of a Doubt*. Universal.
—— (1944) *Lifeboat*. 20th Century–Fox.
—— (1946) *Notorious*. RKO.
—— (1948) *Rope*. Transatlantic.
—— (1949) *Under Capricorn*. Transatlantic.
—— (1951) *Strangers on a Train*. Warner Bros.
—— (1953) *Dial M for Murder*. Warner Bros.
—— (1954) *Rear Window*. Paramount.
—— (1955) *The Trouble with Harry*. Paramount.
—— (1959) *North by Northwest*. MGM.
—— (1960) *Psycho*. Paramount.
—— (1966) *Torn Curtain*. Universal.
—— (1972) *Frenzy*. Universal.
Jackson, W. dir. (1937) *The Old Mill*. Disney.
—— *et al*. dir. (1953) *Peter Pan*. Disney.
Kramer, S. dir. (1959) *On the Beach*. United Artists.
Kubrick, S. dir. (1956) *The Killing*. James B. Harris/United Artists.
—— (1957) *Paths of Glory*. Bryna/United Artists.
—— (1960) *Spartacus*. Bryna/Universal.
—— (1962) *Lolita*. MGM.
—— (1964) *Dr. Strangelove; or, How I Learned to Stop Worrying and Love the Bomb*. Columbia.
—— (1968) *2001: A Space Odyssey*. MGM.
—— (1971) *Clockwork Orange*. Warner Bros.
—— (1999) *Eyes Wide Shut*. Warner Bros.
Langton, S. dir. (1995) *Pride and Prejudice*. BBC.
Lubitsch, E. dir. (1932) *Trouble in Paradise*. Paramount.
—— (1940) *The Shop Around the Corner*. MGM.

Lumet, S. dir. (1964) *Fail-Safe.* Columbia.
Luske, H. and B. Sharpsteen. dir. (1940) *Pinocchio.* Disney.
Musker, J. and R. Clements. dir. (1989) *The Little Mermaid.* Disney.
Sharpsteen, B. supervising dir. (1940) *Fantasia.* Disney.
—— dir. (1941) *Dumbo.* Disney.
Trousdale, G. and K. Wise. dir. (1991) *Beauty and the Beast.* Disney.
Welles, O. dir. (1940) *Citizen Kane.* RKO.

Adaptation and Autobiographical Auteurism: A Look at Filmmaker/Writer Doris Dörrie

Margaret McCarthy

Doris Dörrie's films and literary texts demonstrate a non-hierarchical approach to adaptation, revealing an artistic sensibility highly respectful of both genres. The way Dörrie's characters evolve from text to film and back again conjures the illusion of floating, mutating particles which she adapts in unexpected ways. Dörrie's films and texts also often contain structuring autobiographical elements, revealing the highly subjective filter through which she transports her characters. Her auteurism is, however, tempered by the overall other-directedness of her artistic practice: not only does Dörrie decentre her authorial presence in commentaries on her books and films, but she also situates her practice in relation to larger conventions and constraints, even as she strives for her own unique vision. Likewise, the male protagonists of her two films *Männer* (1985) and *Erleuchtung garantiert* (2000) and her novel *Was machen wir jetzt?* (1999) struggle to adapt pre-given forms of masculinity and evolve into something better.

Film vs. Literature: Top Dogs and Losers

Scholarship on filmic adaptation is currently labouring towards sophisticated theories and capacious metaphors for rethinking relations between literary texts and filmic adaptations, hitherto fraught by film's long history of unrepentant infidelity towards literature. Entrenched assumptions and pre-programmed responses unite academic scholars and movie-goers, who have long bemoaned film's presumed inability to truly understand and respect its better half. Instead, it eschews monogamy with an author's singular voice for a film crew's collaborative vision, plus panders to the bigger pay-off at the box office than the bookstore. The cosmic unfairness of it all underpins Spike Jonze's 2002 film, *Adaptation*, embodied in Nicolas Cage's identical, but constitutionally contrary twins. Personality traits suspiciously reminiscent of literature and film undermine the fantasy of a perfect clone: the tormented twin, Charlie, is highly introspective, his voice-over monologues giving us the interiority that film purportedly lacks, while his dim-witted *Doppelgänger*, Donald, exhibits the transparent nature traditionally associated with film. Not surprisingly, it is the dope who writes a successful screenplay, netting a girlfriend in the process. If *Adaptation* gives us a bald-faced version of literature as sentient loser to film's witless top dog, it also adds one important twist: Charlie outlives Donald in the end, making us wonder why the auteur is not dead and how he survived when he clearly was not the fitter of our twins.

Wrapped up in a witty parody are, in fact, compelling metaphors, beginning with the way evolution as metaphorical backdrop to the entire film reminds us that all things change over time. Evolution's glacial pace picks up considerably, however, in the highly subjective, autobiographically inflected imperatives that underpin the adaptation process throughout the film. Significantly, Charlie understands very little about either marketability or following the conventions that net Donald a successful screenplay. Rather, his script evolves according to his own highly unstable states of mind. And far from being an autonomous creator and control freak, Charlie works within a chain of subjectively filtered texts inspired by a source, a rare orchid, whose exquisiteness gets mostly lost in translation. So much for the sanctity of origins, because the orchid evolves into something completely different, if not superfluous. More important, it is the auteur, Charlie, who becomes part of what is nonetheless cast as a life-sustaining process, while Donald's screenplay on a serial killer mostly relies on inert conventions.

Auteurism that adapts pre-existing phenomena, rather than bears the fruit of its own unique vision, corresponds with the current direction of adaptation theory. To move beyond the conceptual impasse of origin and deficient copy, critics have begun looking to Mikhail Bakhtin's dialogics, or the notion that all texts are actually intertexts which quote or embed fragments of earlier texts. Part of an infinite play of endlessly disseminated texts, filmic adaptations, as Robert Stam writes, 'are caught up in the ongoing whirl of intertextual reference and transformation, of texts generating other texts in an endless process of recycling, transformation, and transmutation, with no clear point of origin' (2000: 66). The bad marriage of text/origin and film/copy that generated moralistic metaphors of betrayal becomes, in this formulation, something much more free-wheeling and carnivalistic. If the author seems to disappear in the process, the anxious twin, Charlie, reminds us of the highly individual psyches through which texts pass as they evolve into something new. When texts are adapted into film, of course, a director's subjective distillation of pre-existing material is only one piece of a very collaborative process, one also known to be influenced by convention and audience expectations. In general, this process challenges the supreme control traditionally associated with auteurs and gives us a pragmatic multitasking in the face of many forces, external and internal. If multitasking implicitly turns macho auteurism into something more womanly, then German filmmaker and author Doris Dörrie is a figure worthy of close attention.

Auteurism Squared: Doris Dörrie as Writer and Filmmaker

Born in 1955, Doris Dörrie has been making films in Germany since the early 1980s. After graduating from Munich's film school, she found early success with her 1985 international hit *Männer* (*Men*), viewed world-wide by more than six million people. For better or worse, the success of *Männer* and subsequent films have made Dörrie 'the mother of German comedy' for many, particularly given the ascendancy of German popular film in the 1990s. Altogether, Dörrie has made ten feature films, many of them based on her own screenplays or adapted from her short stories and novels, which she began writing in the late 1980s. In what looks like a process of cross-pollination, Dörrie's literary figures are often fleshed out in her films, only to reappear in subsequent stories. Conversely, some characters devolve across texts and films into a mere shadow apparition of their antecedents. Either way, an always vaguely familiar Dörrien cast of uptight Germans function as floating, mutating particles which she transports and adapts from work to work.

At first glance, Dörrie's output as both filmmaker and author looks like auteurism squared—a steady, consistent body of work across a twenty-year span, which has sometimes been awarded prizes. Yet her status as adaptor in the widest sense complicates things, particularly if one considers the commercial aspects of Dörrie's work. One should praise, first off, her equitable relationship with literature

and film, which lacks the air of indiscretion traditionally associated
with adaptation. Despite playing fast and loose with her own characters, one could hardly accuse Dörrie of 'betraying' her literary texts.
Yet critics who know Dörrie's entire oeuvre wonder why some of the
more difficult aspects of her short stories tend to disappear when
adapted for film. Peter McIsaac, for instance, questions why German-
Jewish relations and the legacy of the Holocaust seem to have been
systematically 'cleansed' in the film version of Dörrie's short story
collection *Bin ich schön?* (*Am I Beautiful?*) (1998). Even though he
recognises the film's complexities and praises its 'non-trivial insights
into German national identity' (2004: 341), McIsaac also concurs with
critics who place Dörrie in the general trend of German comedies
towards uplifting, conventional story lines.

When pressed in interviews to account for her filmic happy
endings, Dörrie tends to fall back onto the essentialising notions of
literature and film which critics have begun to challenge. Literature,
Dörrie claims, is faster: it can not only span time within the space of a
sentence, but also express and then quickly retract ambivalence
towards a character (Jasper 2001). Film she describes as sluggish in
comparison. Once a character is depicted in a particular way, it is hard
to show other feelings for him. Dörrie's distinctions here are both odd
and striking. On the one hand, she ascribes each medium a tempo that
one would associate with its counterpart—classically, literature has
been understood to move at its own contemplative pace, whereas film
presumably zips around to accommodate its audience's more limited
attention span. Yet Dörrie's distinctions have a lot to do with the
challenges of presenting a character in a sympathetic light. Invoking
the classic advantage that literature supposedly enjoys over film, she
argues that a character's interior point of view can be more radical in
literature, meaning it can jump around in all its idiosyncratic inconsistencies without losing the reader's sympathy. Of course, a consciousness laid bare in textual form is no more a guarantee of sympathy than
the nuance, gesture and uttered speech of film. What is more, neat
typologies of ambivalent literature and optimistic film not only break
down in practice, but really do not do justice to the complexity of
Dörrie's own films. Her happy endings notwithstanding, Dörrie gives
us films with as much metaphoric heft as her novels. Indeed, her
novels tend to explain their metaphors, whereas her films wisely let
them resonate in ways that conjure manifold meanings.

Given her observations, it would be easy to fault Dörrie for essentialising each genre in order to rationalise the commercial tendencies in her films. That she is concerned with depicting her characters sympathetically in each medium does smack of commercial imperatives, but it is part of a general other-directedness in Dörrie's work that can also be read in a positive light. This tendency is integral, paradoxically, to the way she presents herself as auteur. As I will discuss further below, Dörrie tends to decentre her authorial presence in interviews, describing her writing process, for instance, as simply being with her characters and describing what she observes. The way her characters float from text to film and back again, evolving in their own quirky, unpredictable ways, sustains again the illusion of a consciousness that Dörrie merely filters and sustains. Couched this way, Dörrie more convincingly embodies her role as sympathetic observer of German Angst and desire all their evolving forms. Neither auteurist swaggering nor commercial concerns tallies with such a pose.

Yet it is precisely the way that Dörrie embodies such anti-thetical camps that deserves close analysis. In fact, she has made it her *modus operandi* to produce commercially viable cinema from the vantage point of a European sensibility. To this end she has at times adapted classic Hollywood film genres and conventions. Comedies, buddy films, road movies, and noirish crime thrillers, for instance, have provided Dörrie with a frame for reflecting on German identity. Not surprisingly, the mainstream look of her films has rankled film critics and scholars alike. German film critics generally associate Hollywood with deficient artistic merit, while many Anglo-American film scholars still actively mourn the passing of New German Cinema, the alternative films of Fassbinder, Herzog, Kluge, Wenders, *et al.* Of course, nostalgia for these 'precursor texts', as Bakhtin would call them, not only invokes the pre-programmed sense of loss familiar in the adaptation process, it also sets up a divide that in practice breaks down in significant ways. For Dörrie's other-directedness is highly attuned not only to Hollywood as omnipresent other, but also to key elements of Rainer Werner Fassbinder's legacy.

What she shares with him in particular is a desire to 'create a union between something as beautiful and powerful and wonderful as Hollywood films and a critique of the status quo' (Fassbinder quoted in Gemünden 1994: 55). Generally speaking, Dörrie does give us a kinder, gentler version of Fassbinder's ugly Germans indulging in unappealing acts and extreme behaviours. In the three artistic products that I will analyse in this chapter, Dörrie is quite uninhibited about depicting the aggression, callousness and sexual foibles of German males, even if her men retain a mainstream look compared to Fassbinder's cultural underdogs. She also shares Fassbinder's highly savvy ways of procuring funding despite having even less control over the system than the vaunted auteurs of New German Cinema enjoyed. At the same time, Dörrie's auteurist identity takes again an other-directed form. Alasdair King's work on Dörrie rethinks auteurism not as a 'mode of directorial expressivity', but rather as a 'commercial strategy for organizing audience reception, as a critical concept bound to distribution and marketing aims that identify and address the potential cult status of an auteur' (2002: 4). If Dörrie's writerly pose casts her as mere observer of German identity, the stories that she tells about herself in film-promoting forums aim for a similar decentring of self. She often emphasises her desire to work with small film crews and independent production companies that facilitate a collaborative process. Dörrie also views herself not as the sole author of her films, but as part of a non-hierarchical team. Lastly, Dörrie always plays up multitasking that is the hallmark of modern motherhood: in many interviews she has described how her writing takes place in the space of time that her daughter is in school.

Equally important, Dörrie's texts and films often contain structuring autobiographical elements. Sudden death and Buddhism as existential salve are frequent themes in her literary and filmic output after her husband and cameraman, Helge Weindler, died of cancer in 1996. Auteurist control in Dörrie's work is more accurately at times an autobiographical grappling with unpredictable turns of life. She has compared the autobiographical traces in her writing and films to mosaic tiles, which again links her to a larger structure of which she is only a part. Dörrie's metaphor, of course, jives well with the way she continually positions herself within a larger nexus of conventions, expectations and constraints. Part to whole, however, does not erase the contours of a unique vision, one which aims to transform convention into something better. Significantly, the three examples which I analyse below—the 1985 film *Männer* (*Men*), the novel *Was machen wir jetzt?* (1999) (*What Should We Do Now?*), and the 2000 release *Erleuchtung garantiert* (*Enlightenment Guaranteed*)—continually reprise the metaphorical rubric within which Dörrie situates her artistic practice. In all three we find a decentred consciousness that adapts and struggles with pre-given forms of masculinity, yet sometimes strives to evolve into something better. What Dörrie wears as a badge of honour—a fully relational self who paradoxically strives for an individual voice—comes to some of her men and only after much hard-bitten struggle. Dörrie in fact at times deposits her own autobiographical traces in them, setting them on a path where the markers of progress can be distinctly feminine.

Ying/Yang vs. Enlightened Masculinity

The template for all three pieces is a ying/yang doubling which recalls the mirror as trope of adaptation, but also, where Buddhism is a shaping force, pointing to the possibility of change over time. In *Männer* a callous, bourgeois husband and a fading hippie labour under the effects of a zigzagging *Zeitgeist*, or the passing of 1968 ideals into the money-mongering 1980s. *Was machen wir jetzt?* welds the jerks of *Männer* into the first-person singular voice of Fred Kaufmann, once a gloomy film student dressed in black, now unhappily evolved into a husband, father, and proprietor of bagel shops in Munich. Much more the salesman that his German name signals, Fred's unhappy conventionality is offset by the presence of other feminised, spiritual 'softies', the German designation for wimps. In what seems like an ironic subtext on the whole notion of adaptation, Dörrie's third reflection on masculinity, *Erleuchtung garantiert*, gives us the same actor who played the hippie in *Männer*, now transformed into a callous, bourgeois husband. The bourgeois husband of *Männer* appears briefly as the antithesis of his macho forerunner, playing a foppish queen in search of feng-shui enlightenment. More importantly, masculinity in flux sometimes moves beyond the logic of the mirror and its dualities to suggest the possibility of an evolving identity en route to points unknown.

In the analysis of Dörrie's reflections on masculinity that follows, I would like to examine the ways that novel and film do, in fact, do things differently, although not necessarily because of diverging essences or the formal limitations of discrete genres. It should be pointed out up front that the novel *Was machen wir jetzt?* gives us an unabashedly happy ending, while both films end on a more ambivalent note. What we find throughout is a mixed bag of filmic and literary techniques that cross over into their twin's domain. Fred Kaufmann's first-person singular interior monologues reveal again and again, for instance, a subjectivity shaped by Hollywood films. *Männer* and *Erleuchtung garantiert* also reveal the imaginary bases of selfhood, whether the mirror where men posture or in the opaque wisdom delivered by a Japanese sensei. Each film, too, exhibits a talkiness that one would associate more with solely verbal art forms. Both the two films and the novel thematise heterosexual men stripped bare of their identity, cuckolded and/or ousted from their homes. By constantly revealing the imaginary bases of identity which fill the void, Dörrie again recalls Fassbinder, specifically his ardent refusal 'to naturalize identity by concealing its external scaffolding' (Silverman 1989: 58).

Männer, which Dörrie both directed and wrote, explores the vexed, often volatile relationship between Julius, a yuppie manager, and his hippie rival, Stefan, who is having an affair with Julius's wife. At the start of the film, Julius retools his identity into the jeans and t-shirt-clad 'Daniel' and moves in with the unknowing Stefan in order to systematically transform him into a jerky yuppie like himself.[1] Dörrie's script, so the story goes, was based on fieldwork in Munich bars where she eavesdropped on men's conversations. The anthropological tinge of this set-up gives us the sense of an origin untampered with. The film then offers up Dörrie's notes in monologues which carry the force of the first-person singular voice so persuasive in literary texts. Dörrie thus would seem to function less as a shaping artistic presence than a scribe who charts masculinity in unadulterated form, even if her film is very much in the spirit of the classic buddy flick. And much in the same way that Dörrie captured floating bits of conversation in her notebook, the male protagonists doggedly cling to the German script of masculinity, with its tortured dichotomy of machos and softies.

An early scene shows Julius living in a hotel room where we watch him shower, a man fully dispossessed of his former identity and

---

[1] Strikingly, the scenario played out here is reduced to a single anecdote in *Was machen wir jetzt?*, when Fred describes editing a fellow film student's overlong, but artistically sophisticated film down into something thoroughly as banal, pale and normal as he views himself. Such compression of the film's entire plot is surprising, given the expansiveness one usually associates with literature.

belongings. According to the logic of the mirror as the film's visual centrepiece, antithetical types like him and Stefan are merely inverted images of one another, not truly different. Stefan, for instance, is revealed to be the boss of his roommates, and both he and Julius unmagnanimously dump a lover in the film's early scenes. For his part, Julius occupies the job of 'creative director' at his firm, which links him to Stefan the artist, as does his brief time in art school and his uncharacteristic defence of the ethos of 1968 in one scene. Likewise, the passage of time invariably turns hippies into managers because, according to the logic of the film, seemingly incompatible lifestyles are mere role-play. The line 'es bewegt sich nichts' (nothing moves) uttered in one scene and the film's final image of Julius's and Stefan's confrontation on a paternoster suggest some sort of eternal sameness, or what goes around, comes around.[2] Masculinity, even if revealed as a pose, remains unable to move beyond a range of predictable positions. At the same time, *Männer* shows us Julius manipulating the signifiers of masculinity to his advantage: his makeover of Stefan into himself is less a product of cutthroat managerial tactics than of his 'creative' ability to manipulate the categories of macho and softie to his advantage.

When Julius asks his wife what she finds attractive in her new lover, he speculates aloud: 'He attacks you and bites your throat, tells you something sweet and is a wild animal'. Ironically, Julius often seems to play the *Wilder* in his attempts to 'seduce' Stefan, or usher him into the world of Rolexes and Maseratis. Several times, Julius not only physically assaults Stefan, but also in one scene almost castrates himself as he hides a knife presumably meant for his new roommate. In a similar vein, Julius ends up gnarling on a bag of peanuts in an earlier scene as he presents presumably consumer-friendly packaging to prospective clients. Sometimes, as Julius slowly learns, playing the *Wilder* simply makes one look *affig* or ridiculous. Stefan's weakness, by contrast, consists not so much of the femmie attributes of a softie, but his willingness to try on any role in willy-nilly fashion. In the infamous 'Manager Test' scene, Julius tricks him into making a newspaper hat, putting it on his head, and standing on a table. Being

---

[2] A paternoster, which one generally finds in Bavaria and Austria, is an open-door elevator that continuously rotates around an axis, obliging passengers to hop on and off as it passes a particular floor.

the more flexible and therefore mouldable character, Stefan finds himself continually seduced and humiliated, whereas Julius the manipulator mostly gains the upper hand in their relations.

Yet his success is not merely a matter of exposing Stefan's inner bourgeois conformist, but instead manipulating the creativity, experimentation and role-playing associated with the generation of 1968. For the film charts his transformation as much as Stefan's, from a cuckolded macho who flubs an important business presentation through his discomfort before the mirror in jeans and t-shirt. If along the way he gets in touch with his younger self circa 1968, Julius's reverse *Bildung* also seems a clumsier version of the highly polished business ethic he shares with Stefan as they spruce up his portfolio for a job interview. 'Ich bin ein Spieler' ('I'm a gambler'), he announces, revealing his willingness to try on a range of arbitrary roles to gain advantage. For as much as both men often look *affig* as they slip all over the signifiers of machos and softies, Julius's ultimate triumph comes from learning to play either side of the equation if it helps his cause, while Stefan must be seduced, cajoled and manipulated into trading places, while never truly internalising the wily ways of the *Spieler*.

In this sense, the film is less a critique of the ethos of 1968, I would argue, than an exposé of successful masculinity across two warring epochs. To be sure, co-opting the spirit of 1968, here reduced to a set of variables in the game of masculinity, for the more selfish *Zeitgeist* of the 1980s is only marginally better than merely rejecting it. Yet duelling ethos are challenged during Stefan's and Julius's vociferous ride on the paternoster by a man in the foreground sporting both a business suit and a ponytail. Planted as an audience stand-in, he positions us to think, what is the big deal?, while giving us an unconflicted amalgam of what Julius and Stefan represent. If hippies inevitably turn into managers, perhaps two seemingly antithetical identities can complement, if not benefit one another, giving us a synthesis which counters the stagnation of 'es bewegt sich nichts'. To the film's credit, it never asks us to feel sorry for men because of the quick-change artistry which masculinity seems to require. But at the same time the mirror as base does not oblige the two leads to find themselves across truly discomforting differences. Equally significant, successful masculinity in *Männer* is about dominance, or winning *das Spiel*. Women remain entirely marginal to this game, even if the film subjects men to the same specular conditions that have long been recognised as a pre-given of femininity.

To use the parlance of colloquial German, Fred Kaufman, the protagonist of Dörrie's novel, *Was machen wir jetzt?*, is an unrepentant *Sack* (bastard). Half the allure of the book is being inside the *Sack*, which is chock full of very unmarketable things: racist, bestial porn fantasies and politically incorrect words for the female anatomy, evident in Fred's penchant to compare vaginas to well-fitting shoes. The plot itself features his teenage daughter's late-term abortion, plus the death of a major character midway through the story. There is also a fair amount of unapologetic aggression, plus many moments when Fred is simply an instinct-driven, sexist pig. Yet his Hollywood-inspired sense of self, which leans on monstrous machos like Travis Bickle, is shown to be in a constant state of fluctuation. For Fred repeatedly imagines himself at times not only as a killer or an asshole, plain and simple, but also just as often as a hero. While such unimaginative, formulaic categories may explain Fred's lack of success as a filmmaker, they also point up a sense of self that is very much tied to whoever is in Fred's orbit at the moment. As much as the novel plays out the paradigm of the buddy movie, Fred has no one buddy to offset his selfhood. At various times, the overlapping admiration and antagonism of the buddy film emerges in Fred's relations with his wife, Claudia, his daughter, Franka, with the sorry softie, Norbert, whom he and Franka pick up on their road trip, and with his wife's lover, Theo. All of them enable Fred to live out the complicated permutations of intersubjective dependence on another. In fact the novel's title, 'what should we do now?', alludes to the mutual dependencies of all its players.

Film technology, particularly the slow-motion effect that Fred often conjures in his mind, helps readers to slow down and reflect on the various forms of identification that engender Fred's sense of self. Initially, however, Fred defines himself as much through opposition as psychic affinities, being unable to recognise the personhood of those around him, particularly women.[3] Describing sex with his mistress,

---

[3] The same ying/yang doubling gets played out in male/male relations, including Fred's comparisons between himself and the softie, Norbert, and his wife's lover, Theo, plus later in reflections on the artist Vincent van Gogh and his brother, Theo. Such relations set the stage for the antagonistic brothers of *Erleuchtung garantiert*

Fred again spins an elaborate comparison between vaginas and shoes, both of which provide him with a womblike-cradle of self while never rising above the status of a thing. As much as one smells a macho rat here, Fred's extensive reflections elsewhere on shoes and clothes as shaping presences at different points in his life gives us a decidedly feminine dynamic. Despite undiluted animosity towards his wife and her control-freak tendencies, the binary oppositions that Fred leans on to define their relations eventually elevate her status: if he is the gloomy film student in black, she is the 'white cook', the rescuer and saviour. More tellingly, she clearly seems the parent at times to his helpless child, or the 'driver' in their relationship: 'Claudia sits at the wheel and knows where to go, she moves unceasingly forward' (Dörrie 1999: 258). If Fred's own real and psychic flight takes the form of much aimless cruising at the wheel of his car, his final act in the novel is literally driving a man off the *Autobahn* who has suffered a heart attack and then administering artificial respiration. As much as Fred is metaphorically unconscious at the wheel throughout the novel, it is Claudia as rescuer who inspires his very goal-oriented, 'driven' ability to rescue another and finally convincingly embody the role of hero.

Equally striking are the complicated permutations played out in Fred's relationship with his daughter. Franka's mercurial teenage self, as opaque and annoying as it, initially bears, however, distinct affinities with Fred's less appealing masculine traits. She thinks, for instance, 'with the lower part of her body' (Dörrie 1999: 49), and Fred's comparison between her and a chimp recalls the metaphorics of *Männer*. Later, when Fred confronts the boy who got Franka pregnant, vacillating in his own mind between being a monster and a hero, his observation that she 'sought out a monster' (Dörrie 1999: 43) in her brief sex partner also underscores Franka's psychic affinities with her father. Finally, Fred's sense that Franka has lost the uniqueness she exuded as a child echoes his present sense of self as shameless conformist. At the same time, Fred also imagines himself at times in their relations as the petulant child to her parent, revealing not only his fluctuating selfhood, but also the general the way that adulthood can be a very unreliable state of mind. By the end of the novel, however,

---

who may be polar opposites, but who achieve peace and balance by the end of the film.

Franka is deeply in love with a Buddhist acolyte, which in some sense clearly inspires his return to Claudia, the ardent Buddhist. Just as Claudia inspired his heroism on the *Autobahn*, Franka's actions in the end also inspire a heroic act on his part. When Claudia's lover, Theo, dies unexpectedly, Fred marvels at the way Franka very unselfconsciously takes Theo's grieving wife into her arms. Immediately thereafter, Fred volunteers to drive her back to Holland, and those present subsequently treat him 'like a hero, wish [him] much strength and a good trip, as if [he] were Orpheus driving into the underworld' (Dörrie 1999: 240).

Fred's slow transformation is also clearly inspired by the shaping influence of Buddhism and by various forms of enlightenment that enable him to rise above duellist thinking and his own physical desires and limitations. Initially, however, for Fred to identify with rather than be repelled by others, he must bring them down to his own level, which he does with crass contrasts and comparisons. Yet as often as not, the opposite can happen, with Fred rising above a limited point of view to achieve some kind of spiritual and psychic affinity with others. One senses such affinities in those brief moments where Fred revels in the lyrics of Bob Dylan, which he also confesses to never really understanding, which suggests the way that enlightenment is a rather precarious state, a brief *Augenblick* or moment of insight, like the neon light which flashes on and off in an Amsterdam hotel room towards the end of the novel. Alternately, it enables Fred to briefly float above things, rather than remain entrapped in his car in constant motion. Overall, it bears resemblances to the filmic concept of identification, which is never as straightforward as characters identifying with one another in an affirmation of sameness. Rather, it comes and goes and can tip in any variety of directions that enable the spectator to abandon his or her own limited purview. If Buddhism is based on the possibility of change at any moment, it relies not on the fixed nature of identification, but its profound instability, evident in the way Fred waffles between monsters and heroes as identificatory anchor. Form is emptiness and emptiness form, the novel tells us, again in an affirmation of Buddhist belief which also has ramifications for identity more generally. For the signifiers of masculinity and femininity are essentially arbitrary, which opens up the possibility not only of trading places, but of briefly floating above the forms that anchor identity, if not evolving into something different.

Concretely, such insights help Fred to ultimately imagine female anatomy not in terms of a womblike loss of self in another.
Rather, Fred's startling encounter with a three-breasted woman, which
would seem like nirvana for a macho rat, opens up other metaphoric
possibilities. It is reprised in an image of three peas in a pod which
inspires Claudia's brief moment of happiness, plus the threesome of
which their family is comprised. Ultimately, one senses Fred's ability
to recognise the unity and parity of himself, his wife and child.
Equally significantly, Fred's evolution in the novel is signalled not
only in key moments that revolve around his defining activity of
driving,[4] but the way enlightenment enables him to evolve into the
sensibility of a filmmaker, someone capable of floating above,
achieving a bird's eye view which sees connections inspired by
empathy. Ultimately, again, it is Claudia, not Clint Eastwood, who
inspires a heroism based on connection and which reveals Fred's
evolution beyond the estrangement which initially defines his relations
with others. The stagnation of 'es bewegt sich nichts' in *Männer* gives
way to decidedly evolved masculinity in *Was machen wir jetzt*.

Erleuchtung garantiert taps into the themes and metaphors of
its two predecessors, yet its masculinity is far less scripted by convention, since the film was largely improvised by actors using their own
names. The mirror, with its self-same logic, also falls away as central
prop, and we leave the insular confines of a German milieu, as the
film's two leads, Uwe and Gustav, travel first to Tokyo and then to a
Zen centre in an outlying province. If *Männer* and *Was machen wir
jetzt* showed us men defining themselves within the confines of
machos and softies, monsters and heroes, *Erleuchtung garantiert*
complicates such simple inversions. Instead, it gives us masculine
identity in relation to things more uncomfortably other, as differences
between Eastern and Western culture are played out. It would be easy
to assume that our macho/softie polarity merely finds geographical
nodal points here, with domineering westerners claiming their space in
a feminised, exotic world of spirituality. Dörrie's observation in an
interview, however, that the filming in Japan put them all in the

---

[4] After arriving at a Buddhist camp in France, Fred runs over and kills and owl. Later,
he becomes a passive witness when he discovers Theo dead of a heart attack by the
side of the road. And finally, he, of course, saves the man who had a heart attack on
the *Autobahn*.

position of Alice in Wonderland helps us to appreciate a different dynamic. *Erleuchtung garantiert* gives us men as children, perpetually bewildered and disadvantaged in an unfamiliar environment. The imaginary bases of identity available to the two male leads are as overwhelming as a chaotic Tokyo street and as physically painful as an early morning meditation session. When enlightenment does ultimately come, it remains as opaque as the untranslated words of a Japanese sensei and as aloof as the airborne crow that seems to follow them from Germany to Japan.

The film begins on familiar Dörrien territory: we witness not only a callous husband dumped by a fed-up wife, but also a confused spirituality with a profoundly materialistic base. In Dörrie's plots, material possessions are almost always central to selfhood—in *Erleuchtung garantiert* we watch Uwe's wife fussing over an expensive, leaky indoor fountain as he meditates in the foreground, plus enlightenment packaged in the form of Gustav's feng shui consultation sessions. We see a grey, wintry Germany where Gustav and his wife sit stone-faced in black overcoats on the subway, plus Gustav standing and bolting a meal on a wintry Munich Street. The implicit critique of Germany and Germans poises us, of course, to expect something better in Japan. Yet Japan does not make good on what have become conventional, Merchant-Ivory-inspired expectations, i.e. uptight, alienated tourist appropriates an exotic foreign backdrop to tweak him/herself back into form, rather than redefine selfhood along entirely different lines. As Alice in Wonderland stand-ins, the male leads are unable to monkey around and dominate in a game of differences, but instead like children can at best learn by route and without understanding, evident every time they attempt to master Japanese chants and the rituals of the Zen Centre.

Predictably, however, a materialistic toy is in tow along the way, as Uwe brings a video camera to record every moment of their odyssey. If it seems merely a portable, high-tech version of *Männer*'s mirror, or a favoured object in a global environment where Japanese products flood German markets, it functions, I would argue, in a different fashion. It becomes, for instance, the means through which Uwe continually speaks to the absent wife who dumped him, thus turning the looking glass into a window onto another. It also records the Japanese woman who reads Uwe's palm, which a compatriot must later translate for him. The Sensei's words of wisdom also remain initially untranslated in individual sessions with Uwe and Gustav, but later we see each of them on videotape paraphrasing for us in German, which leaves us at a multi-layered remove from the already foreign forms shaping selfhood here. (Interestingly, even when they read the aims of Zen in German from a guide book, neither Uwe nor Gustav seems to really understand what the words mean). For as much as the film does play out the dynamics of machos and softies, with Uwe the overbearing brother to the sensitive, often teary-eyed Gustav, ultimately both men define themselves in terms far removed from an otherwise insular, self-same dynamic. Equally important is the way these terms are internalised in entirely subjective ways, evident each time Uwe and Gustav mediate their own version of what the sensei said. Along similar lines, we later see them mulling over their relationship to that airborne crow, which to each of them at different times seems to articulate, 'ja ja', 'nein, nein', or 'so so'. As acoustic mirror, the bird remains at a distance, and thus only partially serves as an easy extension of self like the mirror.

Ultimately, what exactly inspires profound changes—Uwe seems finally able to accept the uncertainty of the future around his departed family, and Gustav announces that he is gay—remains opaque to the spectator. The film closes with the men chanting in Japanese, shielded from view, unlike Julius and Stefan displayed on the paternoster, in a tent erected on a Tokyo tennis court. Missing as well is an audience stand-in to demonstrate an unconflicted, easy synthesis of East and West. Compared to Dörrie's other films, the ending in *Erleuchtung garantiert* is only provisionally a happy one. Significantly, the film does not circle back on itself, but leaves us on open ground, indeed 'unenlightened' as to what exactly has altered our male protagonists. What we have witnessed along the way reverses the traditional power dynamics in which masculine, western selfhood defines itself by dominating in a game of difference—indeed one scene shows Uwe and Gustav earning money by sporting *Lederhosen* and serving beer in a restaurant, playing to Japanese expectations of Germanness. More important, the two men remain unable to co-opt difference to gain advantage, since power remains consistently in the hands of others. Instead we witness a much more childlike, searching, tentative relation to difference, one which ultimately does profoundly alter our protagonists beyond, say, the purely cosmetic pairing of business suit and ponytail. With reference to that omnipresent political touchstone of German identity, or the ideals of 1968, we do witness here a kind of experimentation and role-playing that alters selfhood along more desirable lines. Again, it embraces difference without seeking to dominate or co-opt it. Less laudable, perhaps, is the way this process serves entirely personal needs and development, rather than fomenting larger political change. Yet given our global context, the idea of a non-dominating, respectful relationship to difference does carry important and larger political ramifications. Given the opaque, subjective nature of the way West meets East here, what emerges is highly individual and unpredictable and thus also unavailable for easy, wholesale co-optation. It reminds us that as we travel swiftly and easily across borders these days, we can acquire something other than duty-free electronic equipment, namely highly individual, idiosyncratic forms of enlightenment not available for resale.

Ultimately, a number of reasons seem clear for giving Dörrie's commercially-oriented artistic practice its due. Hopefully this chapter has demonstrated that its mainstream look co-exists with sophisticated, relevant reflections on German identity, providing readers and spectators with as much pleasure as it does scholars fodder for analysis. And beyond the various forms of other-directedness detailed earlier in this essay, plus the way the two films and the novel reprise them metaphorically, Dörrie gives us prose highly respectful of film and film highly respectful of prose. Equally important, such equitable relations lack a mirroring imperative and instead provide an overall artistic eco-system in which Dörrie's characters can either evolve or wither, as she sees fit. Moreover, she enjoys tilling one medium with the tools of the other in order to cultivate the whole process. In the current boom of adaptation theory which both lauds and makes change its object, Doris Dörrie deserves lots of attention.

Bibliography

Bakhtin, M. M. (1981) *The Dialogic Imagination: Four Essays by M. M. Bakhtin.* M. Holquist (ed.) and C. Emerson and M. Holquist (trans.). Austin: University of Texas Press.
Dörrie, D. (1999) *Was machen wir jetzt?*. Zürich: Diogenes Verlag.

Gemünden, G. (1994) 'Re-fusing Brecht: The Cultural Politics of Fassbinder's German Hollywood', *New German Critique* 63, 55-75.

Jasper, D. (2001) 'Interview mit Doris Dörrie', in *Dirk Jasper Filmstarlexikon. Deutsches Entertainment Magazin.* Available HTTP: http://www.filmstar.de/entertainment/stars/d/doris_i_ 01.html (10 August 2004).

King, A. (2002) 'Doris Dörrie and the Commerce of European Auteurism', conference paper presented at 'Screening Identities: 2nd European Cinema Research Forum', University of Wales, Aberystwyth.

McIsaac, P. M. (2004) 'North-South, East-West: Mapping German Identities in Cinematic and Literary Versions of Doris Dörrie's *Bin ich schön?*', *German Quarterly* 77 (3), 340-62.

Phillips, K. (1998) 'Interview with Doris Dörrie: Filmmaker, Writer, Teacher', I. Majer O'Sickey and I. von Zadow (eds.) *Triangulated Visions: Women in Recent German Cinema.* Albany: State University of New York, 173-84.

Silverman, K. (1989) 'Fassbinder and Lacan: A Reconsideration of Gaze, Look and Image', *Camera Obscura* 19, 55-84.

Stam, R. (2000) 'Beyond Fidelity: The Dialogics of Adaptation', in J. Naremore (ed.) *Film Adaptation.* London: Athlone, 54-76.

Filmography

Dörrie, D. dir. (1985) *Männer.* Olga-Film/Zweites Deutsches Fernsehn.

——— dir. (2000) *Erleuchtung garantiert.* Bernd Eichinger/Megaherz TV Film und Fernsehen.

Jonze, S. dir. (2002). *Adaptation.* Columbia/Intermedia Films.

CONTEXTS, INTERTEXTS, ADAPTATION

John Huston's vs. James Joyce's *The Dead*

Manuel Barbeito Varela

This chapter deals with some of the main differences, including technical devices and thematic changes of emphasis, between James Joyce's short story 'The Dead' (1914) and John Huston's film (1987), and shows the ways in which the latter invites its audience to contemplate death, thus performing a cultural feat by going against the grain of the current widespread tendency to make death invisible. Huston's treatment of the Western myth of passionate love, the attention paid to historical issues in the film, the camera's relationship with the protagonist, and the carving out of a temporal dimension to which the audience belongs within the time of the film's action, all contribute to engaging us in Gabriel's final meditation on death as the horizon of an ordinary life which contrasts sharply with the intensity of the passionate lovers' ecstasy.

Adaptation as Creative Re-enactment

Starting with a comparison between the relationship established by the camera with Gabriel in John Huston's *The Dead* (1987) and by the narrator with the same protagonist in James Joyce's short story, composed in 1907 and published in 1914, this chapter examines some of the most important differences between these two texts and the strategies the film deploys in order to involve its contemporary audience in the situation that the protagonist faces at the end of the film—a situation created by the contrast between the great Western myth of passionate love, which ends in the lovers' death in their prime, and a life that faces death after the coming of age. The differences between short story and film and the strategies used in the latter are decisive as regards the interpretation of each text at the historical moment of its creation, one at the beginning of the twentieth century and of Joyce's career, the other—Huston's last film—at the end of the same century. This chapter emphasises the greater historical realism of

Huston's film, its minimal concern with the protagonist's education compared to Joyce's story, and especially the meaning of the camera's assumption of Gabriel's point of view at the final moment of his meditation on death. Huston's film has often been considered his last will and testament, although he stated that the proximity of his own death was not relevant to the film. This seems true in the sense that the camera does not simply adopt an individual's private point of view, but rather a representative if unconventional one: as it assumes Gabriel's point of view, the camera offers a counterpart to current attitudes towards death, which paradoxically conjugate its social oblivion with its becoming a spectacle in the mass media.

The thorny issue of fidelity is often implicit in value judgements made of films based on literary texts, particularly so when they are 'great classics'. Does fidelity mean that the film should reproduce the text as closely as possible? If so, Huston's film is only partly successful, given that it differs from Joyce's story at certain crucial points. For example, Joyce subverts the tradition of the Quest Myth by placing the beginning of the protagonist's journey at the end of the story (Barbeito 2004: 254), while Gabriel is already well into his 'journey westward' at the end of Huston's film. That is the reason why his realisation that 'The time had come for him to set out on his journey westward', though it was still there in the third draft of the screenplay (Hart 1988: 34), disappeared from the film to the distress of some critics (Gerber 1988; Pilipp 1993). However, if we no longer understand fidelity in terms of identity but relate it to the possibilities which arise when a text is re-enacted in a different scenario, translated into another time, space and artistic medium, then Huston's The Dead, which tackles a contemporary issue that is related to but not identical with the one addressed in Joyce's story, may be considered to be much more successful.[1]

---

[1] When conceived in terms of identity, as is too often the case, fidelity is used to degrade the film to the status of a 'copy' of the source text. Robert Stam (2000) offers a thorough criticism of fidelity-as-identity, but leaves unexplored the possibilities of the trope when detached from the notion of identity.

The Camera vs. the Protagonist

There are a few major changes in Huston's film regarding the camera's presentation of the protagonist as well as the role of the protagonist himself. The position of the camera at the beginning and at the end of the film is a case in point. At the beginning, it is outside, static, like an onlooker watching the front of a house in which a party is already going on; at the end it is inside, showing what Gabriel sees and imagines is occurring outside and will occur in the future. Joyce begins the story, on the contrary, with the narrator inside and paying attention to Lily as she ushers the guests into the scene. At the end, Gabriel's thoughts are reproduced in both cases, but with one major difference: in the film, Gabriel is standing by the window perfectly awake as we listen to his interior monologue in voice-over, whereas in the story he is sleepy, lying in bed beside his wife as the narrator reproduces his thoughts in free indirect speech (cf. Barry 2001: 73-7). Joyce has very carefully punctuated this: when Gretta falls asleep Gabriel is in bed 'leaning on his elbow'; after observing her and her things 'unresentfully', he thinks about his own 'riot of emotions' and imagines the wake of Aunt Julia in the near future; then 'the air of the room chilled his shoulders. He stretched himself cautiously along under the sheets' (Joyce 1972: 218, 219).[2] All this time Gabriel is looking out of the window in Huston's film. Furthermore, while at the end of the short story all music has ceased except that of language, in the film some background music accompanies Gabriel's voice-over.

The use of voice-over while the camera adopts Gabriel's point of view—a technique that replaces the free indirect speech used in the text—is related to the decision to present him fully awake, instead of letting the rhythms of language lull him into sleep as in the story's famous final paragraph. Lea Baechler and A. Walton Litz have criticised the change which takes place at the end of the film by saying that 'the final voice-over, which makes Gabriel's thoughts unexpectedly explicit, is startling and unsatisfactory' (Baechler and Litz 1988: 522) because up to this point Gabriel's inner life has been approached only indirectly through a 'partially successful medium of expression and gesture' (1988: 523). In so far as the change is simply from Gabriel's exterior to his interior, this is a valid criticism. In this sense,

---

[2] Subsequent references to Joyce's text are made by mentioning the pages in brackets.

there is little reason to privilege Gabriel's point of view because until the last scene the focus is on Gretta rather than him, which according to these critics is the film's great successful innovation and its main difference from Joyce's text (Baechler and Litz 1988: 524, 527; see also Hart 1988: 13, and Gerber 1988: 531). Not everyone, however, acknowledged this focus on Gretta to the detriment of Gabriel; for Hinson, for instance, 'Gabriel is the self-conscious centre of the movie. We see the events of the night, and the characters' actions, through his eyes' (1987).

One may indeed argue that Gabriel continues to be the main protagonist in the film, not because the camera adopts his point of view, as Hinson suggests, but on the contrary, because it plays a game of proximity and distance as regards him and offers us shots, whether taken from his position or not, that show what he is looking at, even if they rarely reproduce exactly what he sees or imagines, except at the very end of the film.[3] Although the camera does offer shots from the position of other characters as well, it does not engage in this game of proximity and distance with them. A clear and relevant example of this is when Gretta stops to listen to Bartell D'Arcy's song: Gabriel looks at her and the camera shows her, but what we see is not exactly, nor only, what Gabriel is seeing. This game begins as soon as Gabriel enters the house. At this moment the camera leaves its favourite recess by the stairs, with the banisters tracing a diagonal on the screen, and follows Lily—for the first and last time—to receive the two much-expected guests. After Gabriel blames Gretta for the delay, she goes past the camera, which remains with Gabriel as he watches her through the glass window on the door; but when Gabriel moves, the camera stays put, thus making it clear that it does not identify with Gabriel's point of view. This is a unique shot in a film full of repetitions. One important consequence of this game is the contrast between

---

[3] Jakob Lothe (2000) studies the relationship of proximity and distance between the narrator and the protagonist in Joyce's story and exemplifies how this is transferred to the screen at the end of the film. According to him, the objectivity of the camera compensates for the subjectivity of Gabriel's vision (Lothe 2000: 154-5). Lothe thus tries to answer Stanzel's criticism that the 'shift from third to first person reduces the dimension of meaning from near-universal validity to Gabriel's subjectively limited personal view' (Stanzel 1992: 121). Lothe, though, does not develop the idea of the relationship between the camera and the protagonist in the film's own terms. In order to do be able to do this, one must take the audience into account.

the camera's and the protagonist's perspectives on Gretta: the camera is captivated by the spellbound Gretta as she is deep in her memories, whereas Gabriel, overly concerned with the speech he has been commissioned to give, is unable to fathom the depths in which his wife is immersed.

This distance from the protagonist's point of view allows room for the creation of another salient quality of the film, the importance awarded to the lives of other characters (Baechler and Litz 1988: 526). Even the cabman has a little story to tell that adds to those allusions to the west of Ireland that Hart finds slightly excessive (1988: 13). And it is not only Freddy Malins that receives special attention at the party, but even Mrs Malins, who is almost inconsequential in the story, becomes much more relevant: her unending talk becomes an ordeal through which Gabriel's good manners clearly fail to sustain him, and she assumes briefly, yet incisively, the matriarchal role played in Joyce's story by Gabriel's mother when, while looking at 'her photograph [that] stood before the pier-glass' (184), he broods over her objections to his marriage with Gretta. Of utmost importance is the recording of the effect that the allusions to passionate love have on the young girls; they become fascinated with the poem 'Broken Vows' read by Mr. Grace, who honours his name by inspiring the strong emotion that carries them away as it does Gretta, whose 'enigmatic beauty pours from her like that of a fine unsentimental picture of the Annunciation' (Huston's screenplay, quoted in Hart 1988: 27). Equally important and thematically related to this is the flirtation between D'Arcy and Miss O'Callaghan, yet another of Huston's inventions.

Huston's Historical Sensitivity

At one point in the film, Huston appropriates Joyce's symbolism in order to establish a significant difference between film and story as regards Gabriel's role. In the story, Lily reserves three potatoes for Gabriel, thus symbolically—the number three, the potatoes—tying him to an Irish identity he is at odds with. In the film, she adds one potato to the slice of goose he has put on a plate, which is then passed from hand to hand and is closely followed by the camera. In this way, Huston suggests a link, Irishness, among all the characters, instead of specifically alluding to Gabriel's individual relationship to it. Here as elsewhere, the attention paid to other characters compensates for the low level of concern with the protagonist's education, and results in a higher degree of historical realism in Huston's film. Though humbling encounters with women—Lily, Miss Ivors, Gretta—also take place in the film, they are no longer part of a general process of education which runs throughout the story until it ends in the complete demolition of the self-centred position of the hero. Furthermore, Hart, who acted as literary advisor for Huston's film, thinks that Joyce's 'The Dead' 'is best understood in relation to the preceding stories in *Dubliners*' (1988: 7), and that because the film does not elaborate on this it 'is more engaged than the story, more immediately poignant, more concerned with realism, less with artistic transformation' (1988: 16). There are two salient instances of Huston's attention to historical detail in this film: the relationship between Catholics and Protestants, and the concern with the New Woman. In dealing with both, a marked emphasis along with a subsequent change in focus is introduced.

In Joyce's story the tension between Catholics and Protestants can be seen in Aunt Kate's attitude towards Mr Browne, but a sort of harmony prevails in keeping with the Irish hospitality celebrated by Gabriel in his speech. In Huston's film, this is much more precarious and the Protestant Browne starts at the top only to eventually go downhill. Browne begins by ascending the stairs and announcing the Epiphany (Palacios González 1999: 1110);[4] but he ends up alone, drunk and snoring in the men's dressing room at the bottom of the stairs. Those moments in Joyce's story when Browne cooperates with the others have been elided; instead, he is shown drinking, sometimes alone and rather heavily, and provoking Freddy by insisting on calling him Teddy (as he does in the story but without any negative consequences). Whereas in Joyce's text Freddy and Browne use drink as a way of bridging the distance between opposite factions, in Huston's film the role of crossing social boundaries is exclusively reserved for

---

[4] According to Palacios González, this is one of those anticipations that Huston, in contrast with Joyce, likes to make. Jolanta W. Wawrzycka (1998: 68) gives the example of the presentation of Gretta: 'the first-time viewers of Huston's *The Dead* ... will immediately recognise the importance of the character she plays', whereas 'it will take the readers by surprise to discover Gretta Conroy's function in the story'. Lothe (2000), though, points out a good number of prolepses in the story that the reader can find on second reading.

Freddy, who is not tied to any definite social niche—frustrating as he does his mother's expectations of marriage. He makes efforts to explain the life of Catholic monks to Browne; he uses the ladies' dressing-room instead of the men's; he praises a black tenor while the other guests all speak of white grand tenors; he drinks with a Protestant; and he plans to go to the monastery where the monks sleep in their coffins, thus moving between lay and religious life. By portraying Freddy positively and Browne negatively, Huston, unlike Joyce, seems to reproduce Catholic bitterness against Protestants. This does not mean that Huston's film is restricted to problems specifically related to being Irish; on the contrary, he balances these with more general concerns. For example, Miss Ivors's nationalism is balanced with her feminism, and feminism crosses the barriers of class, nation and race. Similarly, the story of passionate love, of Celtic origins, has transcended the borders of one country and become a central myth in Western culture. Finally, by facing Gabriel with issues that transcend frontiers—such as feminism or, as discussed below, consumerism and the concealment of death in advanced societies—the film makes it clear that his bond with his country does not have to limit him as he fears.

A crucial area where Huston's historical sensitivity is revealed is his treatment of the relationship that Gabriel and especially Gretta establish with Miss Ivors. The Hustons—John Huston's son, Tony Huston, wrote the screenplay—made few but important changes concerning this point. In the film, Gabriel's rude answer to Gretta is exclusively the result of Miss Ivors's attack on him, which reaches its climax when she calls him 'West Briton'. In Joyce's story, while Mary Jane is playing the academy piece, Gabriel contemplates a family picture, remembers—and resents—his mother's objection to his marriage with Gretta, and feels it necessary to defend his choice mentally by arguing that it was his wife who took care of old Mrs Conroy in her last illness. His rudeness towards Gretta when she proposes going to the West as Miss Ivors had suggested is not only a consequence of the state of mind that the latter has generated, but also of his mother's 'presence'—she had en-gendered (masculine) expectations the unfulfilment of which is related to Gretta and her more 'lowly' Irish origins. In Joyce's story, then, under the immediate cause of Gabriel's perturbed state of mind—Miss Ivors's attack—lies a deeper one in Gabriel's unconscious, his mother's rejection of his wife. This disappears in the film, but not because Huston is uninterested in the subject of dominant mothers; on the contrary, instead of presenting it as Gabriel's personal problem, he exposes the institutional role of the mother as represented by Mrs Malins: to impose social conventions, such as marriage, on her children.[5]

In the clash between Miss Ivors and Gabriel during the lancers dance, the gender of the protagonists of the quarrel matters, from a historical point of view, as much as the subject under debate.[6] Apart from their divergent approaches to nationalism, the source of the discrepancy between them is the fact that Miss Ivors, as the representative of the New Woman trying to enter the male public political sphere, poses a challenge for the man committed to playing the part of the patriarch in the enclosed world of the party. As in Joyce's story, Miss Ivors leaves before Gabriel makes his speech (which he had hoped to make use of in order to take revenge on her), thus indicating that she has little time for nostalgic dealings with the past, while she also denies him the alternative to gallantly accompany her home. The difference between film and story is very noticeable at the moment of Miss Ivors's goodbye, where Huston fills in a gap in Joyce's text in a revealing way. Just before dinner, Miss Ivors takes leave at the top of the stairs. In Joyce's text she does not explicitly confirm where she is going, but neither does she deny that she is going home. In Huston's film it is made clear that she is exchanging dinner for a political meeting:

> - If you really are obliged to go, I'd be glad to see you home.
> - I'm not going home. I'm off to a meeting.
> - O, what kind of meeting?
> - A Union one at Liberty Hall. James Connolly is speaking.

In Joyce's story Mary Jane shows 'a moody puzzled expression on her face' (193), which can only be the result of her inability to understand Miss Ivors's hasty departure, and Gabriel, wondering whether her

---

[5] In the film, Mrs Malins points out the contrast between Freddy and Gabriel as she descends the stairs assisted by the latter: she defines Gabriel, who represents the institutional stability of marriage for her, as a firm post which one can hold on to, while Freddy, who 'will never marry', is defined visually by his comic instability as he descends the stairs with a chair for his mother.

[6] Kevin Barry (2001: 50-3) emphasises the issue of nationalism and refers only in passing to feminism.

leaving has to do with their previous clash, 'stared blankly down the staircase' (193). As for Gretta, we can only deduce her attitude in Joyce's text from the sentence, 'Well, you're the comical girl, Molly' (193), and when we read that 'Mrs Conroy leaned over the banisters to listen for the hall-door' (193), a gap is left open as to what this means in terms of her attitude. Just at this moment Huston introduces a powerful variation: he replaces the attention that Joyce's narrator pays to Mary Jane—who is used instead to provide a historically specific detail when she states, 'Sure you'll be the only woman there'—by the camera's focus on Gretta through a series of close-ups with Gabriel in the background. Her attitude, reminiscent as it is of previous close-ups, strongly suggests that she faces a lost opportunity, an alternative to her 'dull existence', as Gabriel puts it, and more specifically to married life. In other words, in the film Gretta not only remembers a lost love, an ideal alternative that has evaporated, but she also ob-serves a historical and contemporary alternative in Miss Ivors. At this moment, then, his lesser concern with Gabriel's education allows Huston to reproduce the historical context more closely or, it might be claimed, more 'faithfully' and pungently for his late twentieth-century audience, inviting them to ponder with historical hindsight what is announced through the figure of Miss Ivors. This is the true moment of Gretta's epiphany in the film, as we see her before two alternatives which are both equally denied to her. The first alternative is an ideal one, but incompatible with everyday life, enacted by the passion and death of Michel Furey; the second is real, historically bound to transform women's lives, but equally beyond Gretta's scope. This takes place in an instant, but the contrast with Joyce's text helps to emphasise it for those familiar with it. Unfortunately, criticism of film versions of literary texts has too often centred on what is lost in the differences between the text and the film, but the way in which these differences may be illuminating, as in this case, tends to be ignored. Indeed, one should take into account the historical audience that induced Huston to this recreation of the literary text. While most of Joyce's contemporary readers would normally react to Miss Ivors as Gabriel or Gretta do in the story, and they would not be anachronistic because the New Woman was still a strange specimen, those members of Huston's audience who reacted in the same way, many as they still may be, would certainly be behind their times.

Despite his presentation of women having often been considered misogynist, by offering Miss Ivors as an alternative, Huston challenges the audience to acknowledge the historical role of the New Woman.[7] Joyce was content with the clash between the patriarch and the political woman, but Huston supplemented this by placing before Gabriel's wife a destiny that does not lead beyond life and death as that of the lovers, but materialises in history. So Gretta is suspended in the film between past and future, an ideal from the past and an ideal for the future. Is Huston simply representing a past situation more 'faithfully' than Joyce could ever do? After the feminist revolution, are women no longer suspended between the two ideals? Or perhaps the 'palaver', to borrow Lily's bitterly dismissive description of men's behaviour, is now much more powerful in so far as it is consumed in multiple ways, while the feminist revolution is all too often taken for granted.

The Structuring Function of the Myth of Passionate Love

In the same way that the potatoes are not reserved for Gabriel in the film, passionate love does not exclusively affect Gretta. The myth of passionate love as the maximum expression of life lived in full is the topic which dominates the party in the film. Full life is experienced by some characters as belonging to the 'old times'—Aunt Kate caught in a close-up, spellbound as she remembers Parkinson, the tenor she heard in her youth—by others as a romantic ideal—the young girls—and by Gretta in both these senses, that is, as an ideal which belongs to the past. Only the woman who is absent, Miss Ivors, has an alternative to it.

It is crucial to note that, in the film, the subject of passionate desire, and also subject to it, is, and is supposed to be, a woman. For the men this idea of love is only an aesthetic object, whose beauty they may use to attract women—as the poetic voice in Mr Grace's poem laments, Lily seems to have already experienced, and D'Arcy is very close to enacting. It is around this centre that all the other actions move in a relationship of parallelism and contrast: D'Arcy and Miss

---

[7] In contrast, Wawrzycka, following Mulvey and de Lauretis, states that 'the character of Gretta, framed by Gabriel's (and the audience's) gaze, is finally "articulated" by Gabriel's look' (1998: 73).

O'Callaghan flirt with the idea, the young girls are fascinated by it—unlike Freddy, as little concerned with it as he is with marriage, and Miss Ivors, who is not enchanted by the past as the other women are. For their part, Aunt Julia and Mr Grace are two vehicles of tradition without being much affected by it: she sings 'Arrayed for the Bridal', stressing the contrast between the message and the messenger even more in the film than in the story, while he plays the role of the intellectual as he recites a poem about a love he has no more experienced than the other intellectual in the party, Gabriel. As for the protagonists, they represent the contrast between married life and the story of passionate love.

The film's rendering of Gretta as she listens to the song 'The Lass of Aughrim' crucially expresses the contrast between passionate love and married life, between a love that transcends human life and an institution that is meant to socially reproduce it. The attraction that Gretta exerts on the camera repeats the fascination of the Western imagination with the story of passionate love that Denis de Rougemont (1983) has thoroughly documented and that the girls' fascination with the poem re-enacts. But while on the one hand the camera repeats the fascination, on the other it shows its dangers. Gretta has experienced the story of love and death that she now revives, and the girls pine for a passionate love whose nature is actually unknown to them. When Hart laments the replacement of Gretta's definition of Gabriel as 'generous' in Joyce's story (214) for 'responsible' in the film, he explains the meaning of 'generous' but not that of the repetition of this word in Joyce's story. The first time it applies only ironically to Gabriel, since Gretta uses it not knowing the reason why he tells her at this particular moment the story of his lending Freddy a sovereign (namely, to show off his generosity as a strategy to attract her). The second time, however, the narrator refers to the true generosity of Gabriel's humble acceptance of his wife's past and of his role in her life. But the 'Generous tears' cannot be filmed; hence no repetition and no word play are possible. The Hustons supplied 'responsible' which, as Hart correctly says, is 'doubtless a good thing in a husband' (1988: 17). Precisely—Gabriel may, and should, aspire to be a good husband, because becoming the subject of the story of passionate love is simply not a possibility for him, and this not because of any quality or capacity he lacks, but because he is a married man, and passion of the Tristan and Isolde kind is at odds with any social convention or institution, and with marriage as their main representative.

The Camera, Gabriel and the Audience

Both Joyce and Huston give great importance to the different ways of performing transitions from one kind of space to another: the stairs connecting public and private sphere,[8] the windows—a point of contact between the exterior and the interior—, the street covered with snow, and the cab that takes the main characters from the party to their room in the hotel, thus separating the intimate sphere of the couple (at least this is what Gabriel expects) from the rest of the world. Huston's camera adds to these traditional symbolic spaces of transition the fade as a device to connect exterior and interior. In the film, the windows at the Morkans' only contribute briefly to the transition from exterior to interior. One can distinguish dancing figures through the windows when the camera shows the front of the house at the beginning of the film, but we never see through them from the inside. There is a moment in the story when, just before his speech, Gabriel wishes to escape and imagines people outside looking up at the windows (199). Gabriel's musings are omitted in the film; instead, the camera takes the place of the people outside watching the front of the house as it did at the beginning. That it is not an imagined person but a camera that actually observes makes a significant difference, because the only people behind the camera belong to the future; in other words, it is the audience who become here the 'people' Gabriel imagines and who perhaps cast as cold an eye on the party as the camera seems to do at this moment.

The camera itself performs the transition from exterior to interior by crossing the wall as the front of the house dissolves into the goose carcass. This is not the only time that the camera replaces Gabriel's imaginings as it performs a transition and that it does so in order to get the audience involved. There is another moment when the camera performs a transition on its own as it slowly ascends the stairs and goes to a room where it shows us objects which seem to be

---

[8] The stairs achieve great plastic force in the film, where we see all the characters performing the transition between the ground and the upper floor, whereas in the story only the protagonists are followed at this moment.

meaningless because the subject for whom they make sense is not there (Gandía and Pedraza 1989: 154). This recalls the Berkeleyan question about the table when there is no one there to see it. Huston seems to be suggesting that when there is no one there, a camera may still be filming; once again, the camera stands in for a future someone. The effect of this is to carve out another time dimension, an indefinite yet future one in so far as it is the time of any audience.

The shot of the perfectly clean carcass does not correspond to anyone's point of view at the table, thus establishing a strong contrast between a mere skeleton and the traditional meaning invested on the wishbone that becomes a part of D'Arcy's and Miss O'Callaghan's dallying. The connection between Gretta's story and the new couple is established after Mr Grace reads the poem: after the camera shows the young girls' fascination in a repeated shot, and just before the applause abruptly awakes Gretta from her daydreaming, D'Arcy tells Miss O'Callaghan that the poem would make a beautiful song. Later, it is Gabriel that gives them the wishbone and finally D'Arcy sings to Miss O'Callagan the song that Michael Furey used to sing to Gretta, thus definitively plunging the latter into her past. D'Arcy and Miss O'Callaghan's romance functions in the film as a pivot between the institution of marriage that Mrs Malins sees fulfilled in Gabriel and the mere 'palaver' that Lily denounces at the beginning. In the latter case, we have the degradation of the story of passionate love, the use of its rhetoric with no true feeling or meaning; in the former, we have its opposite—married life, which, as Gabriel comes to accept at the end, does not achieve the intensity of the mythic lovers' ecstasy. One does not know how the relationship between D'Arcy and O'Callaghan will develop, though they seem rather foolish. As for Gabriel, once he is no longer jealous, though still envious, of Michel Furey, he becomes a companion for his wife and thus in his apparent defeat he offers an alternative to the passionate love relationship. Though it will never achieve the intensity that death invests on the lovers' tragic instant, it will nevertheless be good for living.

During their cab ride to the hotel, Gabriel attempts to direct his wife's attention to an intimate evening far away from their children, but he realises that it is futile and gives up soon, contrary to what happens in Joyce's story, in which his struggle to control his wife's feelings dominates a good part of the scene in the hotel room (Barbeito 2004: 261-3). In the film, this scene begins with the camera crossing a wall again. It is impossible to reproduce the story's introductory ascent of the stairs, nor does Huston attempt to translate it onto the screen. In Joyce's text, the narrator adopts Gabriel's point of view and records his feelings:

> She mounted the stairs behind the porter, her head bowed in the ascent, her frail shoulders curved as with a burden, her skirt girt tightly about her. He could have flung his arms about her hips and held her still for his arms were trembling with desire to seize her … in the silence Gabriel could hear the falling of the molten wax into the tray. (212)

Instead, the camera remains for a moment focusing on the empty stairs and then penetrates into the room across the wall with a fade in of Gabriel's face in the mirror.

Both in the story and in the film the light from the window is decisive. In the film, however, Gabriel does not tell the porter to take the candle away as he does in the story, unconsciously choosing the light from the window with the resulting irony that the 'long shaft [of light] from one window to the door' (213), which determines the very movements of the characters in this scene in Joyce's text, is the 'ghastly light' associated with Michael Furey (Barbeito 2004: 260-1). The light from the window in the film projects prominent shadows on the wall, a sort of radiography of the protagonists. This anticipates the vision of his life that Gabriel is going to have as a consequence of Gretta's story—the 'light' of Michael Furey again—and foreshadows the shades, which he is soon going to experience as his own end. Both the light and Gretta's story come from the outside, precisely the position Furey occupied when he sang his last song to her. After she falls asleep, Gabriel takes his place by the window where he looks out and is looked at by the camera through the windowpane; he remembers and visualises his dance with Aunt Julia, which he observes from the outside through a window, and then imagines her dead. The camera, which has previously taken advantage of its distance from the protagonist to carve out the time dimension inhabited by no one but the audience, now identifies with Gabriel, but also transcends him as the viewers are invited to share in a serene contemplation of death.[9]

---

[9] See Anne Marie Paquet-Deyris (2000). For Carlos Losilla (1989: 152) 'the future does not seem to exist' in the film. As a consequence, he thinks that Gabriel's voice-over becomes 'the voice of a ghost' (153) because it now performs the same function

One may hear an echo here of the end of Wordsworth's 'Intimations of Immortality', where the sunset clouds receive a sober hue from the eye that has contemplated mortality:

> The clouds that gather round the setting sun
> Do take a sober colouring from an eye
> That hath kept watch o'er man's mortality (Wordsworth 1977: 529)

In Wordsworth's poem, the poet enjoys his solitude and, instead of ghosts, there are 'intimations', 'embers' of an immortal life. In both Joyce's story and Huston's film, the sobriety with which Gabriel contemplates death comes from his acceptance of the humble place that he as a husband has occupied in the life of a wife on whose heart an unknown rival has branded unforgettable feelings. The fascination will always remain with the heroic life and with death in the prime of life—'Better pass boldly into that other world, in the full glory of some passion, than fade and wither dismally with age' (219). Such fascination goes back in Western culture to archaic Greece, and since the twelfth century it has been embodied in the love story of life and death. In non-heroic times, when consumerism seems to offer an escape to lives curved under the weight of routine, the power of the story is potentially more alienating than ever. By making Gabriel and his audience learn from the contrast between ordinary life and the story of passionate love, Huston takes advantage of Joyce's text to use the power of the myth in the service of a life that, like Huston's own, does not end in its prime and is to be led with death on the horizon. In contrast with traditional societies where death was mythically invisible yet socially present, advanced societies generally tend to make death invisible. In the postmodern world, death has disappeared from public light (and life) only to reappear as a spectacle. In this sense, Huston's *The Dead* runs against the grain of the widespread social ignorance of death. Therefore Gabriel, in an act of infidelity to the letter of Joyce's text, must be fully awake at the end of the film in order to realise the sober contemplation of death.

---

as the memories of the dead and the voice-over heard by Gretta (Michel Furey's song sung by Bartell D'Arcy).

Bibliography

Baechler, L. and A. W. Litz (1988) 'John Huston. Director. *The Dead*', *James Joyce Quarterly*, 25 (4), 521-7.

Barbeito, M. (1997) '*Dubliners*: "A Style of Scrupulous Meanness"', *Il Confronto Litterario* 14 (28), 606-16.

—— (2004) *El individuo y el mundo moderno: El drama de la identidad en siete clásicos de la literatura británica*. Oviedo: Septem, 251-79.

Barry, K. (2001) *The Dead*. Cork: Cork University Press.

de Rougemont, D. (1983 (1940)) *Love in the Western World*. New York: Schocken Books.

Gandía, J. L. and P. Pedraza (1989) 'John Huston: Una lejana melodía', *Archivos de Filmoteca* 2, 150-3.

Gerber, R. (1988) 'John Huston. Director. *The Dead*', *James Joyce Quarterly*, 25 (4), 527-33.

Hart, C. (1988) *Joyce, Huston and the Making of the Dead*. Gerrards Cross: Colin Smythe.

Hinson, H. (1987) 'The Dead', *Washington Post* (18 December), g01.

Joyce, J. (1972) *Dubliners*. Harmondsworth: Penguin.

Lothe, J. (2000) *Narrative in Fiction and Film: An Introduction*. Oxford: Oxford University Press.

Palacios González, M. (1999) 'Peregrinaxe de James Joyce e John Huston á terra dos mortos', in M. R. Álvarez Blanco and D. Vilavedra Fernández (eds.) *Cinguidos por unha arela común: Homenaxe ó profesor Xesús Alonso Montero*. Vol. 2. Santiago de Compostela: SPUSC, 1107-14.

Paquet-Deyris, A. M. (2000) 'Experiences of Epiphany: John Huston's *The Dead*', in P. Bataillard and D. Sipière (eds.) *'Dubliners', James Joyce. 'The Dead', John Huston*. Paris: Ellipses, 201-8.

Pilipp, F. (1993) 'Narrative Devices and Aesthetic Perception in Joyce and Huston's "The Dead"', *Literature/Film Quarterly* 21 (1), 61-8.

Wawrzycka, J. W. (1998) 'Apotheosis, Metaphor and Death: John Huston's *The Dead* Again', *Papers on Joyce* 4, 67-74.

Stanzel, F. K. (1992) 'Consonant and Dissonant Closure in *Death in Venice* and *The Dead*', in A. Fehn *et al.* (eds.) *Neverending Stories*. Princeton: Princeton University Press, 112-23.

Stam, R. (2000) 'Beyond Fidelity: The Dialogics of Adaptation', in J. Naremore (ed.) *Film Adaptation*. London: Athlone, 54-76.

Walzl, F. (1985) 'Gabriel and Michael: The Conclusion of "The Dead"', in R. Scholes and A. W. Litz (eds.) *Dubliners: Text, Criticism and Notes*. New York: Viking, 423-44.

Wordsworth, W. (1977) 'Intimations of Immortality', in J. O. Hayden (ed.) *William Wordsworth: Poems*. Vol. 1. Harmondsworth: Penguin, 523-9.

Filmography

Huston, J. dir. (1987) *The Dead*. Vestron Pictures.

Politicising Adaptation:
Re-historicising South African Literature
through *Fools*

Lindiwe Dovey

This chapter shows how, through their political and educational goals, postcolonial African film adapters provide a challenge to traditional film adaptation theory. African film adaptations tend to radically re-interpret and re-historicise literary texts written during the 'colonial' era, drawing on history as an additional source in the adaptation process. This process creates infidelities which generate new meaning for contemporary audiences, urging them to see African identity itself as requiring constant re-composition. Briefly situating my claims in the context of postcolonial and film adaptation theory, I move on to analyse the infidelities of one African adaptation, *Fools*, as they exist in the filmmaker's re-presentation, in 1997, of the 1983 novella's scenes of violent crime during apartheid. The powerful choices filmmaker Ramadan Suleman made in transforming South African fiction and history into cinema press for an understanding, on the part of critics, of the political potential of 'unfaithful adaptation'.

The Politics of Film Adaptation

> I looked at the academic impressions [of *Fools*] ... but I also went to the community and said, look, this is the book we're [adapting] and this is the character I'm going to be playing ... When [I] go to [my] community, and the shebeens [township bars] ... I bounce my characters off my fellow drinkers. It's the society I live in, the people I live with ... so I try to give them space to contribute to my artistic interpretations of the characters and story ... It's a completely different impression from the one academics would have. Academics look at things from up here – and [in the township] what I get [is] the soul of the character, which is where I base my perform-ance. Academics too have a soul, but often they do not project the soul—it's just about intelligence.[1]

---

[1] Patrick Shai, lead actor of *Fools*; filmed interview with author, March 2003.

Describing his preparation for the role of Zamani in *Fools,*
Patrick Shai articulates a vital aspect of African film adaptation,
which, I will argue, sets it apart from Western film adaptation, as
many African film adapters grapple not only with the intellectual and
aesthetic questions of how to transfer literature to cinema, but also
with the pressing political problems of how to represent a colonial
past in a postcolonial present, thereby recreating a history and identity,
or, in Shai's words, a communal 'soul'.[2] This reconstructive urge is
described in explicit terms by Senegalese postcolonial critic, Achille
Mbembe, who argues that it is only 'by force of repetition' that
African narratives 'end up becoming authoritative' and that Africa
itself is 'a subjective economy that is cultivated, nurtured, disciplined
and reproduced'. The past, he says, must be 'recycled and imbued
with new meanings' (Mbembe 2002). And Senegalese filmmaker
Moussa Sene Absa draws attention to the role of the African filmmaker as communal storyteller, saying that, 'We [African filmmakers]
have a [different] goal [from Hollywood], which is to educate ... We
think that cinema can help in changing realities ... telling the society,
this is you, look at the mirror like this ... Every country, every
continent has its own goals [in filmmaking], its own way of telling
stories, its own character'.[3]

Through an analysis of Ramadan Suleman's 1997 film adaptation (set in 1989) of Ndebele's 1983 novella *Fools* (set in 1966), I will
argue that it is this—essentially political— function of many African
adaptations that is at the source of their challenge to Western adaptation theory, and that this challenge is manifest in two related areas.
Firstly, it is evident in the way in which African film adaptations
frequently situate themselves in relation to particular historical
moments, using history itself, so to speak, as a source, in addition to

---

[2] While this chapter engages in comparative analysis of novella and film, it attempts
to move beyond 'medium specificity' theorising, whose aesthetic basis—as Sarah
Cardwell points out (2003)—was contested in the 1980s and 1990s by 'culturalists',
intent upon situating film in a broader context. This chapter, although recognising its
own reliance on aesthetic analysis, claims that it is not enough simply to debate
whether literature and cinema own different 'languages': the filmmaker's decisions
beyond those relating to the shift in medium are the ones that carry authority, and thus
potential political consequences.
[3] Filmed interview with author, March 2003.

the literary text. The second, related, challenge is apparent in the ways in which African filmmakers often radically alter their source material, reconstructing the past moment in the present, making it necessary for the adaptation theorist to read each through the other.

Certain theorists, such as Patrick Cattrysse, have begun to confront the way in which history has been largely ignored in film adaptation theory, and to suggest that we replace traditional film adaptation studies with 'source studies'. Cattrysse argues that 'a so-called film adaptation of a literary text generally adapts many other semiotic devices next to the one literary source text' (1997: 223), and that

> [b]y opening up the study of the film adaptation to all possible semiotic devices that may have functioned as models, the film adaptation is analyzed in a larger context, and many new and interesting aspects of the adaptation come into focus. (1997: 229)

In the context of postcolonial African film adaptation, Cattrysse's source study is not merely preferable, but necessary, as the means to taking into account the way in which these films work in and with history as well as with literary texts.

The radical alterations to source material in many African adaptations pose a challenge to film theorists' traditional reliance on the criterion of fidelity. Erica Sheen argues that the prominence of fidelity as a topic of debate within adaptation studies means that it should not be simply superseded, but should instead be explored in new ways so as to highlight its larger discursive function. For, as Sheen points out, 'The way adaptations [that are perceived to be 'unfaithful'] produce not just animosity, but incoherent animosity, suggests that what is at stake is institutional definitions and *identities* rather than textual forms and contents' (Sheen 2000: 3 [my emphasis]).

While Sheen refers to the implicit construction of Western institutional identities around canonical texts, her argument is useful in drawing attention to the way in which identity is always at stake in acts of repetition and/or interpretation. My own argument is that the liberties taken by African adaptations—their radical infidelities—foreground the ways in which they are working with identity—an identity that is fundamentally to do with Africanity. This is not the kind of Africanity promoted, for example, by the Negritude movement, which implies that a pure African past can be recuperated, but a reconstructing of identity which forestalls closure and invites us to think of Africa itself as potentially revisable and reconstructable.

In relation to the re-historicising produced by the radical infidelities of African adaptations, Gérard Genette's notion of the 'hypertext' is also useful, defining, as it does, a situation in which 'a new function is superimposed upon and interwoven with an older structure, and the dissonance between these two concurrent elements imparts its flavor to the resulting whole' (Genette 1997: 399). Genette's comprehensive taxonomy of literature that rewrites previous literature, as set out in *Palimpsests*, has recently been seen by many film adaptation theorists as providing not only an extremely valuable set of shared terms, but also an approach to film adaptation grounded in the notion of transtextuality. Genette identifies five types of transtextuality,[4] and places film adaptation in the category of hypertextuality, which he defines as 'any relationship uniting a text B ... the *hypertext* ... to an earlier text A ... the *hypotext* ... upon which it is grafted in a manner that is not that of commentary' (Genette 1997: 5). It can be argued, however, that the mode of adaptation practiced by African filmmakers does in fact embrace commentary (the domain of metatextuality, according to Genette) and thus results in their creating hypertexts that also operate as metatexts—as commentaries on texts and history operating from within that history, rather than as a form of critique from an assumed position outside of history.

In discussing hypertextuality, Genette makes an important distinction between 'formal transpositions' and 'thematic transpositions'. He distinguishes the former as 'transpositions that are in principle (and in intention) purely *formal*, which affect meaning only by accident or by a perverse and unintended consequence' (Genette 1997: 213) and the latter as 'transpositions that are overtly and deliberately *thematic*, in which transformation of meaning is manifestly, indeed officially, part of the purpose' (Genette 1997: 214). African film adaptations, I would argue, could generally be classed as thematic rather than formal transpositions, since they tend to be deliberately unfaithful to their sources' content and methodologies in order to generate new interpretations of African texts and contexts. They

---

[4] These are intertextuality (Genette 1997: 1-2), paratextuality (3), metatextuality (4), architextuality (1), and hypertextuality (5).

require the adaptation theorist to perform what Genette calls a relational reading:

> That relational reading (reading two or more texts *in relation* to each other) may be an opportunity to engage in what I shall term, with an outmoded phrase, an *open structuralism*. Indeed, two kinds of structuralism coexist, one of which is concerned with the closure of the text and with deciphering its inner structures ... The other kind ... demonstrates how a text (a myth) can, with a little help, 'read another'. (Genette 1997: 399)

Without intending to adopt a structuralist approach (open or closed), I hope that my discussion of *Fools* will reveal how this South African adaptation requires the critic to undertake just such a 'relational reading'—to move back and forth between book and film, and the historical moments encompassed by the times in which they are embedded and the times they represent.

The Case of *Fools*

Although set in 1966 and written at the height of the South African apartheid resistance movement in the mid-1980s,[5] Ndebele's novella refuses to engage directly in an anti-apartheid, anti-white critique. Instead, as Graham Pechey has pointed out, Ndebele's writing contributed to the creation of a post-apartheid rather than an anti-apartheid perspective on South Africa, even though it was produced in the time of apartheid. Pechey distinguishes the practice of anti- and post-apartheid discourse as follows:

> Anti-apartheid discourse demands tactical simplifications, ethico-political short-cuts and makeshifts of the kind that Ndebele's post-apartheid perspective readily understands but *always exceeds*. Post-apartheid discourse is in this sense not a new orthodoxy of 'liberation' ... [but] the critical interlocutor of all projects for democratic renewal; and its theme is nothing less than the (re)composition of the whole social text of South Africa. (1994: 3-4 [emphasis in original])

As Pechey's analysis suggests, Ndebele's aim has been to develop an autochthonous black critical project, conscious of the overarching

---

[5] Apartheid is generally considered to have run from 1948, when D. F. Malan became the President of the Nationalist Party, until 1994, the year of South Africa's first democratic elections.

structures of apartheid, but focused on appraising the black South African community, and thereby 'recomposing' it.

In his critical essays, Ndebele has concentrated on the shortcomings of protest literature, long considered the only satisfactory response by black South African writers to the apartheid regime. When asked whether he agrees with Pechey's assessment of his work as falling within the domain of 'post-apartheid' discourse, Ndebele said:

> [Yes] ... in the sense that the reason that I broke with ... the protest tradition ... was that I was trying to deliberately focus on the individual experience as opposed to the tendency of the system to massify. What the system did was to treat people— black people—as a big mass of people to whom you could *do* things ... And the impact of that is to devalue the person ... So, I think that what is likely to happen in South African literature in a post-apartheid condition is precisely that [i.e. valuing the individual]—the matter of reconciliation is not a public spectacle.[6]

The violent act at the heart of Ndebele's novella, a black-on-black rape, is—unlike the politically- motivated white crimes represented during apartheid through both protest literature and liberal humanist writing—essentially personal.[7] Furthermore, the narrative is focalised through the consciousness of the black protagonist, Zamani, who performs this act of brutality against one of his pupils, Mimi. In this way Ndebele takes on the role of 'critical interlocutor'—to use Pechey's term—of his community, re-valuing the individual even as he shows this character coming to grips with his violent crime against one of his own people.

The rape, recounted as flashback, occurs extra-diegetically, while the diegesis follows the interaction between Zamani, a middle-aged schoolteacher and disillusioned former anti-apartheid activist, and Zani, Mimi's brother, whom Zamani recognises as a younger, lost version of himself, and who is returning home for the first time since the rape occurred. The story concludes with Zani, a budding activist, protesting against a township celebration of Dingaan's Day, which— as he rightly claims—represents the defeat of Dingaan's black

---

[6] Filmed interview with author, May 2003 [emphasis in original].

[7] The writing of white South African liberals about the suffering of black South African individuals—typified in the work of Nadine Gordimer and Alan Paton—is generally labeled 'liberal humanist'.

warriors by white Afrikaners and thus should not be cause for festivity.[8] Zani's headmaster tries to chase the boy away from the celebration by hurling a stone at him. The stone misses Zani, but hits the car of a passing Afrikaner, who, enraged, takes a whip out of his car and proceeds to lash Zamani. While everyone else scatters, Zamani remains, bearing punishment on Zani's behalf and thereby atoning for his own crime against Mimi. Although Zamani's crime is not directly decipherable in political terms, the metaphors throughout the novella allow us to understand that it is Zamani's sense of powerlessness under apartheid that has led him—a victim—to seek someone even more powerless than himself as a scapegoat for his anger and pain.

Suleman's decision to adapt this novella into film in 1997 is interesting in itself, given that black-on-black violence has escalated in post-apartheid South Africa, which currently has one of the highest levels of violent crime and rape in the world. Suleman's adaptation adheres to the novella's story as recounted above, but deviates from it in certain crucial respects, both content-wise and methodologically, creating infidelities which will be the focus of my analysis. The filmmaker was inevitably to lose Zamani's interior voice— 'devocalization' (Genette 1997: 290)—in the transformation from book to film,[9] but he also made choices that have little to do with the constraints of shifting a narrative from one artistic medium to another. It is these choices that are significant in demonstrating his authorial voice and his re-historicising of his source(s).

The representation of rape from the perspective of the rapist is fraught with danger, running the risk of encouraging the reader to identify imaginatively with the rapist, or at least to occupy the position of the voyeur, and thus to become an accomplice to the violence. In the novella, Ndebele has Zamani describe the rape in a way that does not allow the reader to visualise the act of violence against Mimi's

---

[8] Dingaan's Day, 16 December, was the name used by black South Africans during apartheid for what the Afrikaners celebrated as the 'Day of the Vow', the day on which—in 1838—464 heavily armed 'Boers' fought and defeated 10,000 Zulus (under Dingaan's leadership) at the Ncome River, due to land disputes. The clash has become known as 'The Battle of Blood River', but in the New South Africa the day of commemoration has been renamed 'Reconciliation Day'. In 1998 a memorial was resurrected for the 3,000 Zulus who died; not a single 'Boer' lost his life in the battle.

[9] The use of voice-over is, of course, the method by which filmmakers frequently attempt to preserve the first-person voice, but Suleman rejected this option altogether.

body—Zamani uses language strangely centred on the act of seeing and being seen, at the same time as being a surreal poetic description of sowing and harvesting:

> 'Here is the chicken', she says.
> We stand up at the same time, and I see her move towards me. I cannot see her eyes; I cannot see her cheeks; I cannot see her lips; I cannot see the bulge of her breasts beneath the dress ... I'm talking to her, but I do not understand my words, for words have yielded more vividly to endless years of seeing ... See, floating on the water, thousands of acorns, corn seeds, wheat and barley, eyeballs winking endlessly like the ever changing patterns on the surface of the water ... I want to come into the water, but I can't ... The pain of heaving! The frightening screams! ... And I break through with such a convulsion. And I'm in the water. It is so richly viscous ... Like the sweetness of honey. And the acorns, and the corn seeds, wheat and barley sprout into living things. And I swim through eyes which look at me with enchantment and revulsion. (Ndebele 1983: 194-5)

While Zamani is made to list the parts of the girl's body that he *cannot* see, Ndebele is simultaneously asking the reader to visualise these parts—the eyes, cheeks, lips, bulge of the breasts—that draw attention to the fullness of her feminine humanity. Zamani cannot see Mimi, but he sees and is seen by a disembodied multitude of 'eyeballs', which seem to approximate the mass of people to whom the apartheid system could do things.[10] Ndebele thus seems to desire the judgement of Zamani's act of rape as the character's attempt to differentiate himself, to 'break through' into an individualised state, but simultaneously as an act of violence against the mass to which he belongs.

The girl, Mimi, brings Zamani a gift of a live chicken, which, after the rape, Zamani describes as squawking 'like a voice of atonement' (Ndebele 1983: 195). In self-recognition, and self-destructive shame, Zamani tears off the chicken's head, releasing it 'to flutter to death freely in the dark' (Ndebele 1983: 195). Zamani's recollection of the rape is, in fact, framed by the metaphor of the chicken, since the recollection is set off by Zamani's visit to Mimi's home, to deliver Zani, who has been stabbed for remarking that one of the township men has 'the mind of a chicken' (Ndebele 1983: 179), to his family. Zamani—on arriving at the scene, ready to help—describes Zani as

---

[10] Ndebele; filmed interview with author, May 2003.

'breathing hard and fast like a chicken that is being slaughtered with a blunt knife' (Ndebele 1983: 181). It is thus the men who are compared to chickens, and it is also through this metaphor that Ndebele presents Zamani's rape of Mimi as a turning in of violence against his own community, and against himself.

Ndebele, in the medium of written language, had to resort to the trope of 'sight' to achieve this outcome, but Suleman, working in the visual medium of film, had the challenge of depicting the rape in a way that would not allow the viewer to occupy the position of voyeur. Stephen Prince, in examining the history of violence in *Hollywood* films, reaches the conclusion that creating a witness instead of voyeur out of the spectator is impossible, since the 'aesthetic contract that the filmmaker must honor with viewers entails that screen violence be made to offer sensory pleasures' (Prince 2000: 29-30). In spite of Prince's argument, Suleman's rape scene in Fools induces only pain and revulsion in the spectator.

Suleman's attempt to represent the characters' emotions through the mise-en-scène renders an interesting sense of 'embodied consciousness'. He cuts to the rape—as flashback— directly after a close-up of Zamani's apprehensive face, thus indicating that the memory of the rape is unravelling within Zamani's consciousness. The manner in which the rape scene is choreographed and edited is thereby 'attributed' by Suleman to *Zamani* (as opposed to the film-maker himself). Inevitably, however, the rape itself (in its cinematic 'presentness') is shown from the camera's point of view—a position external, in an immediate sense, to the consciousness of Zamani.

Suleman does use the camera, nevertheless, as an 'embody-ing' device in one shot during which the camera assumes Zamani's point of view—the camera handheld, and tracking towards Mimi's face—encouraging the viewer to identify with *her* consciousness rather than his. At this point it is not Zamani's *consciousness* (his psychological space) that the viewer is encouraged to inhabit, but his *perception* (his anatomical space). Ndebele has spoken of his shocked reaction to this moment in the film, recalling 'the terror on the face of Mimi … and the realisation that there was a violation of her trust',[11] thereby registering his extreme discomfort as spectator. Held simulta-neously in the physical space of the rapist and the psychological space

---

[11] Filmed interview with author, May 2003.

of victim, the viewer cannot take voyeuristic pleasure in this violation of the child by the man.

In the film the chicken, instead of being compared through simile to a 'voice of atonement', now becomes a witnessed object that we *hear* squawking painfully as Mimi tries to escape. After the camera has assumed Zamani's perceptual space, as described above, Suleman discloses in wide shot Zamani pushing Mimi onto his couch and forcing himself onto her. A close-up of Mimi's distraught face follows, occasionally blocked by her hands, strenuously attempting to repel her rapist. At the moment of penetration Suleman cuts to a shot of Zamani's window—the window the community will break with rocks in the following sequence—and to the sound of a baby crying, highlighting Mimi's youth and foreshadowing the baby she will bear as a result of the rape. After Zamani's window has symbolically been broken, Zamani echoes the community's sentiment by breaking the chicken's neck, causing its blood to spray all over his face, in a gesture which also mirrors the self-referentiality of the stream-of-consciousness scene in the novella. Zamani is shown to be both perpetrator and victim: in violating the girl who came to him in trust, bearing a gift, he has also violated himself and his people.

The chicken's anguished cry is transformed into an aural motif by Suleman who, using a technique that Genette calls 'augmentation' (1997: 254), embellishes Ndebele's story by revealing Zani listening to Mimi give birth. (In the novella, in contrast, Ndebele does not describe the birth, but introduces us to the child of the rape already as an infant). In this way Suleman further emphasises the suffering of women in communities where the impotence and self-hatred of the men is unleashed on those who have least power.

In the novella, this kind of abuse of women by their own menfolk is generalised through the figure of the madman, 'Forgive Me', who is invoked only once, in a letter written to Zani by his girlfriend, Ntozakhe:

> [Zamani] reminds me of the man who lives alone about five houses away from us … Some say he killed his mother, others say it was his wife he killed; some vow he raped his niece … But for as long as I can remember, he has been getting up very early in the morning, and going up and down our street three times, all the while shouting: 'Forgive me! Forgive me! Forgive me!' [...] Nobody knows his real name; but we all call him, 'Forgive

Me'. Now isn't that an example of someone for whom atonement has become the very condition of life? (Ndebele 1983: 253-4)

Like Zani, who represents Zamani's younger self, but also like the
naive young men of the township, 'Forgive Me' is a foil, gesturing
towards the atonement which Zamani must live out, having recognised
the significance of his violation of the girl who was his pupil. Suleman
augments this slight but powerful reference to 'Forgive Me' into an
important, omnipresent character. The film opens with an establishing
wide-shot of 'Forgive Me', in half-silhouette against the sunset,
climbing down from the hillside to the township; throughout the film,
'Forgive Me' re-emerges, wandering the streets or stoking his smoking rubbish heap; in the denouement, 'Forgive Me' comes to Zani's
aid by trying to distract the angry Afrikaner.

     In the film, then, 'Forgive Me' represents not personal atone-
ment, as he does in the novella; he represents, rather, political atonement on behalf of the entire black *and* white community. For the film
version of 'Forgive Me' is not the perpetrator of a crime against his
own family but—as one of Zamani's friends explains—a victim of the
'German war'. Suleman's 'Forgive Me' does not chant for his own
absolution; he prays on behalf of an unknown people, eerily transfig-
ured in paintings of distorted faces on the wall behind his lair—
possibly the white people who co-opted him into the war, possibly the
Germans, possibly the black people of Charterston. He calls out:
'Forgive *them*, God, for they know not what they do' [my emphasis].
His role thus changes from that of the traitor, receiving protection
from his community in return for attempting to atone for his sins
against them, to a victim of white violence in a far-removed society,
and a scapegoat disburdening all humanity of its sins, personal and
political.

     Rather than remaining a local character with a local meaning,
'Forgive Me' appears to have been fashioned into a traditional African
griot or storyteller, partially inside the story and partially without. His
role, particularly at the end of the film, seems to be to deflect attention
away from Zamani's individual crime to humanity's crimes, and
perhaps to situate the black-on-black violence in South Africa in the
larger context of the vast scale of the white-on-white violence of the
Second World War.

     In the first scene of the novella, Zani reminds Zamani of how
he used to whip a schoolchild 'until his skin peeled off' (Ndebele

1983: 161). In the novella's closing scene, Zamani describes being whipped by the Afrikaner in precisely the same words: 'It was *as if my skin was peeling off'* (Ndebele 1983: 275 [my emphasis]). After this moment in which Zamani has borne physical pain on behalf of Zani (the instigator of the Afrikaner's rage), the latter—who has not witnessed the whipping since he runs away—waxes into a naïve speech. As the wounded Zamani approaches Zani, the older man notes, 'I had expected to see pain in his eyes, but I found instead, a pensive look' (Ndebele 1983: 277). In such a way, Ndebele-as-author implies that Zani has not yet crossed the threshold of pain, the threshold beyond which there is nothing left to *say*. For Ndebele, pain brings silence—all that Zamani can do is '[stand] silently next to [Zani]' (Ndebele 1983: 277), and Mimi (the ultimate victim) is the quietest character in the story.

This insight would accord with what Elaine Scarry writes, in *The Body in Pain*, about the fundamental 'unsharability' of pain and thus pain's resistance to language. Those who speak in certain situations, Ndebele suggests, have not experienced the kind of pain that resists language. Zani, oblivious to Zamani's present agony, remarks: '"I suppose they are still dancing, drinking, singing, and fornicating ... And that's the point of it all ... We're just drifting. All without the liberating formality of ritual"' (Ndebele 1983: 277). What Zamani has scarcely performed represents precisely the 'formality of ritual'—of submitting himself to becoming scapegoat so as to restore communal balance, even if in this case the perpetrator is a 'false' one, from outside the community.[12]

Suleman cites part of Zani's speech to Zamani in this closing scene as a postscript to the film: '"The sound of victims laughing at victims ... And when victims spit upon victims, should they not be called fools?"' (Ndebele 1983: 278). Notably, the filmmaker appends *Ndebele*'s name to this quotation, when in fact the words are spoken by Ndebele *through* the character of Zani as a sign of the boy's insight *as well as* his naïveté. Suleman's infidelity on this account to Nde-

---

[12] This is the kind of 'scapegoat mechanism' of which René Girard speaks in *Violence and the Sacred*. Girard uses the term 'sacred violence' to describe forms of ritual practiced in traditional African communities in a 'pre-judicial' condition. By performing such a scene through fiction and film, Ndebele and Suleman speak 'back' to traditional systems of justice in Africa. For them, justice is resolved by the community, not by the state.

bele's ironic authorial tone reveals a discarding of certain nuances in order to reinforce the political thrust of the film. For we cannot ignore the *double entendre* of Ndebele's 'fools'—fools are those who are foolish, and also those who are visionaries, who see more than do ordinary people. Zamani is both—a foolish fool, for enacting his own pain on Mimi, and a visionary fool, since, by the novella's end, he comes to understand the depravity to which he has been driven through his impotence under the system of apartheid, and to take responsibility for his behaviour. In the novella, Zamani sees the complexity of political activism in a way that Zani, being younger and less experienced, does not.

Further to Suleman's abandoning of Ndebele's ironic author-ial tone, Josef Gugler has pointed out how Suleman almost created an incident of collective black revenge violence in the film by rewriting the final scene with 'Zamani defending himself and the Afrikaner dying in a hail of stones [from the black bystanders]' (Gugler 2003: 103). Yet, as Gugler writes, Suleman eventually discarded the idea and 'concluded that Ndebele's was the more powerful image: Zamani's pain symbolising 350 years of suffering endured by Black South Africans, and the white man left to live and, hopefully, regret his deeds' (Gugler 2003: 103-4). Through a close-up of Ntozakhe's hand picking up and then dropping a stone (rather than not showing this action at all), Suleman makes a powerful comment about the need, in post-apartheid South Africa, for black South Africans to reject the desire for physical violence against whites. This image implies that, despite the brutality they have endured at the hands of whites, blacks must refuse to be brutalised as Zamani was.

Commenting on the way the whipping scene is presented in the film, Ndebele points out that:

> [O]ne of the things that [black] African viewers found disconcerting ... is how one white man with [a whip] gets all those people running away ... And there were many people who felt, surely it wasn't this bad. But in fact it was, because what you had were three million white South Africans with a very well-trained army ... and I think it came through very well in the movie that if you have the monopoly of instruments of violence and destruc-tion, you can control large numbers of people who don't have those things.[13]

---

[13] Filmed interview with author, May 2003.

Ndebele's words bring to mind Naomi Segal's definition of violence, and her assertion that it is institutionalised violence that incites scapegoating, since 'abstracts cannot bleed and the symbolic (the fathers) are what they are by being abstract ... That is why the body-blow is always against an other who can be hit ... the child, the animal, the woman. No one can hit the fathers: they are the abstraction and institution of power' (Segal 1994: 142). The way in which Ndebele describes the Afrikaner, as 'someone who wielded absolute power and did not even doubt that things would always remain so' (Ndebele 1983: 273) summons this image of the abstracted, omnipotent 'father' who represents state injustice. Similarly, Suleman seems to perform such abstraction of the Afrikaner in visual terms—for instance, by framing him with low angles, making him seem distant and looming— an overwhelmingly oppressive individual.

The novella concludes with Zamani seeking out his wife Nosipho, who is childless, a nurse (a symbol of *personal* healing), and the daughter of a priest (signifying the importance of private rather than public redemption). One is led to imagine that he will seek forgiveness from his wife as representative of the suffering women of the community. In the novella, Zamani does not escape his outcast status in the community—Mimi and Ntozakhe shun him after the whipping, and it is *Zamani* who stumbles away to search for *Zani*, before he sets out at last on his 'long, painful walk' (Ndebele 1983: 280) to find Nosipho. In the film, it is Mimi, Zani, and his girlfriend, Ntozakhe, who search for Zamani, in what appears to be the film-maker's desire to stage reconciliation between the generations. Zamani, however, scrambles away from them, up the hillside to where the film begins, either to assume the mantle of, or ask pardon from, 'Forgive Me', as the community's most recent victim of white brutality and the scapegoat of the Afrikaner's misdirected wrath.

Made in 1997, in the post-apartheid era that Ndebele had to conjure through his imagination, the film reverses the orientation of the novella's closing gesture. Under apartheid, Ndebele's protagonist has to learn how to escape the process of 'massification' imposed on him by the system; he has to realise his individuality, his full person-hood, by refusing to allow the system to destroy even his soul, and he has to take responsibility and atone for what he has done. In 1997 and beyond, Suleman's film seems to work in the opposite direction, reminding young people—the generation that was not exposed to, or is already forgetting, the worst atrocities of apartheid—of their *collective* history and responsibilities. Through Mimi and Zani's reconciliatory gesture, the film seems to urge the viewer to try to understand the origins of the brutalisation of a black character such as Zamani, although not condone it. The tragedy thus becomes one of *public* redemption in which the violator must be drawn back into the community *by* the community.

Conclusion: Re-historicising through Infidelities

If one of the intentions of African writers and filmmakers is to try to turn their readers/spectators into compassionate witnesses, the way they choose to describe/depict pain and violence is crucial to this endeavour. Through the public medium of film, available to those who cannot read novels, Suleman publicises and re-politicises the violence represented in the novella. His cinematographic and editing choices in the rape scene, in particular, seem intended to provoke viewers into considering their role in current South African society, especially in the context of widespread physical and sexual abuse of women and children in black communities.

At the same time, Ndebele's comment on black African viewers' responses to the white violence in the final scene indicates that the adaptation has already been important in educating viewers and providing them with a sense of their shared history of suffering and oppression under apartheid. Indeed, in relation to the dilemma of how to represent the violent *white* perpetrator in South African fiction, Ndebele—in true post-apartheid vein—writes: 'Artistic compassion only situates the villain within the domain of tragic acceptance, which, in practice, translates itself into moral or political rejection. We cannot wish away evil; but genuine art makes us understand it' (Ndebele 1984: 35).

Whereas the novella asks us to turn away from apartheid to individual life and consciousness, to reflect on the way individuals within an oppressive and violent political environment can keep their soul alive, the film asks us not to focus on the individual at the expense of forgetting apartheid and its continuing legacy. This chapter has attempted to explore the nuances of Suleman's infidelities to the novella, and to suggest that they have allowed him to create an adaptation that re-historicises a past moment in order to politicise and mobilise the consciousness of contemporary South African viewers.

Bibliography

Cardwell, S. (2003) 'Theorizing Adaptation, Temporality and Tense', *Literature/Film Quarterly Online* 31 (2), 82-92.

Cattrysse, P. (1997) 'The Unbearable Lightness of Being: Film Adaptation Seen from a Different Perspective', *Literature/Film Quarterly Online* 25 (3), 222-30.

Genette, G. (1997 (1962)) *Palimpsests: Literature in the Second Degree*. Trans. C. Newman and C. Doubinsky. Lincoln and London: University of Nebraska Press.

Girard, R. (1972) *Violence and the Sacred*. Trans. P. Gregory. Baltimore: Johns Hopkins University Press.

Gugler, J. (2003) *African Film: Re-Imagining a Continent*. Oxford: James Currey.

Mbembe, A. (2002) 'Africa in Motion: An Interview with the Postcolonialism Theoretician Achille Mbembe' by C. Höller, in *Springerin* 3/02. On-line. Available HTTP: http://www.springerin.at (15 October 2003).

Ndebele, N. (1983) *Fools and Other Stories*. Johannesburg: Ravan Press.

—— (1984) 'Turkish Tales and Some Thoughts on South African Fiction', in G. Pechey (ed.) *South African Literature and Culture: Rediscovery of the Ordinary*. Manchester and New York: Manchester University Press, 17-40.

Pechey, G. (1994) 'Introduction', in G. Pechey (ed.) South African *Literature and Culture: Rediscovery of the Ordinary*. Manchester and New York: Manchester University Press, 1-13.

Prince, S. (2000) 'Introduction', in S. Prince (ed.) *Screening Violence*. London: Athlone, 2000, 1-46.

Scarry, E. (1985) *The Body in Pain: The Making and Unmaking of the World*. New York and Oxford: Oxford University Press.

Segal, N. (1994) 'Who Whom? Violence, Politics and the Aesthetic', in J. Howlett and R. Mengham (eds.) *The Violent Muse: Violence and the Artistic Imagination in Europe, 1910–1939*. Manchester and New York: Manchester University Press.

Sheen, E. (2000) 'Introduction', in E. Sheen and R. Giddings (eds.) *The Classic Novel: From Page to Screen.* Manchester: Manchester University Press, 1-13.

Filmography

Suleman, R. dir. (1997) *Fools.* Produced by Jacques Bidou. Distributed in South Africa by the Film Resource Unit.

Adaptation, Appropriation, Retroaction: Symbolic Interaction with *Henry V*

José Ángel García Landa

This chapter approaches adaptation from a hermeneutic perspective, specifically from a post-structuralist hermeneutics of discourse informed by symbolic interactionism. The intertextual relationship between a cultural product (e.g. a play) and its screen adaptation(s) is analysed as a performative intervention on an existing discourse formation which includes both the original product or text and the discourses using it, originating it, deriving from it or surrounding it. This intervention amounts to both an interpretation and an appropriation of the original text. Like other intertextual modes (translations, critical readings), adaptations produce a retroactive transformation of the original, not in se, but rather as it is used and understood in specific contexts and instances of communicative interaction. These theoretical issues are explored with a special focus on Shakespearean film adaptations, more specifically on the major *Henry V* films, Laurence Olivier's (1944) and Kenneth Branagh's (1989), and their treatment of violence and war in a variety of contexts. A case for a 'resisting' approach to Shakespearean adaptation is put forward.

Shakespeare and Adaptation

As late as 1994, a collection of studies on Shakespeare on film began with one of the editors' statement that 'theatre remains the legitimate expressive medium for authentic Shakespeare' (Davies 1994: 1). Such certainty as to what is 'legitimate' and 'authentic' is clearly dissolving fast by now, and the study of both theatre productions and film adaptations of Shakespeare's plays is given a prominent place in some contemporary editions, as film and film criticism are nowadays major cultural discourses for the diffusion and 'recycling' of Shakespeare. Film adaptations effect both interpretations and appropriations of the plays, in order to channel (part of) their existing cultural potential in a given direction, combining it in effect with other discourses.

There is no question, then, of privileging faithful over other types of adaptations as a matter of course. Instead, the adaptation should be seen as having, by definition, a different agenda from the original (aesthetically and ideologically speaking), even if a reuse of the original is included in that agenda. There results also—and here the image of the hermeneutic circle is relevant—a retroactive transformation of the original, not in se, but rather as it is used and understood in specific contexts and instances of communicative interaction—an aspect of significance more adequately studied from the standpoint of social semiotics, ideological critique and reception studies rather than through formalist or aesthetic analysis.

Like any other word, 'adaptation' serves to direct our attention to a common element present in the diverse phenomena it is applied to. In any given case, however, differences between the instances so named may prove to be as relevant or interesting as the similarities between them. That is, each filmic adaptation adapts an original text in a unique way, depending on the specific problems encountered, the solutions given to them, and the different priorities of the adapters besides their common interest in adapting a text. For one thing, an adaptation is an adaptation only if you consider it from the point of view of adaptation. Nothing can come of nothing, and any film script, however 'original', may be analysed from the point of view of the way it adapts previous stories, texts, discourses, myths. That is, me may thrust the issue of adaptation upon any film, although it must be admitted that some films become adaptations once we look at them twice, and some, of course, are born as adaptations.

Shakespeare films would seem to fall into the latter category. But then, what is a Shakespeare film? Consider the ever more diffuse Shakespearean status of Orson Welles's *Macbeth* (1948) and *Chimes at Midnight* (1966), Michael Almereyda's *Hamlet* (2000), Ken Hughes's *Joe MacBeth* (1955) and William Reilly's *Men of Respect* (1990), Jocelyn Moorhouse's *A Thousand Acres* (1997), and Disney Productions' *The Lion King* (1994). A working distinction may be adopted here: Shakespeare films identify themselves as adaptations of a previous text through a title which connects them with the source play—more or less tenuously, of course, and more indirectly through allusions to Shakespeare in the promotional material surrounding the film (prominent references in *A Thousand Acres*; practically none in *The Lion King*).

An aesthetic classification of film adaptations of playtexts popularised by Jack Jorgens usefully sets up three reference points, the 'theatrical', 'realist' and 'filmic' modes (Jorgens 1977: 7-10), in what is arguably a continuum. That is, while Olivier's *Henry V* and *Richard III* (1955) are both 'theatrical', they are not theatrical in the same way, and they are certainly not theatrical in the same way as David Giles's *Henry IV* (1979) for the BBC Shakespeare. Besides, other dimensions of adaptation should be considered, beyond the aesthetic one. The ideological dimension of adaptation could also be assigned three benchmarks: consonant reading, critical re-reading and parodic deconstruction of the original, for instance. Here, as elsewhere, trying to establish neatly watertight categories, and trying to force any one film into any one of these categories, risks oversimplifying the issues (which is not to say that such oversimplifications may not be useful in a given pedagogical or exploratory context). Likewise, fidelity as a criterion to gauge the quality of an adaptation may well be 'misguided' (McFarlane 1996: 22), but still some notion of homology between original and film version must be preserved in order to make them comparable, much more so when the film is defined by its makers as an adaptation, and when it is studied as an adaptation.

Arguably, there is a specific quality in Shakespeare films as against other adaptations. They seem to belong in a choice select group of adaptations with very few equivalents among adaptations of other classical authors—as is to be expected, since Shakespeare is the leading canonical author in the Anglophone sphere, and as such has a unique position in the world's leading film industry. Adaptations of the greatest literary classics may give rise to a number of different films based on the same text. This is a distinct phenomenon, different from sequels (e.g. *Henry V* as distinct from *Rocky IV*), and different as well from adaptations of popular myths (see e.g. the analysis of the Batman films in Brooker 1999: 196). Remakes are yet another phenomenon, insofar as their reference point is the earlier film, rather than the fiction or play on which that film was based. Remakes tend to focus on box-office spectaculars or, again, on popular fiction or myth. If in films of popular myths and in remakes the original text is usually bypassed, in the adaptations of classics it remains a crucial reference point—and usually a crux as well. This is especially so in the case of adaptations of classical drama. Austen, Scott or Dickens adaptations are a comparatively minor phenomenon, and besides they are adaptations of novels, a medium which arguably has a less vitiated relationship to film than drama has. Adaptations of dramatic works start from a medium which, in the light of semiotic and linguistic parameters, is arguably closer to film than novels. Still, many critics have emphasised the different spatial and perspectival dynamics which may turn theatre into a 'false friend' for film, with the novel paradoxically allowing the filmmaker a greater scope in reinventing his or her own aesthetic strategy in filmic terms. A significant part of the text of a play can (should/might/had better not) be used directly in the film script, while most of the text of the novel is simply suppressed (as text) and recoded through mise-en-scène and acting. As is well known, thanks to their swift scenic movement Shakespeare's plays are to some extent 'cinematic' and avoid the stifling theatricality of many films based on 'regular' plays confined by the three dramatic unities.[1] Still, the challenge of successfully transposing Shakespeare's speech has often been noted as a major stumbling block for actors and directors alike.[2] Different traditions of mise-en-scène and acting styles in drama and film usually add to the difficulty of successfully adapting drama to the screen.

The major Shakespeare plays have given rise to a number of variant films, with the earlier versions serving as the 'theatrical' reference point which allows later versions to explore more 'realistic'

---

[1] On Shakespeare's 'cinematic' qualities, see Ball (1968: 38) and McDonald (1980). They are emphasised by Olivier—Shakespeare 'in a way "wrote for the films"' (Olivier 1984: v). For Kracauer, 'Shakespearean plays ... are relatively transparent to unstaged nature, introducing characters and situations which might as well be dispensed with in a strictly compositional interest; and these seeming diversions and excursions evoke, somehow, life in the raw—its random events, its endless combinations' (1997: 219). This would seem to make Shakespeare in a way already cinematic, not theatrical, with his plays finding a most adequate expression in the cinematic medium—or in the TV medium (Coursen 1984, quoted in Davies 1994: 12). Lehmann (2002: 58-9 *passim*) puts forward a far-fetched and well-argued claim to make Shakespeare a cinematic auteur *avant la lettre*—or *avant la caméra*, rather.

[2] Walker (1953: 470-1), quoted in Jorgens (1977: 9): 'the poetic drama does not thrive on photographic realism ... [which] has the effect of making the poetry sound unnatural and self-conscious'. Davies (1988: 5-25) stresses the very different theatrical and filmic approaches to the treatment of space, a serious obstacle to successful adaptation.

or 'filmic' solutions, as well as more critical or deconstructive readings of the play, once the 'straight' (or conventional) one has been appropriated by a previous film. For instance, Franco Zeffirelli's realist *Romeo and Juliet* (1968) both exploits and transcends George Cukor's more theatrical version (1936), and it exhausts the ground in such a way that a major *Romeo and Juliet* after it—e.g. Baz Luhrmann's *William Shakespeare's Romeo + Juliet* (1996)—needs to be more transgressive both aesthetically and ideologically in order to make its mark. The adaptive moves—in setting, costume, present-day reference, stylisation and intermediality—of Luhrmann's film are therefore far more daring.[3] 'Belated' adaptations, while not necessarily anxiety-ridden, tend to present themselves more explicitly as 'a reading of the text' rather than as 'the text, adapted to the medium of film'.

The existence of previous film versions thus produces a retroactive effect, inviting comparison not just with the original but with previous adaptations as well. According to Russell Jackson (2001: 145), a new Shakespeare film, being an adaptation of Shakespeare's text, is not understood to be a 'remake' of a previous film of the same play. Still, for Imelda Whelehan, it is a 'commonplace observation that subsequent adaptations often refer to earlier versions (either critically or as homage) as much as they "return" to the original' (1999: 14). Thus, Branagh's *Henry V* (1989) measures itself against Olivier's *Henry V* (1944) as much as Branagh against Olivier himself, as noted by several critics (e.g. Buhler 2002: 107ff; Kliman 1989). Actually there is not an either/or dynamics at work between adaptation and remake, here or elsewhere. Shakespeare adaptations have multiple intertextual dimensions, connecting them—unlike most adaptations, or remakes—to the original text, to previous films of the same play, to stage productions—which in turn have an intertextual history of their own—and to other discourse formations which appropriate 'Shakespeare' (academic criticism, popular culture, nationalist propaganda, and so on).

---

[3] More daring approaches than mere 'contemporaneity' are thinkable, and they are visible in Luhrmann's film. They are more prominent in Julie Taymor's *Titus* (1999). But some things no one has risked doing yet—e.g. a gay all-male all-naked *Twelfth Night,* an all-black *Othello* with most of the cast in whiteface, a *Julius Caesar* in Hollywood Renaissance costume. Or a Hitlerian Henry V.

Thus, Shakespearean adaptation involves a complex intertextual dynamics. A film's screenplay is of course an adaptation of Shakespeare's play, but in addition many such films are based on a specific theatrical production, which was already an interpretation of the text. This is the case with some of the most celebrated Shakespeare films—Orson Welles's *Macbeth,* Richard Loncraine's *Richard III* (1995), Kenneth Branagh's *Henry V* or *Hamlet* (1996), Julie Taymor's *Titus* (1999). Originally, Shakespeare's dramatic text itself was not a primary means of communication, even if it has subsequently become 'literature' or 'poetry'—in Shakespeare's original conception, it was subordinated to performance, although a play might be published if successfully performed. Moreover, the play was itself an adaptation, a version of a previous literary or historical text written for another medium (most obviously print—e.g. Holinshed's *Chronicles* in the case of *Henry V*).[4] The privileged position of Shakespeare's text as a nexus in the intertextual network may arguably be short-circuited. On the one hand, this might give rise to adaptations which are actually remakes of another adaptation rather than of the Shakespeare play. Shakespeare himself is perhaps too imposing to provide clear instances of this, but there have been films inspired by *Kiss Me Kate* (1953) rather than by *The Taming of the Shrew*. Or, to stick to musicals, Gérard Presgurvic's *Roméo & Juliette: De la haine à l'amour* (2001) seems inspired by Franco Zeffirelli's film rather than by Shakespeare's play. On the other hand, we may find what Michael Anderegg (2000: 155) calls 'retroadaptation', by which the Shakespeare play is reduced to the simple and brief narrative from which it derives—particularly when it is stripped of any trace of Shakespearean language, as in many of the early silent films chronicled by Ball (1968).

Finally, a later adaptation always alters, retrospectively, our perception of both the original play and of previous adaptations, bringing into relief the possibilities of some scenes, or their problematic nature, and the treatment they were given by the earlier adaptation—forcing us, intentionally or unintentionally, to re-read and revaluate.

---

[4] This intertextual continuum is already noted by Jorgens (1977: 14). Cf. the 'five Henry V's' in Hedrick (2003: 215-16).

The Interactionist Theory of Meaning

The late twentieth-century paradigm shift away from formalism and structuralism in the direction of reader-response criticism is familiar enough by now to allow me to presuppose it as a basis for the following discussion. Suffice it to note that another prominent paradigm shift, in the direction of cultural studies and ideological criticism, shares much common ground with the shift towards reader-response, as it is through response that the ideological issues of (visual) texts are generated, brought to light, and played against one another. What I would wish to emphasise is a neglected theoretical connection of reader-response criticism: symbolic interactionism, as theorised in the field of social studies already from the first half of the twentieth century by G. H. Mead and H. Blumer. The symbolic interactionist theory of meaning holds that meaning inheres not in the object, or in the mind, but in a social process of interaction. This proposition can be used as the foundation of a theory of reading and interpretation, and also of related intertextual/interactive phenomena like translation and adaptation. The meaning of a 'source' text, like the meaning of any object, is constituted through interaction—it is not predetermined by what is brought to the interaction and certainly not by a formalist or grammatical grid. Meaning is, then, not objective (not 'in the object'), but it is not subjective either, as it cannot be restricted to the subject's isolated mental processes:

> Symbolic interactionism [...] does not regard meaning as emanating from the intrinsic makeup of the thing that has meaning, nor does it see meaning as arising through a coalescence of psychological elements in the person. Instead, it sees meaning as arising in the process of interaction between people. (Blumer 1986: 4)

Blumer's opposition to the notions of either an 'objective' or a 'subjective' anchoring of meaning, if applied to literary interpretation, yields the revolutionary insight—taking into account that this is a mid-twentieth century theory—that the meaning of a literary text is neither stable nor arbitrary; rather, it is remade for use every time through an interpretive process involving social interaction (1986: 5). That the use of meanings involves an interpretative process means that they are not taken as ready-made: 'The actor selects, checks, suspends, regroups, and transforms the meanings in the light of the situation in which he is placed and the direction of his action' (Blumer 1986: 5)— 'actor' meaning here of course, when applied to film, not just actresses but also directors, scriptwriters, spectators and critics. The transcendental status of the Shakespeare text as a privileged object for adaptation is a function of just a possible context of action, Shakespeare studies, but other social contexts and projects may focus on different aspects of the resulting film. That is, there is a certain validity of the discourse which demands fidelity to the source text, but that validity is defined in that discourse's own terms, and there is no warrant to establish the absolute priority of that discourse over other discourses surrounding the phenomenon of film.

As a matter of fact, adaptation studies as a whole have moved from a formalist paradigm, still prominent in Brian McFarlane's *Novel to Film* (1996), towards a more ideologically, culturally and contextually informed theory of meaning-making. For instance, Robert Stam's (2000) approach to the dialogics of adaptation usefully complements the approach outlined above. A parallel shift away from formalism can be detected in theoretical approaches to other intertextual phenomena—e.g. the theory of translation resisting formalist assumptions of translation understood as an instrumental decoding and new encoding of meaning. Instead, a hermeneutic approach to a whole ('thick') cultural and historical context needs to be undertaken in assessing the adequacy of a translation. A further connection might be drawn between these developments and the integrationalist critique of formalist theories of text and language (Harris and Wolf 1998). The integrationalists too emphasise the agency of the 'observer's position', drawing attention to the role of the analytic approach in the constitution of the meaning being studied—with the current communicative context bringing along its own unpredictable contingency.

As critics are not neutral observers, caught as they are in the process of meaning recycling and ideological production, there is arguably a built-in bias in the criticism of filmic adaptations, as it is a form of discourse which addresses a different audience from that of the adaptations themselves—even if there is a partial overlap—and which has of course a distinctly different ideological agenda. There is no possibly 'neutral' analysis of the rightness or otherwise of an adaptation; any judgment is mediated by the critical project, and any response to that judgement—e.g. a response to a paper discussing the adequacy or otherwise of Laurence Oliver's solutions in *Henry V*—is playing on the interface of the critic's ideology and that of the reader of the critical text. A text's ideology is not a pre-existing content packaged in the text, but rather a process of communicative interaction between the text, its critic, and the critic's audience.

Intertextual Retroaction and Appropriation in *Henry V*

Classical literary texts are burdened by their reception history. Adaptations of such texts are not, we have seen, a solitary confrontation between an auteur and an author. Quite apart from the collective dynamics of filmmaking, the hydra-headed 'auteur' is confronting not so much what the text was, as what it has become: the text is surrounded by an intertextual complex of criticism, of attitudes towards the historical period it is set in, etc.[5] As noted above, interpretive retroaction brings to light elements in the text being interpreted which were subdued or subordinated by previous representations. Critical discourse may be more or less aware of its own retroactive bias on this intertextual complex. At least five theoretically distinct levels of interpretive retroaction can be noted in the critique of an adaptation: the retroaction inherent in the interpreter's reading of the source text, in the interpreter's reading of the adaptation, in the interpreter's reading of the adaptation's reading of the text, in the interpreter's reading of earlier texts of which the source text is an adaptation, and in the interpreter's reading of previous critical approaches to all these texts.

An adaptation, or a critical reading, may be valued for the way it brings out valuable elements in the original, retroactively generating a hitherto invisible virtual dimension of the text, of which the original may come to appear as only one possible expression—and an imperfect one at that.[6] This selective revamping may be used, in the case of

---

[5] Cf. Whelehan: 'the adaptation process … is already burdened by the weight of interpretations which surround the text in question, and which may provide the key to central decisions made in a film's production' (1999: 7). On appropriation as competition, updating and newfangledness, see also Kamps (1999: 27 *passim*).

[6] Cf. Walter Benjamin's theory of translation (1969), according to which a translation illuminates imperfectly realised elements of the original—or Pound's injunction, 'Don't translate what I wrote', instead, 'translate what I meant to write' (quoted in Jorgens 1977: 14). Cf. McFarlane on adaptations from novels: 'there is also a curious

Shakespeare, to make him more Shakespearean than he actually is (or was). But one man's Shakespeareanisation is another man's sanitisation—as when Kenneth Branagh makes King Henry weep as he hangs his former friend Bardolph. Here Shakespeare gives us only Henry's words, 'We would have all such offenders so cut off' (Shakespeare 1992: 138), unpunctuated by tears. Branagh tries to give us a more palatable Henry, a Henry for our times—an all-out appropriation. From Branagh's admission that he 'was probably cautious/nervous/cowardly about doing something that might provoke the wrong kind of reaction to the character' (Wray and Thornton-Burnett 2000: 172), it is apparent that in his view any attitude on the part of the audience short of emotional siding with Henry—a critical questioning of his motives, for instance—would be 'the wrong kind' of reaction. In making Henry more likeable, Branagh—like Olivier before him—makes the overt, jingoistic dimension of the play more acceptable, while it is arguable that a more interesting reading (or adaptation) would concentrate on the *less* likeable and more problematic aspects of both the character and the play. As Alan Sinfield argues, Shakespeare 'has been appropriated for certain practices and attitudes, and can be reappropriated for others' (1985: 137). The virtual dimension of the text to be brought out through interpretive retroaction need not be one which makes Shakespeare more like us or more palatable (or one consonant with an idealised authorial intent), but one which makes him more disquieting (perhaps by deconstructing the text's ideological articulations, or by resisting idealisations of the authorial intent).[7]

Let us take, and provide, a fuller example of such appropriative retroaction: Olivier's *Henry V*, and more specifically the ideological justification of aggressive war in the first scene of the (filmed) play. Much of the Shakespeare text in this scene is cut, and what remains becomes a comic scene in which the issue is settled quite arbitrarily by an honest King's reliance on the learned Archbishop's

---

sense that the verbal account of the people, places, and ideas that make up much of the appeal of novels is simply *one* rendering of a set of existents which might just as easily be rendered in another' (1996: 7). On such 'virtual' dimensions generated by intertextuality or intermediality, see also my 1998 paper.

[7] Cf.: 'One of the merits of a significant Shakespeare film is its capacity to illuminate structures that are not immediately apparent, but which underpin the action in the Shakespeare play' (Davies 1994: 208, commenting on an idea of Lorne Buchman's).

word—although an earlier scene has shown us the King was aware the Archbishop intended to use the war on France in order to buy the Crown's support against a bill which would deprive the Church of many possessions.

Shakespeare's text is notoriously ambivalent at this point, as is his presentation of Henry throughout (see e.g. the various views collected in Quinn 1969; Greenblatt 1985). It is indisputable that Shakespeare is aware of the dubiousness of Henry's political manoeuvres, although he chooses to deal with this issue ambiguously and between the lines, without emphasising the dubiousness of Henry's own legitimacy. As noted by Katherine Eisaman Maus, 'Henry employs against the French a principle that, if it were enforced against him, would strip him of both English and French kingdoms. Yet the point is made so obliquely that only a spectator cognizant of the tangled Plantagenet genealogy is likely to catch it' (Shakespeare 1997: 1449-50). That is, Shakespeare is not exempt from the accusation of Harry-hailing and time-serving, even if he winks at the cognoscenti as he beats the drum.

At first sight Olivier would seem to preserve, in spite of his cuts, the original play's ambivalence as to the King's motives. In fact, though, what is ambiguous in Shakespeare is here conjured away due to a number of factors, of which I will only name a few:

1. Olivier's 'straight' playing of Henry as honest, heroic, open and sincere.[8]
2. The pre-existing dramatic tradition in which Henry was played just thus, with spine-chilling single-mindedness—see Andrew

---

[8] Manheim, however, detects a benign Machiavellian side in Henry, resulting from Olivier's artificial mannerisms and controlling presence, which together intimate 'the idea of Henry as actor and image-maker, as creator of political illusions' (1994: 125). This effect results, I would argue, from Olivier's internalisation of Henry's (rather than Shakespeare's) project, not from a critical or ironic views on his part. As Manheim notes, Olivier's 'very 1940s leading-man dash' has dated, which (retrospectively) brings out the lineaments of some of the contained violence in the play (1994: 122). But Manheim wants to keep his cake and eat it, attributing to Olivier some effects which he nonetheless says arise with historical distance. Another variety of 'middle of the road' reading can be found in Jorgens (1977: 126-7), who ascribes his own skeptic view of Henry to Olivier's filmic treatment, giving the film (and perhaps the play too) more ironic credit than it deserves as a critique of Henry's wars.

Gurr's account of the stage history of the play (Shakespeare 1992: 37-55).

3. Olivier's cutting of many later passages which show Henry in a dubious light, and which could have added to the first scene to provide an ironic comment on Henry (see Geduld 1973: 48-49 for a detailed list of such passages).

4. The fact that Olivier's film begins with a filmed reconstruction of a theatrical performance set in 1600, rather than with an unmediated 'contemporary' performance of the play. This would seem to make allowance for an ironic ideological distance, but only until that distance and its potential for irony are suppressed as the filmed play dissolves into a film which makes the play's ideological conceptions its own.

5. Acting out the text (and filming it) involves an interplay between what is spoken and what is shown on the stage or screen. In Oliver's film, there is ideological consonance rather than dissonance, so that the gestures, acting and setting do not add an ironic inflection to Henry's decision to follow the Archbishop's counsel.[9] The Dauphin's insult to Henry is then used to make Henry the best player in the rhetorical tennis game—and from pleasurable identification with a speaker's rhetorical blows we are led insensibly to condone actual violence on a massive scale. Olivier's film provides a neat transition from the symbolic to the actual (Davies 1988: 31)—but it does so in more than one sense.

Now, how is this issue dealt with by critics of the film? Let us take Harry Geduld's commentary as a representative case. According to Geduld:

> Olivier does not want us to become too aware of the duplicities and complex motivations behind the 'justifications' that the Archbishop offers for Henry's invasion of France (Raymond Durgnat has reasonably objected to this scene on the grounds that it gives moral license to jingoism). In addition, Olivier does not wish to bore us with a deadly serious presentation of

---

[9] The issue has seemed different to some in Branagh's rendering of the same scene: here the clerics are presented as repulsive characters who manipulate the king, as their mutual gaze of good understanding at the close of the scene seems to confirm. But the Branagh film drops the subject after this scene, and Branagh too plays a 'straight' Harry who is neither manipulated nor Machiavellian—although this treatment of the character is itself highly manipulative.

the Archbishop's long and important but dramatically very dull speech on
the Salic Law. So the prelates become amusing characters and the long
speech is almost lost amid the buffoonery over the documents. And so too
Olivier actually leaves in the specious justification for Henry's invasion, but
plays the scene so that we hardly notice its speciousness amid the comedy.
By the time the French ambassador arrives, somehow or other Henry's
forthcoming campaign seems to have been 'justified' without our noticing
precisely how. (Geduld 1973: 28-9)

That is, ideological fog is thrown over the very issue which should
decide whether Henry's war is legitimate or an act of wilful aggression, and, presumably, whether the audience is to identify with Henry
or look upon him as a dangerous bully and manipulator—a matter of
some weight in an ideological approach to the film. Note that both
Shakespeare and Olivier can be said to bury the issue under the
dynamics of theatricality. Now, the same is usually done by their
critics in discussing the episode: whether it is Shakespeare's or
Olivier's aesthetic treatment that is discussed in an appreciative way
by the critic, there can never be a way the moral ugliness of Henry's
war may surface long enough to hold our attention in a critical
discussion. The crucial ideological point becomes lost amid the
theatrics, which is not to say that an ideological effect is not produced,
namely the jingoism alluded to by Geduld before he loses sight of the
issue, as ideological criticism is not among his priorities—after the
passage above Geduld goes on to provide a 'consonant' reading of
Olivier's film's aesthetics in dealing with Shakespearean material.

In an ideologically informed critical approach like the one put
forward here, the existence of rhetorical fog used to justify aggressive
war is a crucial aspect of the study of *Henry V* and of the intertextual
complex surrounding it. No doubt critics who deconstruct the discourse of aggression in *Henry V* do so because of their own political
agenda, and it is with reason too that they point out that there is a
political agenda involved as well in those approaches which take for
granted the play's jingoism and further it with their own unquestion-
ing acceptance.[10] In any case, the interactional context must be taken
into account. Olivier's film was a patriotic film made and released in
time of war, when Hitler's aggressive policy was such a pressing

---

[10] For 'resisting' rather than 'consonant' readings of *Henry V*, see Greenblatt (1985),
Dollimore and Sinfield (1988), Holderness (1995).

concern that any film promoting British patriotism was sufficiently justified by it: all the more so one depicting an invasion of France 'like' the one which was taking place as the film was released in 1944. While not losing sight of the terms of Shakespeare's play, Olivier's film has an intended topical reading—England (and its allies), representing right and justice, invading a France whose weak, decadent rulers deserve no better.[11] It is perhaps a shame that the dynamics of aggressive patriotism seems to cut both ways, and that in the absence of a clearly defined Hitler for the French King's Pétain, Henry embodies to some extent both the aggressive justice of the Allies and the aggressive madness of the Nazis—a reading of the film which no doubt would be highly unwelcome to Olivier.

At the end of a 'Kiss me Kate' scene which draws some intertextual energy from Shakespeare's own *The Taming of the Shrew*, a smug Henry addresses Princess Catherine, the embodiment of conquered France, as follows: 'I will tell thee aloud, "England is thine, Ireland is thine, France is thine"' (Shakespeare 1992: 205). The allusion to Ireland in between France and England is revealing. Shakespeare's own symbolic analogue for Henry was the Earl of Essex, the subject of a rare allusion to contemporary politics in Shakespeare. The play was to provide some patriotic bolster for Essex's 'pacification' of Ireland in 1599. Ironically enough, Essex, whom the play imagines 'from Ireland coming,/Bringing Rebellion broachèd on his sword' (Shakespeare 1992: 191) got his comeuppance at the hands of the Irish 'rebels' shortly after the staging of Shakespeare's play—the first step on Essex's way to an unworthier scaffold. Not surprisingly, both the 1600 Quarto of *Henry V* and Olivier's film (and, perhaps with better reason, the Irish-born Kenneth Branagh) avoid any allusion to Essex or the Irish rebels—although it is just such

---

[11] Gil-Delgado sees in Olivier 'un ingenuo tono de propaganda' ['a naïve propaganda tone'] and a call to patriotic bellicism (2001: 69, 73), while Branagh's film, on the contrary, is 'un tremendo alegato antibelicista' ['a tremendous anti-war statement'] (2001: 73). This view probably reflects the most widespread attitudes to these two *Henry V* films, and it is grossly misleading as to the ideology of Branagh's film. Holderness (1995), Buhler (2002: 107-11), Lehmann (2002: 161-212) or Hedrick (2003) provide far more alert perspectives on Branagh's appropriation of *Henry V*, although they insufficiently stress the extent to which Branagh's engagement with Henry's ideology of aggressive self-promotion glorifies aggression *tout court* as the shortest way to a sense of self.

problematic elements in Shakespeare's play that an adaptation willing to deeply engage with it, instead of sanitising it, or providing patriotic pap, would focus on.

An analysis of subsequent critical involvements with *Henry V* has to keep in sight both the play and the films' original context of production *and* the current context of critical discussion, which once again will not let the issue of aggressive war go away—witness, in the present case, the fact that as this volume was being put together both Britain and Spain were actively supporting the US policy of open-ended aggressive war and invasion against 'the invisible enemy', a war which involves of course its own measure of rhetorical fog, manipulation of evidence, and unmentionable interests.[12] The recent turn towards an international order resting on the right and might to aggression, instead of the right not to suffer aggression, is noticeable, perhaps more so in the countries in which it has already cost many lives. And it looms large as the background of any context we may decide we are addressing.[13]

A critical approach which is aware of cultural icons' treatment of the ideology of violence—or, which is the same, a critical approach wishing to draw attention to this matter—will note the ideological emphases, omissions and choices which emerge in the intertextual and interactional dynamics of meaning-making, whether through adaptations or critical readings. The emphases, omissions and ideological choices in our own approach emerge for others, and are for others to point out. I will conclude by adapting T. S. Eliot's dictum, and argue that it is the fate of any appropriation to be appropriated again. Or, to put it otherwise: never trust the teller, trust the tale—but not the one you have been told: trust *the whole tale*.

---

[12] See e.g. Eno (2003) and Nagra (2003).

[13] For instance, close to home: on the days before the Iraq war, Spanish Anglists chose by majority vote, or rather by majority silence, to disregard a petition I sponsored to make the Spanish Society for Anglo-American Studies address the Spanish government and the Anglo-American embassies, in order to oppose these allies' advocacy of preventive war as an instrument of the new world order after 9/11. Whatever academics do or fail to do is, 'everybody knows' (Cohen 1992), irrelevant. War on terror will go on, although it is also a well known fact that the deepest terror lies behind mirrors (behind 'mirrors of all Christian kings' too).

FIG. 1 A retroactive avatar of Henry V's band of brothers: Alexander the Pig foreshadows Bush's Desert Storm II in Oliver Stone's *Alexander the Great* (2004)

Bibliography

Anderegg, M. (2000 (1999)) 'Welles/Shakespeare/Film: An Over-view', in J. Naremore (ed.) *Film Adaptation*. London: Ath-lone, 154-71.

Ball, R. H. (1968) *Shakespeare on Silent Film*. London: Allen and Unwin.

Benjamin, W. (1969) 'The Task of the Translator', in W. Benjamin. *Illuminations*. New York: Schocken, 69-82.

Blumer, H. (1986) *Symbolic Interactionism*. Berkeley: University of California Press, 1-60.

Brooker, W. (1999) 'Batman: One Life, Many Faces', in D. Cartmell and I. Whelehan (eds.) *Adaptations: From Text to Screen, Screen to Text*. London and New York: Routledge, 185-98.

Buhler, S. M. (2002) *Shakespeare in the Cinema: Ocular Proof*. Albany: State University of New York Press.

Cartmell, D. (1999) 'The Shakespeare on Screen Industry', in D. Cartmell and I. Whelehan (eds.) *Adaptations: From Text to Screen, Screen to Text*. London and New York: Routledge, 29-37.

Cohen, L. (1992) 'Everybody Knows', in L. Cohen, *The Future*. CD. Madrid: CBS/Sony.

Coursen, H. R. (1984) 'Why *Measure for Measure?*', *Literature/Film Quarterly* 12, 65-9.

Davies, A. (1988) *Filming Shakespeare's Plays*. Cambridge: Cambridge University Press.

—— (1994) 'Shakespeare on Film and Television: A Retrospect', in A. Davies and S. Wells (eds.) *Shakespeare and the Moving Image: The Plays on Film and Television*. Cambridge: Cambridge University Press, 1-17.

Dollimore, J. and A. Sinfield (1988) 'History and Ideology: The Instance of *Henry V*', in J. Drakakis (ed.) *Alternative Shakespeares*. London: Routledge, 206-27.

Eno, B. (2003) 'Lessons in How to Lie about Iraq', *Guardian Unlimited* (17 August). On-line. Available HTTP: http://observer. guardian.co.uk/comment/story/0,6903,1020303,00.html   (9 October 2003)

García Landa, J. A. (1998) 'Understanding Misreading: A Hermeneutic/Deconstructive Approach', in B. Penas (ed.) *The Pragmatics of Understanding and Misunderstanding*. Zaragoza: Universidad de Zaragoza, 57-72.

Geduld, H. M. (1973) *Filmguide to Henry V*. Bloomington: Indiana University Press.

Gil-Delgado, F. (2001) *Introducción a Shakespeare a través del cine*. Madrid: Ediciones Internacionales Universitarias.

Greenblatt, S. (1985) 'Invisible Bullets: Renaissance Authority and Its Subversion, *Henry IV* and *Henry V*', in J. Dollimore and A. Sinfield (eds.) *Political Shakespeare: New Essays in Cultural Materialism*. Manchester: Manchester University Press, 18-47.

Harris, R., and G. Wolf (eds.) (1998) *Integrational Linguistics*. Oxford: Elsevier-Pergamon.

Hedrick, D. K. (2003) 'War Is Mud: Branagh's *Dirty Harry V* and the Types of Political Ambiguity', in R. Burt and L. E. Boose (eds.) *Shakespeare the Movie II*. London and New York: Routledge, 213-30.

Holderness, G. (1985) 'Radical Potentiality and Institutional Closure: Shakespeare in Film and Television', in J. Dollimore and A. Sinfield (eds.) *Political Shakespeare: New Essays in Cultural Materialism.* Manchester: Manchester University Press, 182-201.

—— (1995) '"What Ish My Nation?": Shakespeare and National Identities', in I. Kamps (ed.) *Materialist Shakespeare.* London: Verso, 218-38.

Jackson, R. (2001) 'Hamlet's Worlds: Thoughts on Kenneth Branagh's *Hamlet* and the "Competition"', in T. Fischer-Seidel and F.-K. Unterweg (eds.) *Shakespeare: Text-Theatre-Film.* Düsseldorf: Droste, 145-66.

Jorgens, J. J. (1977) *Shakespeare on Film.* Bloomington: Indiana University Press

Kamps, I. (1999) 'Alas, poor Shakespeare! I knew him well', in C. Desmet and R. Sawyer (eds.) *Shakespeare and Appropriation.* London: Routledge, 15-32.

Kliman, B. (1989) 'Branagh's *Henry V:* Allusion and Illusion', *Shakespeare on Film Newsletter* 14 (1), 9-10.

Kracauer, S. (1997) *Theory of Film.* Princeton: Princeton University Press.

Lehmann, C. (2002) *Shakespeare Remains.* Ithaca: Cornell University Press.

Manheim, M. (1994) 'The English History Play on Screen', in A. Davies and S. Wells (eds.), *Shakespeare and the Moving Image: The Plays on Film and Television.* Cambridge: Cambridge University Press, 121-45.

McDonald, N. (1980) 'The Relationship between Shakespeare's Stagecraft and Modern Film Technique', *Australian Journal of Screen Theory* 7, 18-33.

McFarlane, B. (1996) *Novel to Film: An Introduction to the Theory of Adaptation.* Oxford: Clarendon Press.

Nagra, A. (2003) 'Update 2: Case Study Iraq: Oil as an Instrument of Geopolitical Domination', in *Znet Interactive.* On-Line. Available HTTP: http://zena.secureforum.com/interactive/content/display_item.cfm?itemID=4964 (9 October 2003).

Olivier, L. (1984) *Laurence Olivier's Henry V.* New York: Lorrimer.

Quinn, M. (ed.) (1969) *Shakespeare: Henry V.* Basingstoke: Macmillan (Casebook Series).

Shakespeare, W. (1992) *King Henry V.* Ed. A. Gurr. Cambridge: Cambridge University Press (New Cambridge Shakespeare).
—— (1997) *Henry V.* Introd. K. E. Maus, in S. Greenblatt *et al.* (ed.) *The Norton Shakespeare.* New York: Norton.
Sinfield, A. (1985) 'Give an account of Shakespeare and Education...', in J. Dollimore and A. Sinfield (eds.) *Political Shakespeare: New Essays in Cultural Materialism.* Manchester: Manchester University Press, 134-57.
Stam, R. (2000) 'Beyond Fidelity: The Dialogics of Adaptation', in J. Naremore (ed.) *Film Adaptation.* London: Athlone, 54-76.
Walker, R. (1953) 'Look Upon Caesar', *Twentieth Century* 154, 470-1.
Whelehan, I. (1999) 'Adaptations: The Contemporary Dilemmas', in D. Cartmell and I. Whelehan (eds.) *Adaptations: From Text to Screen, Screen to Text.* London and New York: Routledge, 3-18.
Wray, R. and M. Thornton Burnett (2000) 'From the Horse's Mouth: Branagh on the Bard', in M. Thornton Burnett and R. Wray (eds.) *Shakespeare, Film, Fin de Siècle.* Basingstoke and London: Macmillan, 165-78.

Filmography

Branagh, K., dir. (1989) *Henry V.* Renaissance Films/BBC.
Olivier, L., dir. (1944) *Henry V.* Two Cities.

Inf(l)ecting *Pride and Prejudice*:
Dialogism, Intertextuality, and Adaptation

Mireia Aragay
Gemma López

This chapter examines the network of cross-references among Jane Austen's classic, *Pride and Prejudice*, and its metamorphoses into three quintessentially late twentieth-century popular modes of entertainment: a TV mini-series (the 1995 BBC *Pride and Prejudice*), 'chick lit' (Helen Fielding's *Bridget Jones's Diary* and *Bridget Jones: The Edge of Reason*) and the cinematic sub-genre of the 'chick flick' (the films of *Bridget Jones's Diary* and *Bridget Jones: The Edge of Reason*)—all of which share both a common theme, romance in relation to notions of femininity and masculinity, and a common anticipated female audience. Starting off from Julia Kristeva's concept of intertextuality, derived from Mikhail Bakhtin's notion of dialogism, it is claimed that adaptation is a prime instance of cultural recycling, a process which radically undermines any linear, diachronic understanding of cultural history, proposing instead a synergetic, synchronic view of the mutual inf(l)ection between 'source' and adaptation(s). Ultimately, this approach reveals the need to decentre the notion of fidelity in discussions of adaptation.

Diachrony into Synchrony: The Return to/of *Pride and Prejudice*

Kristeva's rendering of Bakhtinian dialogism gives rise, as is well known, to her own concept of intertextuality. In the classic formulation in 'Word, Dialogue and Novel', Kristevan intertextuality regards any text 'as a mosaic of quotations ... [as] the absorption and transformation of another' (Kristeva 1986: 37).[1] Thus, rewriting, in

---

[1] 'Word, Dialogue and Novel', originally entitled 'Bakhtin, le mot, le dialogue et le roman' (1967), was included as the fourth chapter of *Semeioteiké* (Kristeva 1969). It was not translated into English until 1980 (Kristeva 1980: 64-91). We quote the essay

Kristeva's view, is all-pervasive. Authors read con-texts and texts so as to rewrite them in their own act of creation.[2] As opposed to Barthes's proclamation on the 'Death of the Author', for both Bakhtin and Kristeva the author performs as a conduit through whom 'textuality enters into dialogue with other determining elements [...] The author is not dead, but *in rememoriam*' (Orr 2003: 26, 32 [emphasis in original]). With authors as mediators, all texts function as rejoinders in an ongoing dialogue which bypasses simple before-after hierarchies, undermining in turn any simple notion of diachrony:

> Diachrony is transformed into synchrony, and in light of this transformation, *linear* history appears as abstraction. The only way a writer can participate in history is by transgressing this abstraction through a process of reading-writing; that is, through the practice of a signifying structure in relation or opposition to another structure. (Kristeva 1986: 36)

That is, it is by inserting themselves in history and engaging in a dynamic dialogue with other texts that authors, however paradoxically, transcend the concept of linear time by inf(l)ecting those other signifying structures and allowing them in turn to inf(l)ect their own. Intertextuality, in sum, describes the process of cultural recycling: 'it is a permutation of texts [...] in the space of a text, many utterances taken from other texts intersect with one another' (Kristeva quoted in Orr 2003: 27).

Any process of adaptation paradigmatically represents the Kristevan transformation of diachrony into synchrony. More precisely, adaptation sets up a scenario of intertextual dialogues which replaces the binary diachrony/synchrony with a synergy that flows both ways. Seen in this light, adaptation undermines the traditional conception of the 'original' text or 'source' 'as if it were a hermetic and self-sufficient whole, one whose elements constitute a closed system presuming nothing beyond themselves, no other utterances'

---

from *The Kristeva Reader*, edited by Toril Moi (1986). For a more recent appraisal of Kristeva's term and of its reception in both the French and English-speaking contexts, see Orr (2003).

[2] We borrow the term 'con-texts' from Barker and Hulme's 'Nymphs and Reapers Heavily Vanish: The Discursive Con-texts of *The Tempest*', where they argue that con-text with a hyphen signifies 'a break from the inequality of the usual text/context relationship. Con-texts are themselves *texts* and must be *read with*: they do not simply make up a background' (1985: 236).

(Bakthin 1981: 273). Not only is the 'original' text intextextually inf(l)ected by other previous and contemporary texts and discourses, but it is necessarily, as this chapter hopes to demonstrate, open to inf(l)ection by subsequent con-texts. That is, viewed through the lens of intertextual dialogism, the source is neither hermetic, nor self-sufficient nor a closed system. As Robert Stam has recently argued, 'Film adaptations ... are caught up in the ongoing whirl of intertextual reference and transformation, of texts generating other texts in an endless process of recycling, transformation, and transmutation, *with no clear point of origin*' (2000: 66 [our emphasis]). In this light, all creation becomes adaptation as 'Prior text materials lose special status by permutation with other texts in the intertextual exchange because all intertexts are of equal importance in the intertextual *process*' (Orr 2003: 28 [emphasis in original]). Thus, to the social impact of film adaptation—the frequently noticed fact that far more people see the film than read the book, or read/buy the book only after having seen the film—must be added its theoretical dimension, which places adaptation as part of the larger phenomenon of rewriting and of a theory of intertextuality.

This chapter focuses on the intertextual dialogic interactions between the 1995 BBC adaptation of *Pride and Prejudice*, Helen Fielding's *Bridget Jones's Diary* (1996), the film version of Fielding's novel (2000) and Helen Fielding's *Bridget Jones: The Edge of Reason* (1999), all of them presumably feeding from a common source, Jane Austen's *Pride and Prejudice* (1813), which in turn, we will claim, has been and continues to be irrevocably inf(l)ected following its immersion in dialogic heteroglossia in the mid- to late 1990s. This group of texts constitutes a tapestry of conscious quotations and allusions, involving themselves and the reader/viewer in a game of seemingly endless permutations. When asked whether she intended to follow *Pride and Prejudice* from the outset of writing her first Bridget Jones novel, Fielding replied: 'Yes. I shamelessly stole the plot. I thought it had been very well market-researched over a number of centuries' (Fielding 1998). Indeed, *Bridget Jones's Diary* rewrites the plot of Austen's novel to the extent of featuring a male protagonist with the same surname. But the novel also engages in intertextual dialogue with the 1995 BBC adaptation of *Pride and Prejudice*, in which Colin Firth played a memorable Darcy—so memorable in fact that he was chosen to play Mark Darcy by Fielding herself and director Sharon Maguire for the big-screen adaptation of her novel.[3] The intertextual whirl continues in the second Bridget Jones novel, as Bridget is appointed to interview Colin Firth in Rome while negotiating the ups and downs of her relationship with Mark Darcy.

This network of dialogic cross-references is an emblematic example of Bakhtin's point that 'between the word and its object, between the word and the speaking subject, there exists an elastic environment of other, alien words about the same object, the same theme' (1981: 276). In the present case, the common theme shared by the texts and screen adaptations is, we suggest, romance in relation to notions of masculinity and femininity. And, we would add, not only is there a common theme, but crucially, a common anticipated audience: women. Bearing these two aspects in mind, the rest of this chapter addresses the question as to how and why early nineteenth-century, supposedly diachronically distant, notions of romance, masculinity and femininity become synchronic with the late twentieth century, a period which saw itself as post-feminist. It also suggests that the intertextual dialogue established through adaptation/rewriting rejuvenates the presumed source—Austen's *Pride and Prejudice*—while synergetically throwing light on the con-text in which that source is adapted/rewritten. This will ultimately allow us to reflect on the process by which a text that was initially produced as a popular narrative for women—Austen's *Pride and Prejudice*—subsequently acquired the status of a classic, finally to be metamorphosed again into quintessentially late twentieth-century modes of entertainment, that is, a TV mini-series (the 1995 BBC *Pride and Prejudice*), 'chick lit' (*Bridget Jones's Diary* and *Bridget Jones: The Edge of Reason*) and the cinematic sub-genre of the 'chick flick' (the films of *Bridget Jones's Diary* and *Bridget Jones: The Edge of Reason*).

Romance, Female Spectatorship, and Models of Femininity and Masculinity

In an insightful article first published in 1992, 'From *Casablanca* to *Pretty Woman*: The Politics of Romance', Rob Lapsley and

---

[3] Thus bearing witness to the fact that 'In the cinema the performer also brings along a kind of baggage, a thespian intertext formed by the totality of antecedent roles' (Stam 2000: 60).

Michael Westlake point out that at the end of the twentieth century, the spectator 'is no longer able to believe in romance [...] yet at the same time wishes to do so' (1993: 180). As evidence of the pervasiveness of the myth of romance in contemporary Western culture,[4] they quote David Bordwell's 1985 count to the effect that out of a sample of one hundred Hollywood films, ninety-five contained a romantic element, while in about eighty-five, romance was the main plot line—which, apart from anything else, confirms that romance means excellent box office (1993: 190). As mentioned above, Helen Fielding's awareness of the incredible market potential of romance is confirmed by her rewriting of Austen's *Pride and Prejudice*, an all-time romantic best-seller.

In *Pride and Prejudice*, Austen arguably constructs a subversive fantasy of female autonomy through the portrait of Elizabeth Bennett, a heroine endowed with the intelligence and wit that enable her to exert a power of choice denied to women in the context of the social, economic and gender realities of her time (Newton 1994). The operative word here is 'fantasy' in so far as Elizabeth embodies an Imaginary plenitude, a lack of lack. Although she is not wealthy or particularly beautiful, both essential requirements for the construction of Woman as desirable in the early nineteenth century, her intelligence prevents her from experiencing this as lack, and hence as powerlessness. For this reason, Elizabeth is a focal point of identification for female readers. However, for Tania Modleski, as for other commentators, romance is deeply contradictory.[5] On the one hand, the urgently expressed desire on the part of women for open, unambivalent relationships, autonomy and commonality constitutes the utopian dimension of romance—and the utopian function it fulfils for the female audience it addresses. On the other hand, this utopian dimension is a flawed one, in the sense that while romance provides outlets 'for women's dissatisfaction with male-female relationships, [it] never question[s] the primacy of these relationships' (Modleski 1982: 113). To return to Austen's *Pride and Prejudice*, the successful completion of the Elizabeth-Darcy relationship, wedding implicit, encapsulates the dual character of romance—it is the means by which Elizabeth is

---

[4] In this connection, see de Rougemont (1983: 232-5 and *passim*), and Lapsley and Westlake (1993: 185-6).
[5] See Dyer (1981), Jones (1986) and Radaway (1987).

granted access to a utopia of autonomy and community, while simultaneously it signals her inevitable incorporation into the patriarchal
institutions of marriage and the family.

In the first part of Austen's novel, up to Darcy's letter to
Elizabeth, there are numerous occasions where the gaze is as central
as the characters themselves. Darcy's gaze in this part of the novel,
specifically during Elizabeth's stay at Netherfield, could be described
in Laura Mulvey's hugely influential terms as scopophilic (1975: 8).
Inquisitive and possessive, this kind of gaze is a source of pleasure
and power for the onlooker in its commodification of its object. In a
patriarchal culture such as Austen's, men are usually the bearers of the
scopophilic gaze, while women are its passive recipients (Mulvey
1975: 11). But contrary to expectation, Austen's Elizabeth actively
resists Darcy's scopophilic gaze, by means of her wit and sense of
humour and, most importantly, by returning the gaze, to some extent
becoming its subject. The BBC mini-series establishes an intertextual
dialogue with this dimension of the novel to the extent of transforming
the gaze—not only Darcy's and Elizabeth's but, crucially, that of the
female spectator the series obviously anticipates—into a major
structuring principle. Indeed, as Lisa Hopkins demonstrates in 'Mr
Darcy's Body: Privileging the Female Gaze', scriptwriter Andrew
Davies and director Simon Langton introduced a series of additional
scenes and productive camerawork which are worth examining in
some detail precisely because the gaze functions in them as a fundamental structuring motif.

The first episode itself opens with one such added scene. As
Bingley and Darcy ride into view to observe Netherfield, which
Bingley will eventually decide to take, they are oblivious to their
being the objects of Elizabeth's gaze, who watches them from a
slightly elevated plateau. This not only makes Elizabeth the subject of
the gaze within the diegesis, but also, equally importantly, invites the
viewer to share her point of view. This is relevant in so far as it is the
beginning of the construction of Darcy as the object of desire of the
female spectator. Camerawork is also decisive here; although we can
clearly see Bingley's face, Darcy's remains partly hidden throughout,
provoking primarily a desire to see. Gradually, over subsequent
episodes, this man the female spectator desires to see comes to
embody, we would argue, a late twentieth-century Imaginary fantasy
of male completion and self-sufficiency, what has been popularly

labelled the 'new man'. This construction of Darcy is achieved mainly through the added scenes which, contrary to the first one, repeatedly turn *him* into the subject of the gaze he directs at Elizabeth, and simultaneously into the object of the female spectator's desiring gaze. Furthermore, the added scenes also provide insights into Darcy's feelings which the novel, because it is mostly focalised through Elizabeth, does not fully explore.[6] This promotes the female spectators' sympathy towards a hero who embodies a masculinity which differs greatly from that of Austen's Darcy. While the nineteenth-century character remains mostly distant and impenetrable, Colin Firth's 'new-man' Darcy is allowed to express weaknesses, doubts and emotions which the late twentieth century constructed as desirable in a man and which would have been unthinkable in Austen's milieu, the basis of which was an Enlightenment reason-based understanding of masculinity which valued emotional restraint, rather than the new 'cult of sensibility' which favoured the physical display of emotions (Nixon 2001: 25-7).[7]

Elizabeth's unexpected stay at Netherfield during Jane's illness proves the perfect occasion to develop this portrait of Darcy. In three separate added scenes, Darcy's scopophilic gaze is highlighted. In the first one, Elizabeth steps into the billiards room by mistake to find Darcy, who fixes his eyes on her in a desiring regard that lingers for a few seconds and is only broken on Darcy's initiative. In the third one, Elizabeth is unaware of Darcy's intensely gazing from an upper window at her and Jane's carriage as they leave Netherfield. Crucially, in addition to the motif of Darcy's gaze, what these two episodes have in common is the camerawork, which 'frames' Darcy as an object of desire, almost an *objet d'art*, for the female spectator.[8] A triangulation

---

[6] In the novel, the reader is allowed a certain degree of access to Darcy's emotions primarily through the use of irony. For example, we read of the common dislike between Darcy and Elizabeth while understanding that this may not be so. As is well known, Austen sets the ironic tone in the first sentence of the novel.

[7] This is a recurrent motif in Austen's novels; e.g. in *Sense and Sensibility* Willoughby obviously embodies a type of masculinity based on the 'cult of sensibility' which Austen ultimately condemns.

[8] Further, in the billiards-room scene, behind Darcy there happens to hang a huge full-body portrait of a gentleman. In addition to underlining the 'framing' effect, this introduces a contrast between Darcy as he was traditionally read—primarily as a socially-constrained being, mimicked by the gentleman in the portrait who is effectively constrained by its frame—and Darcy as the BBC mini-series constructs

of desiring gazes is thus created, the effect of which Lisa Hopkins describes as:

> What we want to see, I think, is not just Darcy in the abstract, it is Darcy looking—particularly at Elizabeth but also, on other occasions, at images which have contextualized as being poignantly redolent of her absence. These looks too can signify his need. And we look back in a silent collusion, because it is in that need that we most want to believe. (2001: 120)

Returning to Lacan and Mulvey, we would suggest that the need Hopkins refers to can be equated with Lacan's definition of lack. That is, Darcy's scopophilic gaze does not merely imply mastery and domination, but the *desire* to master and dominate, thus signifying lack—which is why when he cannot fix his eyes on Elizabeth, he fixes them on her absence, as he does when she leaves Netherfield with Jane in the episode mentioned above. In addition, we would claim that the female viewer anticipated by the mini-series becomes the bearer of the look, thus complicating Mulvey's theorising of the gaze. According to Mulvey, 'In their traditional exhibitionist role women are simultaneously looked at and displayed' (1975: 11). In the BBC *Pride and Prejudice*, this simultaneity is disrupted: Elizabeth is looked at by Darcy, while Darcy, not Elizabeth, is displayed for the female spectator. The female spectator—not the male, as in Mulvey—becomes the bearer of two looks: on the one hand, the scopophilic gaze which she directs at Darcy; on the other, the narcissistic gaze which signifies her identification with Elizabeth, the object of Darcy's desiring gaze. We would argue that the intense involvement of British female viewers with the BBC mini-series and the 'Darcymania' it gave rise to strongly suggest that the narcissistic gaze by which women fantasised themselves in Elizabeth's place far outstripped the commodification of Darcy afforded by their scopophilic gaze.[9] Mulvey's statement, 'By means of identification with him [the male protagonist in 1940s and 1950s mainstream films], through participation in his power, the spectator can indirectly possess her too [the glamorous, highly

---

him—the late twentieth-century 'new man' in the flesh, far more emotional and sensual.

[9] Mary Ann Doane sees Mia Farrow's 'spectatorial ecstasy' in Woody Allen's *The Purple Rose of Cairo* (1985) as demonstrating 'the extent to which the image of the longing, overinvolved female spectator is still with us' (1987: 1-2).

eroticized female lead]' (1975: 13), could be reformulated as: by means of identification with Elizabeth, through participation in her Imaginary power to make good the lack in man, the female spectator can indirectly be possessed by Darcy, thus making good her own lack. All this bears out the conclusion reached since the 1980s by critics who have attempted to theorise female spectatorship in the wake of Mulvey's germinal essay—namely, that in genres which specifically address women, they occupy a position defined by Teresa de Lauretis as 'the masochist position, the (impossible) place of a purely *passive* desire' (1984: 151 [emphasis in original]). The fact that a television series released in 1995 endorses such a disempowering trope of female spectatorship calls into question late twentieth-century Western culture's view of itself as post-feminist.

In between the two scenes described above, there comes one that provoked numerous sighs among British female spectators when the mini-series was first released. Still at Netherfield, Darcy comes out of his bath and walks to the window, from which he gazes at Elizabeth playing with one of the dogs in the garden. In addition to the interplay of gazes described above, this episode, more blatantly than any previous one, fetishises Darcy's body. In this case, the window works as a 'frame', thus underlining Darcy's partly-revealed body as an object of desire for the female spectator's scopophilic gaze, while simultaneously allowing her an insight into his lack, which is expressed through the lingering look he directs at Elizabeth. Once again, by narcissistically identifying with Darcy's object of desire, a fantasy of power is produced for the female spectator. The bath scene anticipates the climactic episode in the BBC adaptation, namely that in which Darcy, arriving unexpectedly at Pemberley, plunges fully clothed into a pond and walks towards the house with his loose shirt still dripping to come upon an utterly surprised Elizabeth, who has been touring the estate with her aunt and uncle. The pond scene is significantly crosscut with Elizabeth gazing up at Darcy's imposing portrait in the portrait gallery at Pemberley. Far more emphatically than in the billiards-room scene at Netherfield, this self-reflexive gesture creates the impression that the BBC's Darcy has broken out of the 'frames' that constrained him in previous readings, to offer the mini-series's female audience a thoroughly desirable, 'corpo-real' 'new man'.

FIG. 2 Colin Firth's 'corpo-real' Darcy ponders plunge into pond

The tremendously erotic charge of the pond scene centres, once again, on Darcy. It links up not only with the earlier bath scene, but also with previous episodes where he is shown involved in vigorous physical activity in an attempt to control his passions—the fencing scene interpolated at the start of Elizabeth's visit to Derbyshire is a case in point. These added scenes also keep Darcy firmly present in the female spectators' minds, inviting them to wonder about those passions he seems to need to control—why does he mumble to himself, 'I shall conquer this—I shall!', after the fencing match? Why does he plunge into the pond? Further, all these elements contribute to the construction of a far more Romantic Darcy than Austen's generally restrained hero. As Cheryl Nixon notes about the BBC adaptation, 'Darcy's physical actions speak a twentieth-century emotional vocabulary' (2001: 24), one strongly coloured by Romantic notions of demonstration of feelings. The adaptation's economy of the gaze comes full circle when Elizabeth's and Darcy's eyes meet in mutual (mis)recognition in the piano room at Pemberley. Indeed, this would epitomise the fantasy of romance, were it not for the fact that, from the narrative point of view, the story is far from finished. One last difficulty remains to be overcome, namely the consequences of Lydia's elopement with Wickham. The mini-series's treatment of this episode, adding two sequences where we see Darcy fearlessly making his way through London's seedy underworld in search of the couple, bears out Lapsley's and Westlake's argument that, 'The presence of obstacles can ... be explained as a means of both making the object desirable and of preventing its exposure as nothing' (1993: 192). That is, it works to further increase the female viewer's desire for Darcy/to be Elizabeth, and her renewed belief in the Imaginary fantasy of romance, finally clinched by the inclusion of a wedding scene and a passionate kiss. The BBC mini-series, then, fulfils the late twentieth-century Western female spectator's desire to believe in romance—its incredible popularity and success only confirming the persistence of such desire and of its need to be satisfied.

To sum up, then, the BBC 1995 adaptation of Pride and Prejudice engages in an intertextual dialogue with Austen novel whereby it offers an updated concept of masculinity through a trans-formation of Austen's courtship plot into a romance *tout court* which addresses a very specific audience—late twentieth-century Western female spectators. The added scenes in the mini-series, as has been shown, repeatedly eroticise Darcy, increase his presence, provide insights into his feelings and generally construct a model of masculin-ity far removed from Austen's in its emphasis on physicality and emotional expression. This construction of masculinity clearly implies a model of femininity—late twentieth-century Western women, the series strongly suggests, continue to be under the spell of romance, and they desire a man like Darcy, who is handsome, rational, sensitive and in command, and who desires them passionately.

The enormous success of *Bridget Jones's Diary*, both the novel and the film, testifies to the continuing persistence of the myth of romance and its concomitant models of masculinity and femininity. Helen Fielding's *Bridget Jones's Diary* not only bases its plot and its hero's surname on Austen's novel, but it is also directly involved in an intertextual dialogue with the BBC mini-series, which was being broadcast while Fielding was transforming her weekly Bridget Jones columns in *The Independent* into her novel:

Just nipped out for fags prior to getting changed ready for BBC *Pride and Prejudice* [...] Love the nation being so addicted. The basis of my own addiction, I know, is my simple human need for Darcy to get off with Elizabeth [...] They are my chosen representatives in the field of shagging, or, rather, courtship. I do not, however, wish to see any actual goals. I would hate to see Darcy and Elizabeth in bed, smoking a cigarette afterwards. That would be unnatural and wrong and I would quickly lose interest [...] Mr Darcy was more attractive [than Mark Darcy] because he was ruder but ... being imaginary was a disadvantage that could not be overlooked [...] surely Mr Darcy would never do anything so vain and frivolous as to be an actor and yet Mr Darcy *is* an actor. Hmmm. All v. confusing. (Fielding 1996: 246-8)

The speaking voice here, as throughout the novel, is Bridget's, who in her own idiosyncratic way is providing a theory of romance surprisingly akin to Lapsley's and Westlake's Lacanian account.[10] She reveals the paradox at the core of romance, that is, the desire to see Darcy 'get off with Elizabeth' and yet 'not see any actual goals' being achieved. As Lapsley and Westlake put it, romantic narratives in cinema are concerned with deferring the satisfaction of desire precisely and paradoxically as a means of evoking it and of keeping the desired object—in this case, Mr Darcy—at a distance: 'On the one hand the exchange between spectator and film produces a subject who lacks and hence desires [Bridget], and on the other hand objects that will *apparently* satisfy those desires [the BBC's Mr Darcy]' (1993: 192 [our emphasis]). However, interestingly enough, Bridget, *pace* de Lauretis, does not seem to occupy as a spectator the impossible place of passive desire; on the contrary, she is well aware of the *imaginary* status of Mr Darcy and of the fact that the masculinity he embodies and the romance he promises are both performative acts—after all, Mr Darcy *is* an actor![11] Ironically, the implication for the female reader— if not necessarily for Bridget—is that the same points can be made about Bridget's own Darcy and about her fantasy of romance. As is well known, Fielding's novel has been criticised from feminist perspectives as an exercise in 'chick lit' that merely repeats romantic

---

[10] Where Elizabeth was a mere focaliser, operating at the level of colouring (albeit frequently and intensely) the narrative voice, Bridget's voice pervades the novel throughout—it is indeed a diary.

[11] The same actor, as mentioned above, who was later to play Mark Darcy in the film adaptation of *Bridget Jones's Diary*, that is, Colin Firth—but more of this in due course.

clichés and is devoid of a political agenda (Whelehan 2002: 57-63). However, *Bridget Jones's Diary* is so thoroughly steeped in ironic double-coding that its final effect on the reader is, we would suggest, to playfully allow her to have it both ways—that is, to provide the utopian promise of happiness that romance brings while at the same time acknowledging its Imaginary status. It is precisely through such double-coding that the novel involves itself in a playful intertextual critique of the BBC mini-series and of the passive female viewer it posited.

In fact, we would argue that Bridget's nostalgic faith in romance should not be taken entirely at face value. The extract quoted above, to take but one example, is permeated by Bridget's brand of humour, which instantly became one of the trademarks of 'Bridget-ness'. The most frequent target of Bridget's humour is herself—witness her description of what she calls 'date-preparation':

> Being a woman is worse than being a farmer—there is so much harvesting and crop spraying to be done [...] The whole performance is so highly tuned you only need to neglect it for a few days for the whole thing to go to seed. Sometimes I wonder what I would be like if left to revert to nature [...] Is it any wonder girls have no confidence? (Fielding 1996: 30)

Bridget's ironic, self-deprecating description of her trimming of her body to conform to the established standards of beauty culminates in a rhetorical question which subtly interrogates the sexual politics underpinning 'so much harvesting and crop spraying', so much disciplining of the female body with a view to gaining access to the Imaginary status of heroine of romance. In short, this passage, as so many others in the novel, reveals that Bridget is aware of the perfor-mative nature of the femininity implied by late twentieth-century Western conventions of romance.

The film adaptation pursues *Bridget Jones's Diary*'s critique of the BBC mini-series by placing great emphasis on masculinity as masquerade through the already-mentioned casting of Colin Firth, the BBC's Mr Darcy, as Mark Darcy. The film's Mark Darcy is modelled on the BBC character, even as far as his physical traits are concerned. Near the end of the film, Bridget's telling Mark to rethink the length of his sideburns functions as an obvious intertextual reference for the female viewer who, like Bridget herself in the novel, had avidly followed the BBC mini-series and noticed Mr Darcy's spectacular sideburns. Sideburns apart, we would argue that in their insistence on casting Firth—who had become inseparable, in the (female) collective imaginary, from his role as Mr Darcy—novelist and co-scriptwriter Fielding and director Sharon Maguire were trying to (playfully) make a point about the Imaginary and performative nature of the mythical male hero and the romantic completion he promises. Once more, the target audience is a late-twentieth century female spectator who no longer believes in romance yet at the same time desires and even needs to do so. A key scene in this respect is the fight between Daniel Cleaver and Mark Darcy—non-existent in the novel—which parodies the conventions of romance in various ways. The scene is initially set up as the clichéd confrontation between two male rivals for the attentions of the woman, but it immediately turns into farce.

FIG. 3 Darcy's and Cleaver's fight parodies romance conventions

Far from showing a macho-style fight with lots of punching and blood, Daniel and Mark seem to concentrate rather on grabbing at each other, pulling each other's hair and kicking the air. This near mock-fight effect is further enhanced by the soundtrack, which features Geri Halliwell's version of the gay classic 'It's raining men'—all of this parodically undermining the traditional romance concept of masculinity.[12]

Another turn of the dialogic screw comes in the 1999 sequel to *Bridget Jones's Diary*, *Bridget Jones: The Edge of Reason*, where Bridget is sent to Rome by *The Independent* to interview Colin Firth.[13] By way of preparation, Bridget informs us that she has watched the scene where Firth dives into the lake in the BBC *Pride and Prejudice* no less than fifteen times, which leads her to describe herself as a 'top-flight researcher' (Fielding 1999: 158). She obviously overdoes it since, when the actual interview takes place, she obsessively returns to the issue of the wet shirt, much to Firth's exasperation. In fact, Firth is at pains to insist on the distance between his real self and his perform-ance as Mr Darcy, thus highlighting the mythical status of the latter:

> BJ: ... What was it like with your friends when you started being Mr Darcy?
> CF: There were a lot of jokes about it: growling, "Mr Darcy" over breakfast and so on. There was a brief period when they had to work quite hard to hide their knowledge of who I really was and ...
> BJ: Hide it from who?
> CF: Well, from anyone who suspected that perhaps I was like Mr Darcy.
> BJ: But do you think you're not like Mr Darcy?
> CF: I do think I'm not like Mr Darcy, yes.
> BJ: I think you're exactly like Mr Darcy.
> CF: In what way?
> BJ: You talk the same way as him.
> CF: Oh, do I?
> BJ: You look exactly like him, and I, oh, oh ...
> (*Protracted crashing noises followed by sounds of struggle*) (Fielding 1999: 177-78)

In the film adaptation of *Bridget Jones: The Edge of Reason*, where Colin Firth plays Mark Darcy again, the above interview has been suppressed, thus obliterating what, to us, is one of the novel's crucial comments on the gap between the actor and his role as Mr Darcy. This

---

[12] Colin Firth confirms that Hugh Grant and himself 'decided to fight like a couple of wallies ... No big cowboy punches for us' (Firth 2001: 38).

[13] In addition to continuing the intertextual dialogue with the BBC *Pride and Prejudice* and therefore Austen's novel, *Bridget Jones: The Edge of Reason* draws from the plot of Austen's *Persuasion*, thus bringing yet another text into the dialogic interplay.

is in tune with the film's overall approach—some key scenes in the first Bridget Jones film are visually quoted in the second, such as the fight between Darcy and Cleaver, but such repetitions, far from pursuing the intertextual game, are entirely devoid of irony and ultimately prove to be wholly unproductive.[14]

Adaptation as Cultural Dialogue

The adaptation/rewriting of Austen's classic in the 1995 BBC mini-series, *Bridget Jones's Diary* (novel and film) and *Bridget Jones: The Edge of Reason* is not, we believe, an instance of cultural nostalgia, but rather, to borrow Leo Braudy's theorisation of remakes, it is

> ... concerned with what its makers and (they hope) its audiences consider to be *unfinished cultural business*, unrefinable and perhaps finally unassimilable material that remains part of the cultural dialogue—not until it is finally given definitive form, but until it is no longer compelling or interesting. (1998: 331 [our emphasis])

The adaptation/rewriting of *Pride and Prejudice*, that is, reveals that the notions of masculinity and femininity articulated in romance have remained compelling in Western culture as unassimilated material in a self-styled post-feminist *milieu*. With a common anticipated audience in mind, which is female, each of the texts and films discussed in this chapter intervenes in an ongoing cultural and intertextual dialogue while making different emphases. The BBC 1995 *Pride and Prejudice* constructs a model of masculinity which eroticises the male body and highlights the expression of emotions, thus implying a specific model of femininity embodied not in the main female character, but in the mini-series's implied audience. *Bridget Jones's Diary* addresses the same kind of audience in order to offer them a playful intertextual critique of the BBC mini-series and of the passive female spectator it

---

[14] The DVD extras do include the interview. Shot in the studio after the day's work was over, the text has been edited in such a way as to omit the key passage quoted above. Moreover, director Beeban Kidron introduces the scene by claiming that there was no way the interview could have been integrated into the diegesis—unless, we would argue, the filmmakers had chosen to emphasise the performative nature of Darcy's masculinity and to pursue the playful critique of romance present in both Bridge Jones novels and in the first film.

posited, while the novel *Bridget Jones: The Edge of Reason* lays bare, equally humorously, the gap between the fantasy (Mr Darcy) and the reality (Colin Firth), thus epitomising the mythical nature of romance.

The wheel comes full circle when the reader/viewer of these late twentieth-century popular texts/films returns to Austen's *Pride and Prejudice* to realise how it has been irrevocably inf(l)ected by its absorption into dialogic intertextuality at the end of the twentieth century. A fresh light is cast on Elizabeth Bennett when she jostles against the more farcical, self-deprecating Bridget Jones—inevitably, the inauspicious beginning of Elizabeth's and Darcy's relationship at the Meryton ball is coloured by the comically disastrous first meeting between Bridget and Mark Darcy at Bridget's parents' New Year's turkey curry buffet, as depicted both in the novel and in the film. Even more radically, Austen's Mr Darcy is infused with a new dimension as a result of his dialogic crosspollination with the BBC's Mr Darcy and Fielding's Mark Darcy—most noticeably, perhaps, he gains an erotic charge that did not seem to be there in earlier readings. In other words, the significance of rewriting/adaptation stretches well beyond the specific intertextual exchanges it sets up to encompass a radical undermining of a linear, teleological understanding of cultural history in favour of dialogic, synergetic notions of recycling and permutation. From this perspective, the concern with fidelity simply pales out of view.

Bibliography

Austen, J. (1972) *Pride and Prejudice*. Ed. T. Tanner. Harmondsworth: Penguin.

Bakhtin, M. M. (1981) *The Dialogic Imagination: Four Essays*. Ed. M. Holquist. Austin: University of Texas Press.

Barker, F. and P. Hulme (1985) 'Nymphs and Reapers Heavily Vanish: The Discursive Con-Texts of *The Tempest*' in J. Drakakis (ed.) *Alternative Shakespeares*. London and New York: Routledge, 191-205.

Braudy, L. (1998) 'Afterword: Retakes on Remakes' in A. Horton and S. Y. McDougal (eds.) *Play It Again, Sam: Retakes on Remakes*. Berkeley, Los Angeles and London: University of California Press, 327-34.

de Lauretis, T. (1984) *Alice Doesn't: Feminism, Semiotics, Cinema.* Basingstoke and London: Macmillan.

de Rougemont, D. (1983 (1940)) *Love in the Western World.* New York: Schocken Books.

Doane, M. A. (1987) *The Desire to Desire: The Woman's Film of the 1940s.* Bloomington and Indianapolis: Indiana University Press.

Dyer, R. (1992 (1977)) *Only Entertainment.* London and New York: Routledge, 17–34.

Fielding, H. (1996) *Bridget Jones's Diary.* London: Picador.

—— (1998) 'British Author Helen Fielding Discusses "Singletons", "Smug Marrieds" and her Runaway Bestseller, Bridget Jones's Diary'. On-line. Available HTTP: http://www.time.com/time/community/transcripts/chattr061698.html (9 July 2003).

—— (1999) *Bridget Jones: The Edge of Reason.* London: Picador.

Firth, C. (2001) 'Love at Firth Sight: An Interview with Anwar Brett', *Film Review* 605 (May), 36-41.

Hopkins, L. (2001) 'Mr Darcy's Body: Privileging the Female Gaze' in L. Troost and S. Greenfield (ed.) *Jane Austen in Hollywood.* Lexington: The University Press of Kentucky, 111-21.

Jones, A. R. (1986) 'Mills and Boon Meet Feminism' in J. Radford (ed.) *The Progress of Romance.* London and New York: Routledge, 36-44.

Kristeva, J. (1969) *Semeioteiké.* Paris: Points.

—— (1980) *Desire in Language: A Semiotic Approach to Literature and Art.* Ed. L. S. Roudiez. New York: Columbia University Press.

—— (1986) *The Kristeva Reader.* Ed. T. Moi. New York: Columbia University Press.

Lapsley, R. and M. Westlake (1993 (1992)) 'From Casablanca to Pretty Woman: The Politics of Romance' in A. Easthope (ed.) *Contemporary Film Theory.* London and New York: Longman, 179-203.

Modleski, T. (1982) *Loving with a Vengeance: Mass-Produced Fantasies for Women.* New York and London: Methuen.

Mulvey, L. (1975) 'Visual Pleasure and Narrative Cinema', *Screen* 16 (3), 6-18.

Newton, J. L. (1994 (1981)) 'Women, Power and Subversion' in R. Clark (ed.) *Sense and Sensibility and Pride and Prejudice.* Basingstoke and London: Macmillan, 119-44.

Nixon, C. L. (2001) 'Balancing the Courtship Hero: Masculine Emotional Display in Film Adaptations of Austen's Novels' in L. Troost and S. Greenfield (ed.) *Jane Austen in Hollywood.* Lexington: The University Press of Kentucky, 22-43.

Orr, M. (2003) *Intertextuality: Debates and Contexts.* Cambridge: Polity.

Radaway, J. (1987) *Reading the Romance.* London: Verso.

Stam, R. (2000) 'Beyond Fidelity: The Dialogics of Adaptation' in J. Naremore (ed.) *Film Adaptation.* London: Athlone, 54-76.

Whelehan, I. (2002) *Bridget Jones's Diary: A Reader's Guide.* New York and London: Continuum.

Filmography

Langton, S. dir. (1995) *Pride and Prejudice.* BBC.

Maguire, S. dir. (2001) *Bridget Jones's Diary.* Working Title Films.

Kidron, B. dir. (2004) *Bridget Jones: The Edge of Reason.* Working Title Films/Universal Pictures/Miramax Films.

BEYOND ADAPTATION

Beyond Adaptation:
Frankenstein's Postmodern Progeny

Pedro Javier Pardo García

This chapter examines Kenneth Branagh's *Mary Shelley's Franken-stein* (1994) in order to demonstrate how, despite the film's avowed claim to be faithful to the book, it displays important differences with it which are related to other films, not only previous adaptations of *Frankenstein*, but also contemporary adaptations of other texts—Francis Ford Coppola's *Bram Stoker's Dracula* (1992) in particular. After a brief overview of the Frankenstein cinematic myth, the chapter focuses on the elements apparently restored from the book but in fact transformed after Coppola's example, which turn Branagh's film into a romantic *Frankenstein*. Then it moves on to outright additions, elements which have nothing to do with the book but ultimately point to other film versions of the myth, although reinterpreted and trans-formed in order to produce a postmodern *Frankenstein*. The final section discusses the implications of this particular case for a theory of film adaptation and proposes a redefinition of adaptation as cultural intertextuality.

The Frankenstein Myth

When Mary Shelley referred to *Frankenstein; or, the Modern Prometheus* (1818; 1831) as 'my hideous progeny' (Shelley 1993: 197), she could not be aware of how her statement would be prophetic of the cinematic afterlife of her masterpiece. Victor Frankenstein's fears about a race of monsters populating the earth have become reality in the legion of film versions of his monster haunting thou-sands of cinemas and in the imaginations of millions of spectators. Few books in world literature have been so constantly and intensely adapted to film, to such an extent that, as Paul O'Flinn has argued, this ceaseless reproduction has altered the perception of the literary source and engendered a multiplicity of *Frankensteins*, as many as film adaptations have been made: 'The fact that many people call the monster Frankenstein and thus confuse the pair betrays the extent of that restructuring' (O'Flinn 1995: 22). To be exact, however, it is not just the literary source that has been ceaselessly reproduced: most film versions do not take Mary Shelley's text as a point of departure, but previous film versions. In fact, what different versions have in common is not so much the book as the myth created by its dramatic and cinematic reproduction, to the extent that the book has become one more version of that myth—the founding, but not necessarily the most influential one. The mediation of myth in the transference from page to screen must be taken into account in any study of the film adaptations of *Frankenstein*, as the title of this chapter emphasises: it does not refer to *Frankenstein*'s—the book—but Frankenstein's—the myth—progeny. Its topic is the latest adaptation by Kenneth Branagh (1994), a paradigmatic example of this mediation: the film claims to restore the myth to its original purity from the title itself—*Mary Shelley's Frankenstein*—but in fact it adapts the myth as much as the book, and is ultimately one more version of the myth.

The story of the transformation of Mary Shelley's *Franken-stein* into the Frankenstein myth starts very early, with its first drama-tisation by Richard Brinsley Peake in 1823, *Presumption; or, the Fate of Frankenstein.*[1] This is the beginning of the process of omission and simplification characteristic of drama and film adaptations and well summed up by Albert J. Lavalley when he writes that 'we never see Justine and the locket that betrayed her, we never meet Walton, and no one has ever seen the Monster read *Paradise Lost* or Plutarch' (1979: 246). Adaptations, however, also add new elements to the myth: 'a creation scene, a wedding night scene or an abduction of the bride, and a scene of fiery destruction' (Lavalley 1979: 245-6). The process

---

[1] The success of Peake's stage adaptation led to Mary Shelley's father arranging for a reprint of the novel (1823); a new edition, revised by Mary Shelley, was published in 1831. The Oxford University Press edition of 1993 publishes the 1818 text, with an Appendix by editor Marilyn Butler where, previous to the collation of the 1818 and 1831 texts, the types of change made in 1831 are summarised: the characters of Walton and especially Frankenstein are softened and made much more admirable, Frankenstein's scientific education is largely rewritten and he is given an explicitly religious consciousness, and the family and their blood-ties are revised (e.g. Elizabeth is no longer Frankenstein's cousin but a stranger). Shelley's 1831 revision might be seen as part of the very process of rewriting/adaptation of the Frankenstein myth explored in this essay.

of addition is clearly at work in the two classic films by James Whale, *Frankenstein* (1931) and *The Bride of Frankenstein* (1935). The paraphernalia and gadgetry of the laboratory and the creation scene, the presence of an assistant—who provides the wrong brain for the creature—and of a mad scientist, Dr Pretorius, the intervention of the mob chasing the monster and the completion of the creation of a mate, all of them absent in Shelley's novel, recur in most of the later versions and have become part of the cinematic myth. After the Whale films, the myth splits in two traditions, as Martin Tropp explains:

> In fact Whale's two films each inspired its own branch of the Frankenstein tradition. Part One, with its silent Monster and well-meaning but misdirected scientist, became the basis of Universal Studio's many sequels, which in turn firmly established a pattern that would influence science fiction and horror films through the Fifties and Sixties. *The Bride of Frankenstein*, with its articulate Monster and cold, perverse 'Pretorian' scientist, was, for the time being, forgotten. Late in the Fifties, these characters returned to inspire a whole new Frankenstein cycle. (1999: 47)

The new cycle referred to by Tropp was the series of films produced in Britain by the Hammer Studio, which started in 1957 with Terence Fisher's *The Curse of Frankenstein* and ended in 1974 with Fisher's *Frankenstein and the Monster from Hell*, adding up to seven films altogether, as many as the Universal cycle.[2] The Hammer series contributed the recreation of Victor (Peter Cushing) as Gothic villain, and the lush Victorian décor as well as period costume (enhanced by the fine colour photography which replaced black and white); it innovated in the creation scene and the new importance attached to sexuality; and it developed to unexpected extremes the brain motif in a series of brain transplants taking place in succeeding films. After the

---

[2] Tropp's *Mary Shelley's Monster* (1977) remains the most complete survey of the fortunes of Shelley's book on film, and it has been recently (1999) re-issued as a long article that extends the survey to the 1990s—and therefore to Branagh. The other critical cornerstone is Lavalley (1979), which includes interesting sections on nineteenth-century dramatisations and on 'Monsters in Film before the Universal *Frankenstein* of 1931'. O'Flinn (1995) is more selective and focuses on Whale and Fisher, but his views complement Tropp's on the two traditions. Finally, there is the overview in French by Menegaldo (1998), a good summary of previous materials with some interesting contributions, and including short discussions not only of Branagh, but also of the television film produced one year before (Wickes 1993) and of Tim Burton's *Edward Scissorhands* (1990).

Universal and the Hammer cycles, there was a third stage in the development of the cinematic myth aptly characterised by Lavalley as one of excess, parody, and reinterpretation. There was an attempt to retell the myth in new ways, adding a touch of playfulness and self-consciousness, but nonetheless, as Tropp remarks, in line with the two previous traditions. Paul Morrissey's *Andy Warhol's Frankenstein* (1974) revisits the Hammer tradition by taking it to shocking excess, Mel Brooks's black-and-white *Young Frankenstein* (1974) is a parody of the Universal series, and the television film *Frankenstein: The True Story* (1973), directed by Jack Smight for NBC, makes explicit the drive towards retelling and reinterpretation: the 'true' story is not so much Shelley's, but the 'real' story Shelley never told because of its biographical and homosexual implications.[3]

The story of Shelley's *Frankenstein* on film is therefore one of distortion, of omissions and additions, simplification and elaboration, or simply, one in which the myth has supplanted the novel (Tropp 1999: 74), or rather, film has supplanted the novel as a source of myth (Tropp 1999: 39). It is not surprising, then, that after a twenty-year gap without any new adaptation, the latest one, Branagh's *Mary Shelley's Frankenstein*, purported to return to the book from its very title—a move anticipated one year earlier by a television film, *Frankenstein, The Real Story*, directed by David Wickes for Turner Television. Branagh's purported restoration of the novel, however, is only true to a certain extent. It is undeniable that Branagh restores precisely those parts usually absent from film adaptations, as pointed out by Lavalley: the Justine subplot, the narrative frame including Walton and the Arctic setting, and the creature's process of self-education. But the scenes noted by Lavalley as recurrent additions in all adaptations are also present: the creation, wedding-night and destruction scenes. These and other changes discussed below prove that Branagh is well aware of the cinematic tradition of adaptations preceding him and that, in accordance with this tradition, he views Shelley's novel as 'a mythic text, an occasion for the writer to let loose his own fantasies or to stage what he feels is dramatically effective, to remain true to the central core of the myth, and often to let it interact with fears and tensions of the current time' (Lavalley 1979: 245). Apparently

---

[3] A more—although not totally—faithful retelling can be found in another television production of the same year, *Frankenstein*, directed by Dan Curtis for ABC.

Branagh intended—perhaps just pretended—to film a faithful adaptation of the book, but he did not succeed in circumventing the cinematic myth. His film adapts not only Shelley's book, but also the previous film adaptations. In fact, it blends the two central traditions of the myth, its Universal and Hammer elaborations.

And these are not the only traces of previous films in Branagh's *Frankenstein*. In his fake or half-way restoration of Shelley's *Frankenstein*, Branagh is also indebted to Francis Ford Coppola's earlier—and similarly fake—restoration of another Gothic classic, *Bram Stoker's Dracula* (1992). The parallelism in titles entails a parallelism not only in the restoration they announce, but also in the romantic and spectacular rendition of the literary source they effect. Coppola wraps his film in the cultural prestige of the literary text, but in fact carries out an ideological subversion of its meaning and a spectacular visualisation of its content (Pardo García 2003). The Gothic vampire is transformed into a romantic hero, both in the sense of the protagonist of a love story crossing 'oceans of time', as Dracula himself says—and the film credits advertise: 'Love never dies'—and a Romantic rebel-misfit in search of the absolute. The visual spectacle results from a combination of stylised costumes, highly saturated colours, impressive settings, and climactic peaks of frantic action, as well as from the presence of a composite vampire whose metamorphic capacity is used to offer a series of intertextual quotations of previous cinematic vampires. The film thus exhibits a self-conscious awareness of the film tradition particularly conspicuous in the scene of Dracula at the cinematograph. It goes without saying that these strategies ultimately respond to conditions of production, to the Hollywood conception of film as industrial product and the ensuing need to fabricate goods for popular consumption by tuning them to contemporary sensibilities and expectations. Despite the aura of cultural prestige advertised in the title, this is the hidden agenda behind Coppola's adaptation—and behind Branagh's. Coppola's *Dracula*, then, is the second important mediation of film—the first being the cinematic Frankenstein myth—between Shelley's *Frankenstein* and Branagh's *Mary Shelley's Frankenstein*: Branagh adapts Coppola—and Whale, and Fisher—as much as Shelley.

The Romantic *Frankenstein*

Branagh certainly restores the three elements which had been persistently suppressed in previous versions and which endow his film with a much closer narrative kinship to Shelley's novel. In the first place, the Promethean theme of the overreacher who defies God by assuming his power of creating life is brought to the foreground by reinstating the novel's narrative frame, Walton's expedition to the North Pole, which mirrors Victor's Promethean efforts. This theme is developed by narrating in detail the origins of Victor's thirst for forbidden knowledge and his acquisition of it at Ingolstadt. In the second place, the restoration of the creature's autodidactic acquisition of a voice and his later use of it to face his creator on the sea of ice and to narrate his story from his point of view is central to the retrieval of another thematic strain of the story, the monster's vindication of his humanity and of the inhumanity of men, his Satanic—Miltonic—dimension of rebel with a cause. Finally, the recovery of a secondary character frequently sacrificed for the sake of condensation, Justine Moritz, points to a larger motif, that of the natural and familial milieu—to which Justine belongs and from which Victor radically severs himself for the sake of science—and therefore to the female critique of male aspiration subtly articulated by that milieu and by Elizabeth in particular. Furthermore, that milieu is set in the novel's original space and time, thus restoring another Romantic dimension of the book, the sublime landscape, usually erased because of the cinematic habit of presenting the story in more contemporary settings. All three elements identify the dominant trait orienting Branagh's restoration of Shelley's *Frankenstein*: the reanimation of that original Romantic core missing in previous versions. But these elements which are apparently restored are in fact subtly transformed into something different, not wholly Romantic, but rather simply romantic.

As far as Victor's Promethean quest for the secret of life is concerned, this is motivated not just by Romantic aspiration but also by personal reasons absent in the novel. The film presents Victor's decision to create life as the result of the traumatic death of his mother while giving birth—not of scarlet fever, as in the novel—and his desire to prevent women from dying in similar conditions. This is highlighted by the visual conception of the creation scene as procreation, and by the production of the monster as reproduction: a shower of electric eels—spermatozoa—descend from enormous bags resembling testicles to a container of amniotic fluid—a surrogate womb—where the creature is lying and from which he breaks out—the birth waters flood the ground—naked and helpless like a newborn infant—in fact it starts breathing after being slapped. Further, the brain of this creature belongs to Victor's mentor and predecessor in the struggle to create life, Professor Waldman, whose murder triggers Victor's decision to create artificial life. In short, creation for the cinematic Victor is a personal, affective response to the death of his loved ones. There is also a covert attempt to reanimate Waldman—his brain—superimposed on the overt act of artificial birth. This covert conception of creation as resurrection is made overt and developed to its furthest consequences in the making of a female creature, which is not Victor's response to the monster's appeal for a mate, but to the death of Elizabeth and therefore an attempt at resurrecting her. This is the climax of Branagh's transformation of Frankenstein's Promethean quest for knowledge. Victor is basically fighting death; his Promethean rebellion against God springs from his refusal to accept death, not in an abstract sense, but in a very specific one: his mother's, his friend's, his beloved's. Feeling, not intellect, is the force driving him, again not a general love for mankind, but for certain human beings—the love of a dutiful son, a friend, a lover. Branagh's Victor is a Promethean man of feeling, his life a Promethean love story. His grandeur thus decreases, but so does his blame: his sin is not the result of inhuman ambition, but of very human feelings. The changes introduced in relation to the other two elements restored from the book, the humanised creature and Justine, also contribute to this contraction.

The transference from book to film of the creature turned into a monster by the inhuman treatment of humanity is nuanced by two apparently minor additions which turn out to be very significant. In the first place, the creature is given a criminal body. In making him, Victor uses convicts' bodies, particularly that of the murderer of Waldman, which he steals after he has been hanged. This casts new light on the creature's criminal acts, which cannot therefore be explained only in Rousseau's terms as the effect of the corrupting influence of society on a noble savage. The intertextuality contributed by the actor playing both the murderer and the creature, Robert de Niro, well-known for the parts as criminal, gangster and psycho he has played, also adds to this characterisation of the creature. In the second place, the idea of inherited evil is further highlighted when the creature introduces in his speech on the sea of ice a topic which is absent in the novel. His questions—'In which part of me does this knowledge [how to play the flute] reside: in this hand, in this mind, this heart? ... Who am I? ... Who are the people of which I am comprised? Bad people?'—suggest the existence of a kind of 'corporal memory' (Zakharieva 1996: 747) and imply that the creature's body might remember and hence contain its criminal experience, as it does the ability to play the flute. Unlike Shelley, Branagh suggests that evil might be part of his innate nature as much as goodness, that monstrosity is not just a social construct but also a product of heredity. This casts a dark shadow on the creature's self-vindication and his later murderous acts, and also tends to mitigate Victor's responsibility for them, especially because, instead of fleeing his creation and thus letting it loose upon the world, he firstly attempts to destroy it and then, when it runs away, he takes for granted that it will succumb to the plague—another film addition serving well Victor's vindication.

In this respect, Justine is also significant. In the film, unlike the novel, she is not given a fair trial before a court, but is lynched by a mad mob despite Victor's desperate attempts to save her. The difference is not irrelevant. In the book, the creature is presented as Victor's double, embodying in his outer monstrosity Victor's inner or repressed monstrosity, and thus representing the Romantic figure of the *Doppelgänger* (Tropp 1977: 37). In this sense, Victor's inability during Justine's trial to make public the existence of the monster that has actually killed William and thus save her life is representative of his inability to acknowledge his dark, repressed self. It is also an act of cowardice that, despite Victor's protestations, adds to the inconsistencies in the creation of the creature and its mate—he abandons the task for reasons which are no better than his abandonment of the creature for its ugliness. This undermines the image of doomed hero in which he tries to cast himself in his writing, and hence makes his narrative unreliable. But in Branagh's *Frankenstein* he *is* such a hero; both his duplication and his duplicity disappear, the Justine episode being perhaps the clearest indication of this. Another interesting implication of the episode is that Justine is equated to the creature as the mob's scapegoat, as the victim of monster-making and monster-chasing which uses exclusion as community affirmation. The fact that this scapegoat is female, and that her body, like Victor's mother's at the beginning and Elizabeth's at the end, is cruelly destroyed, emphasises the representation of the female as victim of male desire and violence. The female is thus included in the discourse on social victimisation and, again like the creature, is also given a stronger voice. This voice is Elizabeth's, who is a more important character in the film than she was in the novel and is presented as a strong-willed woman (Laplace-Sinatra 1998: 255-6) who makes decisions such as leaving Victor or marrying him, and takes actions such as going to Ingolstadt to fetch him or forcing him to abandon the creation of the female creature. The critique of male ambition originally present in the novel is thus reinforced and developed through female self-assertion and vindication—but only to a limited extent, as will shortly be seen.

As a result of all these changes, the restoration of Shelley's book advertised in the film's title is subverted. What takes place instead is a process of 'romantisation', that is to say, the transformation of the Romantic into the romantic by turning Victor into a hero less complex and obscure, more heroic and one-sided, ruled by human affection rather than Promethean aspiration, the protagonist of a love story involving the other two apexes of the traditional Gothic triangle. The outcome in which the monster competes with Victor for Elizabeth perfectly dramatises both this triangle and his condition as passionate lover rather than overreacher, Pygmalion rather than Prometheus. Branagh does not seem to be aware of Victor's unreliability—of his duplicity and duplication. Elizabeth and the creature, although given the voice that the cinematic myth had denied them, seem to be ultimately subordinated to this romantisation and their traditional Gothic roles: the creature is given a criminal body; Elizabeth is still a woman in love.

In proposing his film as a restoration of Shelley's *Frankenstein* and then subverting it through romantisation, Branagh is following in Coppola's footsteps. Coppola had effected a similar revitalisation of lost elements from Stoker, including a Romantic dimension—which in Coppola was an addition rather than a recovery—and a similar process of narration by a series of different voices—which played an important part in creating the illusion of literary authenticity. The illusion, however, was undermined by Coppola's romantic transformation of Stoker's plot—as is the case in Branagh. The strategies guiding both adaptations—restoration and romantisation—are consequently the same, which is not surprising if we consider that Coppola was actively involved in the production of *Mary Shelley's Frankenstein*, choosing both director and scriptwriter.[4] It would not seem, then, too far-fetched to suppose that Coppola's previous experience in adapting *Dracula*—and making it a box-office hit—weighed heavily on the script. It undoubtedly did on Branagh's visual treatment of that script: the spectacular mise-en-scène is so conspicuous in Branagh's film that it can be considered the third strategy of adaptation derived from Coppola. In turning Shelley's *Frankenstein* into a romantic spectacle, Branagh carries out a similar ideological and visual subversion of the book to Coppola's, under the same cover of restoration. And this creates an analogous conflict between the will to make the film a popular product and the pretension to endow it with the cultural prestige of the literary.

In Branagh, however, there are additional conflicts already hinted at in the preceding analysis. The creator is a blending of the procreator and the re-animator, so the conception of creation vacillates between reproduction and resurrection. The creature is presented both as noble savage and vicious criminal, so there is a hesitation in the presentation of monstrosity as product of environment or heredity. And Elizabeth is strong and outspoken but also submissive and dependent. These conflicts are not restricted to the interiority of the three central characters, but also result from their interaction. The margins—the female and the monstrous—are vindicated, but this vindication, which implies a critique of Victor's inhumanity, selfishness and irresponsibility, collides with and is ultimately submitted to Victor's vindication, to his heroic romantisation, so the critique loses edge. The film thus seems to be a composite product, made up of parts not successfully integrated into a whole, perhaps as a result of its belatedness—with respect to both Coppola's film and the Frankenstein cinematic myth—and ensuing self-consciousness. On the one hand, Coppola's strategies do not seem to have been properly di-

---

[4] Columbia TriStar Pictures, which produced *Bram Stoker's Dracula*, conceived of *Frankenstein* as its sequel so as to cash in on its success, and resorted again to Coppola, who had had a project to adapt *Frankenstein* since the 1970s. Although he eventually declined to direct the film—as did Tim Burton, who was also offered the project—he became one of the producers and chose Branagh instead. Furthermore, Coppola, who was not satisfied with the initial treatment of the story by Steph Lady, chose Frank Darabon to rewrite the original script.

gested; on the other hand, similar tensions can be detected as regards the influence of the cinematic Frankenstein tradition. The examination of the traces left by this tradition makes clear the composite, self-conscious nature of the film, which is perhaps the major symptom of its postmodern nature.

The Postmodern *Frankenstein*

The postmodern affiliation of Branagh's *Frankenstein* is best observed by focusing on three recurring contributions of film versions to the myth or, in other words, three traditional sites of divergence between book and films. If the presence of these sites in *Mary Shelley's Frankenstein* points to the mediation of the cinematic myth in Branagh's adaptation of the book, the way he handles them reveals its postmodern approach to that myth.

The first of these sites is the creation scene taking place in Frankenstein's laboratory and producing a specific visual representation of the monster. After the impact created by the inclusion of these elements in the first version by Whale, they have become the hallmark of all Frankenstein adaptations, a must on which to a certain extent each succeeding version lays its claim to originality and, if not to posterity, at least to recognition.[5] Branagh seems to be well aware of this, since he evokes and blends elements from the two main traditions of the cinematic myth. As in Whale's and the Universal films, the creation involves the vertical ascension of the creature towards the sky as well as the electrical apparatus associated with it. As in the Fisher films, though, the creature is also submerged in a tank of liquid, and eels are used as a source of animation. In this respect, the influence of Wickes's 1993 television version, where the creation takes place in a tank of liquid that duplicates whatever is submerged in it, cannot be altogether discarded. However, as Menegaldo has observed (1998: 54), this technique equates creation and cloning, thus developing the idea of the creature as Victor's double, which is absent in Branagh. In

---

[5] The incorporation of a creation scene is not only the result of the cultural weight of Whale's 1931 film, as Laplace-Sinatra has argued (1998: 261), but it is also related to the visual nature of film. Film is compelled by its visual nature to objectify the creature, and thus forces viewers to face his ugliness, elusively alluded to rather than fully described in the book (Heffernan 1997: 141).

fact, Branagh's visual contribution stresses the differences between creator and creature rather than their affinities. We see Victor frantically moving like a dancer in a carefully designed choreography and exhibiting a naked, muscular bust possibly intended to elicit the spectator's admiration—and probably stealing the creature's traditional centrality in the scene. The creature's body is also naked but, in contrast to Victor's, it is disproportionate and full of stitches, of the scars left by the assembling of body parts, and therefore fragmented or composite. The overall impression left by the scene is therefore that creation is a physical rather than an intellectual activity, an exertion of body—suggesting not only childbirth but also a kind of narcissistic male sexuality—rather than brain. In fact, throughout the film Victor remains quite a physical hero, not only exhibiting his muscles like Schwarzenegger, but also climbing up a vertical ice wall like Stallone, or horse-riding with his pistols on like a Western hero—another echo from Coppola.

The surprising supremacy of body over brain in the creator points to the second site, the relation between the creature's brain and body—the brain motif, once more created by the first adaptation by Whale. Whale's Victor steals the bodies of hanged convicts for his creature, but intends to give him a normal brain, although, as a result of his assistant's mistake, it is replaced by a criminal one instead. Whale thus institutes the motif of the abnormal brain as motivation for the creature's criminal impulses. Branagh is evidently paying homage to this invention, albeit reversing its terms, when he has Victor put Waldman's—a scientist's—brain in a convict's—Waldman's murderer's—body, but in fact he is also alluding to the Hammer films, where the brain motif becomes central as a series of transplants transfer Frankenstein's—a scientist's—and other—usually gifted—people's brains to subsequent creatures' bodies. The brain always determines the creature's personality and behaviour, thus asserting the supremacy of brain over body as the seat of individuality and identity (Tropp 1999: 63-4). Again, Branagh follows this pattern but reverses its implications: in his film, the body seems ultimately to have the upper hand, or at least it is able to rule as much as the brain since, despite Waldman's brain, the creature turns out to be an extraordinarily relentless, bloodthirsty killer.[6] Branagh's film seems to be a response to the Hammer films with their equation of mind and self, their hatred or denial of the body. Branagh—even the creature when he raises the issue of corporal memory—asserts the opposite; in fact, he seems to propose the body as the seat of the soul or, at least, as *one* seat of the soul. It is precisely the creature, with his fractured, composite identity visualised in a fragmented body and face, who raises the question of the seat of the soul when he asks: 'What of my soul? Do I have one? Was that the part you left out?'.

The centrality of the body is confirmed by the third mythic site, the creation of the mate, maybe the most original and interesting turn to cinematic tradition provided by the film. In Whale's *The Bride of Frankenstein*, Victor creates a female companion for the creature and this companion, when confronted with both creator and creature, is appalled by the latter's ugliness and rejects him. The creature, in despair, sets fire to the laboratory with both of them inside. Branagh is undoubtedly making use of that episode when Victor accomplishes the creation of a female creature that is confronted with a similar choice as both the male creature and Victor himself try to gain her for themselves. But he again reverses the situation because, in this case, the female creature is a resurrected Elizabeth, intended as Victor's— not the creature's—mate, who rejects Victor. In this respect, Branagh is again incorporating the Hammer tradition, for example *Frankenstein Created Woman* (1967), where the female creature is the object of the creator's desire, of his sexuality and even necrophilia.[7] This is related in Branagh's film to the powerful presence of a latent, perpetually delayed sexuality—of the body again—in the relationship between Victor and Elizabeth. And it is fully developed in the most original trait of the episode: the mate is, like the creature himself, a composite body, in this case made up by stitching Elizabeth's head— brain—to Justine's body. Although, on the level of the story, this is

---

[6] Zakharieva relates this supremacy of the body in the film to the cholera epidemic that devastates Ingolstadt as the creature is delivered—the plague representing a similar obliteration of the social and the rational by the body and the flesh (1996: 746).

[7] In Branagh's treatment of the creation of the mate the trace of more recent films can also be detected: Franc Roddam's *The Bride* (1986), Roger Corman's *Frankenstein Unbound* (1990), which adapts Brian Aldiss's novel of the same title, and Wickes's 1993 television film, *Frankenstein, The Real Story*.

motivated by the fact that the creature has gored Elizabeth's body by pulling out her heart, the implications are nonetheless significant on a psychological or symbolic level. Since Justine seemed to be in love with Victor, and in the film her body is clearly a more fleshy, desirable one than Elizabeth's, it is perhaps not ludicrous to suggest that Victor, driven by his frustrated sexual appetite, has fabricated his Mrs Right—Justine's better body plus Elizabeth's superior brain—as he did with the male creature. Of course by that point the spectator knows better than Victor, and is aware that the female creature is not Elizabeth—as the male creature was not Waldman—but a fractured individual, a composite body, and that the body, at least as much as the brain, is the seat of the soul. The female creature seems to be aware of it as well and, to Victor's surprise, rejects him and commits suicide by burning herself—and the building, as in Whale. Although this is the most definite instance of female self-assertion in the film (Zakharieva 1996: 750), the explanation for Elizabeth's behaviour, in my view, lies in that awareness, as intimated by her shocked look when she realizes the situation, a look which implicitly poses similar questions to those explicitly formulated by the male creature: who am I? Where is my soul?

The examination of these episodes reveals, in the first place, the extent to which Branagh's adaptation is the result of a dialogue not only with its literary source, but also with previous film adaptations, especially the classic ones by Whale and Fisher, and therefore with the cinematic myth. This undermines the alleged restoration of the book carried out by the film, and reinforces the basic contradiction running through it between the literary and the popular through the added tension between literary source and cinematic tradition. In fact, Branagh's film is a pointed demonstration of the impossibility of 'faithfully' adapting a novel once it has been transformed into a cinematic myth which will necessarily mediate, at least visually, any further adaptation (Tropp 1999: 75). Far from ignoring this fact, and despite the restoration the title misleadingly proposes, Branagh's film self-consciously adds and re-interprets motifs and episodes inspired by disparate film traditions, and it is thus, like the creature, a composite body itself. Behind all these additions and transformations, however, lies not only the burden of cinematic tradition, but also the burden of contemporary cultural concerns or, to be more precise, of the body. In the film, the three traditional sites of cinematic elaboration of the book turn on the question of body and soul, of identity. Identity is a defining theme of the Frankenstein myth, but the film adds a touch characteristic of contemporary culture: the dominance or supremacy of body over brain; the composite body as representation of a fractured identity. The film uses the myth in order to ponder the time-honoured topic of the seat of the soul, but it does so from the perspective on the body afforded by a cultural milieu where the physical dominates, and which is populated by creatures who are first of all bodies, walking collections of body parts and therefore fractured selves. The shattering of the illusion of a unified and coherent self and the dehumanisation which attends the valorisation of body and physical reality over mind and spirit are typical postmodern concerns. We are thus eventually situated at the core of Branagh's reworking of the Frankenstein myth, and also of the significance of adaptation as symptom of a certain cultural system: the film is a postmodern elaboration of the myth, a postmodern *Frankenstein*, whose exploration of the ascendancy of the body and the uncertainty of identity implies a representation of the self not in terms of Romantic inner division, but of postmodern fragmentation and dehumanisation.[8]

Adaptation as Cultural Intertextuality

The complexity of the dialogue between literature and film, as manifested in Branagh's *Mary Shelley's Frankenstein*, suggests the extraordinary possibilities for the study of adaptation once it is freed of certain traditional and obtrusive misconceptions. The first step towards this liberation undoubtedly consists in revising and enlarging the concept of adaptation, so as to refine it and perhaps even redefine it. In particular, three propositions for a theory of adaptation spring from the preceding discussion of Branagh's film. It is evident, in the first place, that film adaptation always implies a transformation, not just as regards the code or semiotic system, but also in meaning.

---

[8] Covert adaptations, not intended as imitations of Shelley's book, revisit the Frankenstein myth with more freedom and originality and use the creature's facet as double/replica in order to carry out a similar questioning of identity, making explicit the postmodern assumptions that are implicit in Branagh's overt adaptation. The most exemplary case is *Blade Runner* (Scott 1982), but *Robocop* (Verhoeven 1987), *Alien Resurrection* (Jeunet 1997), *The Sixth Day* (Spottiswoode 2000), or *Solaris* (Soderbergh 2002) also come to mind.

Adaptation in this sense is always deviation, in varying kinds and degrees. It is also always a reading of the source text; as Michel Serceau puts it, adaptation is not simply 'une transposition, une sorte de décalque audiovisuel de la littérature, mais un mode de *réception* et d'*interprétation* des thèmes et de formes littéraires' (1999: 9-10 [emphasis in original]). Furthermore, as Serceau makes clear throughout his book, other elements apart from the adapted text—myth, genre, character, discourse, and image—converge in this reception or interpretation, so that the study of adaptation cannot be reduced to the comparison between film and source text.

In the second place, adaptation is always acculturation, insofar as the transformations it effects of the literary source are related to— or even motivated by—the cultural system or context in which they originate. Indeed, adaptations not only reflect issues and topics prevalent in a certain culture or cultural tradition—as Branagh's postmodern elaboration of previous versions of the Frankenstein myth demonstrates—but also evince strategies of adaptation active in that system—as the analogies between Branagh's *Frankenstein* and Coppola's *Dracula* testify. This points to a fact which is of paramount importance to a poetics of adaptation: an adaptation is not only influenced by previous adaptations of the same text, which act as a sort of repository of images, motifs and themes, but also by contemporary adaptations of different texts which share a certain approach to adaptation, both visual and ideological, and are therefore also repositories of images, motifs or themes. Adaptation, in this sense, depends not only on the conscious will or intentions of filmmakers, but also on certain strategies, issues and concerns emerging from a specific cultural system. This explains why very poor films in terms of cinematic artistry can make for very interesting adaptations—as is the case of Branagh's *Frankenstein*. This symptomatic value of adaptation is one of the central insights afforded by Patrick Cattrysse's application to the study of adaptation of the polysystem theory of literature and particularly of translation, which implies a shift of focus from the interplay of adaptation and source to the role and functioning of adaptation in the target cultural system that produces the adaptation and generates a series of norms of selection and transposition observable in other adaptations (Cattrysse 1992a, 1992b).

Ultimately, it is evident that film adaptations of literary texts adapt films as well as texts, and they do so in a double way: they adapt films adapting the same text but also films adapting other texts. The concept of intertextuality explains much better than adaptation the complex interplay of sources and the different kinds of relationship involved. This is not just to substitute a new, trendier term for an older one, but to replace the classical conception of adaptation as a one-way relation running from text to film—and therefore, inevitably, characterised by fidelity or betrayal—by a dialogue involving many shades and nuances, and running in both directions: not only from literature to film but also from film to literature, since other films determine in different ways how a certain text is adapted. In a key contribution to the theory adaptation significantly entitled 'The Dialogics of Adaptation', Robert Stam describes adaptation as 'intertextual dialogism', thus referring to 'the infinite and open-ended possibilities generated by all the discursive practices of a culture, the entire matrix of communicative utterances within which the artistic text is situated, which reach the text not only through recognizable influences, but also through a subtle process of dissemination' (2000: 64). Stam exemplifies this approach by applying Gérard Genette's five categories of transtextuality—the relation between one text and other texts—to film adaptations (Genette 1982). Indeed, Genette's transtextual relations are well illustrated by the preceding study of Branagh's adaptation of *Frankenstein*: the film is a hypertextual transformation of the literary hypotext by Mary Shelley. Insofar as the film interprets the book, it can be understood as a metatextual commentary on it from a postmodern perspective, while insofar as it alludes to previous versions, it implies the intertextual presence of other film intertexts as well as the literary hypotext. Finally, the title is both a paratextual indication of the film's intention to restore the book and also, insofar as it evokes Coppola's *Bram Stoker's Dracula*, an architextual generic indication of the kind of adaptation and film one can expect.

Intertextuality, as defined by Stam, is the key term for redefining the concept of adaptation, since it accounts for the three propositions formulated above: (i) it implies both transformation and critical interpretation—Genette's hypertextuality and metatextuality—of the source, as much as the reproduction of that source—Genette's intertextuality; (ii) it suggests the existence of different kinds of adaptation, depending on their hypertextual and metatextual approach to the source, of different sources of the adaptation—other intertexts, including films—and of other architextual relations; and (iii) it includes not only other films as intertexts, but also other kinds of discourse and representation, since it is seen as taking place in a given cultural system. Adaptation can therefore be defined as a practice of cultural intertextuality, and Branagh's *Frankenstein* is an exemplary case in more than one sense: it is not just that the film perfectly exemplifies the concept, but also that its representation of the creature turns it into a walking metaphor of cultural intertextuality. William Nestrick (1979: 294-303) suggests that Frankenstein's creature can be regarded as a metaphor of film since, like film, it is the product of an assembling of parts—montage—and of animation by electricity—light. Branagh's emphasis on the fragmented, composite body of the creature turns it into a perfect embodiment of the composite nature of adaptation as cultural intertextuality, which the film illustrates in an extreme way in its postmodern, self-conscious assembling of fragments from previous films. Adaptation, Branagh's adaptation, and the creature featuring in it, are all patchwork quilts made out of fragments, texts or body parts. There is a perfect correspondence between matter and form in Branagh's film: it is a postmodern hybrid, made of heterogeneous and disparate parts, which ruminates on the hybrid and fractured nature of the self. Branagh produces a composite body in order to talk about the composite body, a fragmented film on fragmentation. It could also be argued, in the reverse direction, that Branagh's creature is a perfect emblem of the composite nature of artistic creation in postmodern times.

Bibliography

Cattrysse, P. (1992a) 'Film (Adaptation) as Translation: Some Methodological Proposals', *Target* 4, 52-70.
—— (1992b) *Pour une théorie de l'adaptation filmique: le film noir américain*. Bern: Peter Lang.
Genette, G. (1982) *Palimpsestes: La littérature au second degré.*Paris: Seuil.
Heffernan, J. A. W. (1997) 'Looking at the Monster: *Frankenstein* and Film', *Critical Inquiry* 24 (1), 133-58.
Laplace-Sinatra, M. (1998) 'Science, Gender and Otherness in Shelley's *Frankenstein* and Kenneth Branagh's Film Adaptation', *European Romantic Review* 9, 252-70.

Lavalley, A. J. (1979) 'The Stage and Film Children of *Frankenstein*: A Survey', in G. Levine and U. C. Knoepflmacher (eds.) *The Endurance of Frankenstein*. Berkeley: University of California Press, 243-89.

Menegaldo, G. (1998) 'Le monster court toujours...', in G. Menegaldo (ed.) *Frankenstein*. Paris: Éditions Autrement, 16-61.

Nestrick, W. (1979) 'Coming to Life: *Frankenstein* and the Nature of Film Narrative', in G. Levine and U. C. Knoepflmacher (eds.) *The Endurance of Frankenstein*. Berkeley: University of California Press, 290-315.

O'Flinn, P. (1995) 'Production and Reproduction: The Case of *Frankenstein*', in F. Botting (ed.) *Frankenstein: Contemporary Critical Essays*. Basingstoke and London: Macmillan, 21-47.

Pardo García, P. J. (2003) 'La adaptación como (per)versión: del *Dracula* de Bram Stoker a *Bram Stoker's Drácula*', in J. A. Pérez Bowie (ed.) *La adaptación cinematográfica de textos literarios: Teoría y práctica*. Salamanca: Plaza Universitaria Ediciones, 141-63.

Serceau, M. (1999) *L'adaptation cinématographique des textes littéraires: Théories et lectures*. Liége: Éditions du Céfal.

Shelley, M. (1993 (1818)) *Frankenstein; or, the Modern Prometheus*. Ed. M. Butler. Oxford: Oxford University Press.

Stam, R. (2000) 'Beyond Fidelity: The Dialogics of Adaptation', in J. Naremore (ed.) *Film Adaptation*. London: Athlone, 54-76.

Tropp, M. (1977) *Mary Shelley's Monster*. Boston: Houghton Mifflin.

—— (1999) 'Re-creating the Monster: *Frankenstein* and Film', in B. T. Lupack (ed.) *Nineteenth-Century Women at the Movies: Adapting Classic Women's Fiction to Film*. Bowling Green: Bowling Green State University Popular Press, 23-77.

Zakharieva, B. (1996) 'Frankenstein of the Nineties: The Composite Body', *Canadian Review of Comparative Literature* 23, 739-52.

Filmography

Branagh, K. dir. (1994) *Mary Shelley's Frankenstein*. Columbia TriStar.

Brooks, M. dir. (1974) *Young Frankenstein*. 20th Century Fox.

Coppola, F. F. dir. (1992) *Bram Stoker's Dracula*. Columbia TriStar.

Curtis, D. dir. (1973) *Frankenstein*. ABC.

Fisher, T. dir. (1957) *The Curse of Frankenstein*. Hammer Studio.

—— dir. (1967) *Frankenstein Created Woman*. Hammer Studio.

—— dir. (1974) *Frankenstein and the Monster from Hell*. Hammer Studio.

Morrissey, P. dir. (1974) *Andy Warhol's Frankenstein*. Braunsberg Productions/Bryanston Pictures/Carlo Ponti Cinematografica.

Smight, J. dir. (1973) *Frankenstein: The True Story*. NBC.

Whale, J. dir. (1931) *Frankenstein*. Universal.

—— dir. (1935) *The Bride of Frankenstein*. Universal.

Wickes, D. dir. (1993) *Frankenstein, the Real Story*. Turner Television.

Me, Me, Me:
Film Narrators and the Crisis of Identity

Celestino Deleyto

This chapter considers a narrative element shared by films and novels although used differently by each: the narrator. Whereas the presence of a narrator (the 'I' who speaks) is inescapable in oral and written narratives, in films narrators are used intermittently, fragmentarily and, very often, to signal 'literariness'. For this reason, this figure constitutes an interesting area of research in studies of the relationships between film and literature. This chapter looks at two recent film adaptations of popular British novels of the 1990s, *High Fidelity* (1995) and *Bridget Jones's Diary* (1996), in order to explore issues of identity, femininity and masculinity. More specifically, it focuses on the tension between the visibility of the narrator and the generic conventions of romantic comedy. As a conclusion, the existence of a sexual imbalance between the two films is detected and this is related to wider representations of masculinity, femininity and sexuality in contemporary culture.

The Increasing Visibility of Film Narration

In Spike Jonze's *Adaptation* (2002), a 'story-structure' guru advises his film students never to use voice-over in their scripts because, as he explains, it is too obvious and 'cheap' a way for a film to translate a character's thoughts into cinema. Being an extremely ironic metafictional story, the film itself does not hesitate to employ not one but two voice-over narrators. In other words, in order to mock current scriptwriting manuals the filmmakers choose the interdiction against voice-over as their target. In this they are echoing not only received opinions among film writers, but also the contempt tradition-ally displayed by film critics against those movies that use the device, especially as a way of adapting novels to the screen. Sarah Kozloff traces this critical attitude back to the theoretical revulsion against

'talkies' when sound was first introduced in films, and relates it to
utopian views of the cinema as a truly popular art which would
overcome the elitist barriers of bourgeois artistic forms like the novel.
As she concludes, for that majority of critics who still believe that the
art of cinema lies exclusively in the images, verbal narration is
nothing short of illegitimate (1988: 12).

However, the history of cinema has often contradicted this
critical and professional bias: from the Japanese *benshi* (storytellers
who accompanied with their narration the screening of silent films,
and whose power in the film industry delayed by several years the
adoption of sound in Japan) to Orson Welles's unmistakable omniscient narrators, the extended use of subjective and tormented voice-
over in *film noir* and the sophisticated experiments of the French
nouvelle vague in the 1950s and 1960s, what Avrom Fleishman has
called 'storytelling situations' (1992: 14) have abounded in films. If
anything, the 1990s have witnessed an increase in the number,
complexity and originality of onscreen and voice-over narrators and
other narrating devices, including their sustained and varied use in the
films of such undisputed *auteurs* as Woody Allen and Martin
Scorsese, and their appearance in a variety of films from blockbusters
and mainstream films like *Titanic* (1997), *The Shawshank Redemption*
(1994) or *The Bridges of Madison County* (1995), to more personal or
independent projects like *Smoke* (1995), *Lone Star* (1996) or *The
Opposite of Sex* (1998). Whether the critics like it or not, the presence
of narrators has become a regular feature in films and one with which
spectators are increasingly familiar.

Although Kozloff rejects the idea that the voice-over narrator
is a literary device (1988: 17), there can be little doubt that these
narrators generally bring films closer to novelistic narratives and,
moreover, as Kozloff herself admits, that they have constituted, since
the 1940s, a common strategy to 'translate' literary texts into film,
immediately having become a shorthand way for films to underline
their 'literariness', to ostensibly present themselves as literary adaptations. In these cases, the filmic narrator may be one more strategy in
the movies' attempts to co-opt the prestige of the originals for their
own viability as industrial projects. However, the situation is slightly
different when the original literary texts do not belong to the pantheon
of 'great works of art', but to the rather more difficult to define realm
of popular culture. Here not only does the tired critical criterion of

fidelity to the original not apply in the same way to the analysis of the filmic texts—fidelity stops being an issue when the original is not greatly admired by the critic: after all, nobody has ever complained about Shakespeare's complete disregard for *his* originals—but, from a purely industrial perspective, the artistic status of the 'great work of art' ceases to be a consideration in the filmic and extrafilmic construction of the adaptation. In this chapter, I would like to explore the pervasive presence of the narrator in two such cases, the recent adaptations of two extremely successful literary examples of 1990s middlebrow British popular culture: Nick Hornby's *High Fidelity* (1995) and Helen Fielding's *Bridget Jones's Diary* (1996). Rather than compare them to their respective originals, I will be looking at how the films *High Fidelity* (1999) and *Bridget Jones's Diary* (2001) signal their 'literariness' through their narrators, and at the ideological consequences of the rather unusual relationships they establish with their spectators in terms of the representation of (gendered) identity. I will therefore relate these narrative figures to issues of self and subjectivity and will discuss the tension between the foregrounding of these issues and the deployment of generic conventions: the films' existence in a space of romantic comedy is seriously compromised by the flaunted centrality of the narrators.

　　Some film theorists and critics use the term 'film narrator' as a synonym of the camera, which, like the novelistic narrator, 'tells the story' (McFarlane 1996: 17), or as an abstract entity which is in control of all the narrating activities of the film (Chatman 1990: 132-4). I, however, will use the concept in a more restrictive sense. Film narratives do not need a narrator. As Fleishman points out, the cinema, like the theatre, is a mimetic spectacle. Therefore, in spite of the 'narrator-effect'—the impression that in the cinema someone is always telling us a story—cinematic stories are not narrated but 'shown' (Fleishman 1992: 2-4). There often is an unconscious and unnecessary tendency to assume that narrative films should work in the same way as novels do, and that the narrator being such an inescapable part of the way in which a story is narrated in a novel, films must also be equipped with equivalent figures, even if their presence is generally not so immediately obvious or necessary. The critics' need to find an anthropomorphic figure behind all the stylistic devices and meanings of a film betrays their unrelenting reliance on the concept of artistic authority and a consequent disregard for the way films work both narratively and industrially. In films there is no need to 'create' the figure of a narrator, that is, an agent that *tells* stories, and it seems more logical to reserve that term for those moments when such figures *do* appear, when an agent actually tells a story. If we are right to criticise traditional adaptation studies for their reliance on the issue of fidelity and their bowing to the artistic superiority of literature over cinema, and we agree with Naremore that such 'inferiority complex' has turned the theory of film adaptation into 'the most jejune area' of film studies (2000: 1), by the same token film narratology should not struggle to find filmic equivalents of novelistic devices paying instead closer attention to the actual ways in which films work, whether they are common or not to other media. In the case of the narrator, the dichotomy telling/showing is sufficient to explain a basic difference between novelistic and filmic narratives: in a novel we need an agent (or several agents) that tells a story; what we need in a film is one or several, internal or external, points of view, but not necessarily a telling agent. Films 'show' stories and only occasionally narrate them.

A film narrator, therefore, is a character or an external agent who uses words (written on the screen or, much more frequently, spoken) to tell a story or, more often, one or several fragments of a story. For Fleishman most films feature storytelling situations even when they are not as a whole narrated (1992: 22). The distinction between narrated and non-narrated films, therefore, can never be absolute. Whether we classify a film as narrated or non-narrated depends on the weight and importance that we give to the storytelling situations in it. Within narrated films, the basic difference is that between external and internal or character-narrators. Whereas the former can generally only address an external narratee, the latter have no qualms about breaking narrative levels (metalepsis) and often address their stories to the audience rather than to other characters. This is the case of the internal narrator of *High Fidelity* and, more ambiguously, of that of *Bridget Jones's Diary*. Fleishman calls those characters who speak directly to the spectator direct internal narrators (1992: 24). Although they usually communicate their stories in voice-over, they can occasionally appear on screen, as is the case of Rob Gordon in *High Fidelity*, or, to mention a more famous example, Alvy Singer (Woody Allen) at the beginning of *Annie Hall* (1977). Other types of internal narrators include dramatised narrators (characters who address their stories to other characters), mindscreen (characters who do not tell the story to other characters but only rehearse it mentally to themselves) and written narrators (characters whose narration consists in the writing of letters or diaries) (Fleishman 1992: 24-27). The narrator of *Bridget Jones's Diary* is a written narrator (she is writing a diary), although, as we shall see, of a more impure kind than that of the novel.

A Fickle Narrator Falls in Love

Bridget Jones's Diary starts with a pre-credit sequence which opens with a medium shot of Bridget (Renée Zellweger) walking in a snow-covered London street as we hear her voice-over as narrator.[1] This is a traditional direct, voice-over internal narrator who, at least for the moment, is telling her story for the benefit of the spectator only: 'It all began on New Year's Day, on my 32nd year of being single. Once again I found myself on my own and going to my mother's annual turkey curry buffet'. This is the type of narrator that we expect to disappear when her voice gives way to the 'story proper', but in this film, as in *High Fidelity*, it is not so easy to get rid of the narrator. Bridget arrives at her parents' house and as soon as her mother (Gemma Jones) has completed the film's first line of dialogue, the narrator is back at it, now introducing the new character: 'My mum, a strange creature from the time when a gherkin was still the height of sophistication'. Narratively, this line confirms the omniscience of the narrator, her power to preside over the story and comment on it, and draws the spectator's attention to the artificiality of the convention—we have had no time to 'get into the story' and the narrator is already 'interrupting'. This second intervention also anticipates that this direct narrator will not be dramatised later: she is

---

[1] I am using the DVD version of the film (Columbia TriStar Home Entertainment, 2001) for my analysis. In her review, Leslie Felperin (2001: 36) refers to a different beginning, which seems to correspond to what in the DVD is the first of the 'deleted scenes'. In it, after a brief exchange between Bridget and a neighbour, we see a long shot of St. Pancras station followed by the medium shot of the protagonist referred to before. The lines of the voice-over narration do not correspond to those of the final cut, and are followed by a sequence inside the station with the train announcer improbably discussing Bridget's thighs on the loudspeakers, which has also disappeared from the DVD version.

addressing only the spectator and not another character in the narrating present. We also know, therefore, that the narrating present is no
more than a convention and hence unlikely to later become part of the
story time. Rather, we understand the narrator to occupy a detached
position outside space and time, close to that of external narrators.
Finally, since the narrator is clearly very important (and very prone to
interfering with the showing), this is also the first indication that the
story will be subordinated to her, rather than, as is more often the case,
the other way round.

    Bridget's next narrating words force us to reassess her posi-
tion once again. When her mother moves to the topic of boyfriends,
the narrator comments: 'Ah, here we go'. Rather than the usual gap
between the time of the narrating and the time of the narration, the
constructed impression here is one of simultaneity, of the narrator
reacting to the events of the story as these unfold and, therefore, of an
agent who is not as much in control of events as we may have thought.
After her dialogue with her mother, Bridget goes upstairs to get
changed and a cut shows her in her new outfit, going into the main
room, where the party is taking place. The narrating voice is immediately back, saying: 'Great. I was wearing a carpet'. The line seems an
impossible combination of the two incompatible positions that
Bridget-narrator has occupied so far: the past tense detaches her from
the narrated events, but the initial exclamation underlines the proximity between both. The spectator is getting accustomed to the
arbitrariness of the film's use of the device and enjoys its comic
effect: this is an ironic narrator whose colloquial, gossiping, self-
deprecating tone will lead viewers not so much through the narrative
of events as through the narrative of the self, to which the story is no
more than a necessary appendage. Spectators will only enjoy the
comedy if they accept the constant play with and disregard for
realistic conventions. The fiction proposed by the film begins to look
like the story told by a technically sophisticated friend of the spectator, who shares with us her frustrations and anxieties about her life as
a middle-class thirty-something single woman in 1990s London and
employs a series of visual snippets from her rather mundane and,
therefore, easily identifiable experiences as illustration of her oral
narrative. At the same time, as we shall see, the emphasis on the self
through the prominence and artificiality of the narrator undercuts the

film's attempts to adhere to the generic conventions of romantic comedy.

After the credits, which now follow, Bridget-narrator reveals the precise nature of the decision that she has made and which she had announced at the end of the pre-credit sequence: to write a diary in order to 'take control of her life' and to tell the truth about Bridget Jones. As the narrator, still in the past tense, explains this, one of the characteristic headings that open each diary entry in the novel, spelling out her weight, calories, cigarettes and 'drink units' consumed, and so on, appears superimposed on the screen in what is meant to be Bridget's handwriting (with the concession for US audiences of substituting pounds for stones, just as, a few seconds later, the narrator uses the US American term 'pants' rather than the original's British 'knickers' to refer to her underwear). As Bridget's voice-over continues, she is also seen writing those very words in her diary, which suggests that what the narrator is going to say from now on corresponds to the contents of this diary. The type of narrator has, therefore, changed without any warning: in Fleishman's terms, from a direct voice-over narrator to a written diary narrator, another convention of long and prestigious tradition both in the cinema and the novel. In theory, this narrator is very different from the direct narrator in that, like a dramatised narrator, it is given a realistic justification. In reality, however, the film will never make much effort to stick to the diary convention. The cut to the next scene, for example, is again accompanied by the narrator's voice who now introduces a new character, Daniel Cleaver (Hugh Grant). As she mentions his name, we see Daniel in close-up with a roguish expression on his face coming into the office and initiating his sexist flirtation with Bridget. Other characters are then presented, following the same convention previously employed to introduce Bridget's mother: the character performing an action and the narrator commenting on it, a stratagem which is well beyond the capabilities of any diary writer. In the course of the film, the diary convention is abandoned or resumed at the narrator's will. For example, at the end of this same scene, when Bridget explains to Daniel that she was talking to F. R. Leavis on the telephone and he ironically asks her whether this is the same F. R. Leavis who died in 1978, the superimposed word on the screen, a long-drawn 'fuuuuuuuuuuck!', again in Bridget's handwriting, is another immediate reaction which suggests not so much the resuming of diary writing as another modality of internal narrator: mindscreen, an amusing way to present Bridget's reaction to the discovery of her *faux pas*. Therefore, what we have seen so far is a narrator both extremely powerful in terms of her mastery over the tale she is recounting and voluble and inconsistent in narrative terms, changing freely from one mode of internal narration to another as the occasion requires (the only one she does not use in the course of the film is the dramatised narrator, the most realistic type). This volubility, of course, reinforces her mastery since she is not bound by any narrative or realistic rules that may curtail her freedom to communicate her feelings, experiences and, above all, anxieties to the audience.

FIG. 4 All by myself: Bridget Jones narrates the female lonely self

The intermittent nature of filmic narrators and the relative autonomy of the image with respect to them work against their control of the textual point of view over the narrated events. In most internally narrated films, the occasional presence of the narrator does not prevent the text from showing the action from the point of view of other characters or from an external point of view, or even from showing a part of the story to which the narrator cannot possibly have access. Film spectators are well accustomed to the convention and do not generally notice the inconsistency. My foregoing description of *Bridget Jones's Diary*'s narrator suggests that the film may be an exception in this respect because of the much closer control that it allows the narrating voice over the image track. However, I have been referring here mostly to the first ten minutes or so of the film and, although Bridget-narrator continues to appear frequently, as the narrative develops her interventions become less constant and her control of the story slackens somewhat, allowing the spectator to settle into a more conventional filmic narrative. Her point of view continues to predominate both through narration and internal focalisation, but the careful spectator will notice breaches of this self-imposed norm quite early on in the film.[2]

An early scene shows Bridget's clumsy but rather funny presentation of a new book at a launch party under the close scrutiny of an onscreen audience which includes real-life authors Salman Rushdie and Lord Archer. For the first time in the film, the visual emphasis here is on Bridget not as subject but as object of the look, her speech working as a comic act which both amuses and embarrasses fictional and real spectators alike. The struggle for control of the narrative point of view between Bridget as narrator and the other characters, particularly Daniel and Mark Darcy (Colin Firth), as focalisers, is momentarily resolved when, after the speech, Bridget stands alone by the bar and we see her briefly from Mark's point of view, while he talks to other people. He is about to go towards her and rescue her from her dejection when Daniel beats him to it and suggests having dinner together. As they leave the party room, we stay with Mark for a second or two, sharing his perspective on them, an intense look which conveys his romantic interest in her, his hatred of Daniel, his disappointment that she prefers the other man and his worry that she will be betrayed. This is a look that Bridget has had no access to and perhaps the first important narrative element that reveals something not controlled by the narrator.

The moment is thematically and generically relevant because it introduces a desire different from Bridget's and consolidates the film's adherence to the conventions of romantic comedy. One of the central tenets of this genre is the articulation of at least two subjects/objects of desire. There is very little romantic hope for a film in which only one point of view and, therefore, only one desire predomi-

---

[2] Fleishman briefly discusses the relationship between narration and focalisation in rather unsatisfying terms (1992: 157-8). For a more thorough discussion of the usefulness of the term for the analysis of film narratives, see Deleyto (1996).

nates. Because of its subject matter—the fulfilment of reciprocal desire in various social and historical circumstances—romantic comedy is, by definition, a more egalitarian genre than most.[3] It follows that the initial format of *Bridget Jones's Diary*, with the total predominance, one would say even tyranny, of Bridget's point of view through her role as narrator (and secondarily as focaliser), is not particularly conducive to the proper consummation of love. It seems logical to speculate, therefore, that the hold of the narrator over the story must loosen before the film can settle into the conventions of romantic comedy, and this is what happens to a certain extent, even though Bridget-narrator continues to direct our attention. It could be argued that, in a sense, the film chronicles the struggle between the narrator and the genre for predominance. It could also be said that the whole point of the great visibility of Bridget as narrator, particularly at the beginning of the narrative, is closely linked to her inability to establish romantic attachments with men: she talks to spectators because she has nobody else to talk to, because only they will listen. For this reason, the film's reliance on an extremely narcissistic narrator becomes part of a neo-conservative ideology which, starting in the USA in the late 1970s, has presented women as frustrated, lonely and unhappy victims of their own ambitions of equality (Faludi 1992). The empowered narrator of *Bridget Jones's Diary* can be interpreted, paradoxically, as a symptom of a cultural female power-lessness. The Hollywoodisation of the novel, particularly through the use of USA star Renée Zellweger to play British Bridget, works towards an universalisation of the trend—'modern women have the same problems everywhere'—and brings important ideological consequences to what was probably, at least on a conscious level on the part of the filmmakers and the producers, only a commercial decision. Conversely, while Daniel's obvious sexist objectification of Bridget was never very promising as a way out of Bridget' histori-cally-specific predicament, Mark's gradually intensified gaze, and its summoning of the conventions of romantic comedy, goes a long way towards counteracting the solipsism of the film's narrative structure. It is significant that the gradual strengthening of both the role of Mark Darcy and the conventions of romantic comedy with respect to the

---

[3] For good accounts of romantic comedy in film, see Neale and Krutnik (1990), Neale (1992) and Thomas (2000).

novel runs parallel to the relative loss of power of the film's narrator, a loss which never happens in the novel, among other things because Mark remains a relatively secondary character and is certainly never given a voice or a point of view. At the end, each spectator will decide which of the two pulls attracts her/him more, but in *Bridget Jones's Diary* a powerful filmic narrator and the fulfilment of erotic desire prove to be incompatible.

Romantic Comedy to the Rescue of the Male Narrator

The film adaptation of *High Fidelity* also stresses the potential for romantic comedy of the original. The story of a break-up between a man and a woman and their final reconciliation is as old as Shakespeare and was, for example, the common subject of a cycle of screwball comedies that Stanley Cavell called 'comedies of remarriage' (1981), even though Rob (John Cusack) and Laura (Iben Hjejle) are not married at the beginning and remain unmarried at the end. However, the hypothetical tension between narrator and genre is resolved here in a different way from *Bridget Jones's Diary*. Sharon Maguire's film, while remaining a 'woman's film' in its overall effect, appears as a conglomerate of disparate narrative blocks in the inconsistency and fragmentariness of its narrator, in its use of a popular USA star to portray a British character, and in the gradual opening up and proliferation of its points of view to accommodate romantic comedy tropes. *High Fidelity*, on the other hand, features a much more disciplined and coherent narrative structure through an internal narrator who is even more pervasive and controlling than Bridget. Unlike her, Rob starts as a direct narrator, sometimes voice-over but mostly on-screen, and remains the same throughout the film. If the filmmakers' decision to transplant the story from London to Chicago is artistically braver and more successful than the casting of Zellweger as Bridget (although the professional press was surprisingly almost unanimous in its praise of the actress's performance), the intensification of the role of the narrator to retain the novel's distinctiveness and appeal is both more inventive and satisfying than in the other film.[4]

---

[4] Predictably, *Bridget Jones's Diary* was much more popular at the box office than *High Fidelity*, although both were produced by the extremely successful British-based 'independent' company Working Title. Made on a budget of $20 million, *High*

Whereas *Bridget Jones's Diary* attempts to ensure the widest audience appeal through highlighting both the romantic comedy dimension and the narrator's role, Stephen Frears's less compromising approach keeps *High Fidelity* on a lower profile while focusing much more intensely on the contemporary male's plight in the field of heterosexual desire. I am suggesting, therefore, that the effect of romantic comedy in this film appears to be seriously impaired for the same reason as it is gradually promoted in *Bridget Jones*. In *High Fidelity* the relationship between Rob and Laura is seen exclusively from *his* perspective. Laura's point of view is either filtered through the narrator or sometimes even imagined by him, as are those of the other characters. Although the specific nature of film language makes it theoretically impossible to suppress the focalisation of characters on the screen and filmic conventions ensure that an external focaliser is always at work even in the most subjective of narratives, there are no moments in this film equivalent to the crucial shift in point of view at the book launch party in Maguire's. In a more decisive way than Bridget, Rob matures in the course of the film, a maturation constantly hindered by his 'infantile' male friends and bolstered by Laura's patience, understanding and compassion, but, unlike in the majority of romantic comedies, this is presented exclusively from his perspective.

The opening segment of *High Fidelity* firmly establishes the narrator's relationship with the story and with the spectator. The first image is a detail shot of the vinyl record playing in the soundtrack. From here the camera pans right following the headphone cable until it finds the back of Rob's head on which it concentrates for a few seconds. This shot already points towards the central conceit of the film: the music can only be heard by Rob and, through his ears, by the spectator, but not by other characters (in this case, Laura, who is also in the house). We, therefore, have privileged access to Rob's subjectivity and will learn very little else apart from his opinions and thoughts. After the cut, a close-up reverse shot shows Rob looking straight at the camera and starting his relentless conversation with the spectator. The similarity with the beginning of a film like *Annie Hall*

Fidelity grossed $27 million in the USA, £4.5 million in Britain and not quite €1 million in Spain. *Bridget Jones's Diary*, for its part, was made on a slightly higher budget of $26 million but grossed $71 million in the USA, an impressive £41 million in Britain and more than €13 million in Spain (Internet Movie Database).

is remarkable but there are also important differences: while the Alvy Singer of *Annie Hall* initially looks like the director himself, perhaps giving an imaginary interview, and therefore introducing the possibility of a dramatised situation and of a diegetic interlocutor (like the interviewer in Allen's later *Husbands and Wives* (1992)), here we are aware from the beginning that Rob is not John Cusack but a fictional character and that he is not talking to anybody but the real spectators. This first address is interrupted by Laura, who is about to leave him, and who, in order to attract his attention, unplugs the headphones. Without any marker of a change of narrative level or return to the fictional world, Rob has a brief conversation with his girlfriend before she goes. He then turns back to the camera to introduce his childish but very amusing distinctive practice of making top-five lists about everything: 'My desert island, all time, top five most memorable break-ups in chronological order are as follows…'. After listing the names of his previous girlfriends, he vindictively shouts at Laura from the window to remind her that their break-up has not even made it into the top five, although the spectator knows that this is not strictly true.

FIG. 5 Top five all time break-ups: Rob-narrator enlists the spectator to his revenge against and later redemption by girlfriend Laura

Then he resumes his dialogue with the camera and starts telling
viewers about those break-ups through a combination of voice-over,
flashbacks and constant returns to direct address to the camera. These
five stories (in the end Laura's *is* included in the top five) constitute
the first narrative segment of the film, but the role and central conceit
of the narrator, established through them, never changes.

The formula admits numerous variations: a 'hypothetical
flashback', when he imagines the dialogue in which Laura tells their
common friend Liz (Joan Cusack) the reasons why she left him; a
mindscreen conversation with Bruce Springsteen with some useful
advice about how to behave with Laura; three fantasised ways in
which he would react 'like a man' when his rival Ray (Tim Robbins)
comes to pay him a visit at the record shop, followed by his real
mumbling, powerless reaction; or direct addresses to camera even
from inside some of the flashbacks. These and other strategies work
because of their subservience to the convention of the direct on-screen
narrator. This technique doubtless enhances the film's artificiality and,
in the words of the Russian Formalists, 'lays bare the device'. Paradoxically, its more specific effect is not so much one of breaking the
illusion but, rather, a simultaneously almost literal and logically
impossible incorporation of the spectator in the same diegetic level as
the fictional characters. In other words, an intense engagement with
the story on our part, as if we ourselves were also fictional characters—or as if Rob were not completely fictional. The repetitiveness
and consistency of the address suggests that there is a character in the
position of the camera, a character that spectators never get to see, an
imaginary confidant of Rob's, who is no other than the spectator
her/himself: an infinitely patient friend who sits and listens to his
ravings. In the first scene, as has been mentioned, Rob moves natu-
rally from addressing the camera/spectator to addressing Laura, as if
both were part of the same world: the girlfriend who abandons him
and the infinitely patient friend who sits and listens to his ravings. In
later scenes, this makes for spotlessly invisible transitions and amusing ambiguities: when standing by the counter in a club, Rob and his
two friends, Barry (Jack Black) and Dick (Todd Louiso), consider
what it would be like to live with a musician as they watch Marie
(Lisa Bonet) perform, and Rob speaks to the camera in close-up—we
cannot be sure whether he is talking to his friends or to us—again as if
the spectator were one more member of the group of friends and

belonged to their same world. At other times, Rob looks at the camera and spectators expect his narration to return, but he is simply meditating and has nothing to communicate for the moment. On these occasions, the illusion of reality is not really broken because, if viewers accept the pact that the film has offered, Rob does not really leave the diegesis to address them. He does not think of us as radically different from the other characters, except that, unlike them, we never talk back (although we would certainly like to). This ensures that the filmmakers can include as many of Rob's thoughts as they like without the film becoming tedious, but it also binds them to Rob's perspective and means that the other characters become ciphers without much real autonomy.[5] Much more than *Bridget Jones's Diary*, *High Fidelity* succeeds or fails on the strength of the believability and the pleasure provided by its protagonist-narrator.

FIG. 6 What men think women think: Rob's behaviour shocks Liz ... in Rob's fantasy

---

[5] Whereas this is true of the film as a whole, the actors' performance can go some way towards counteracting this tendency, and both Todd Louiso and, especially, Jack Black manage to give their characters a life of their own, and turn them into autonomous pleasures. It was probably his performance in this film that opened the way for Jack Black to become the star of later films like the Farrelly brothers' *Shallow Hal* (2001) and Richard Linklater's *School of Rock* (2003).

Both *Bridget Jones's Diary* and *High Fidelity* offer, through the evocation and flaunting of their own 'literariness', almost literally what for Anthony Giddens is the main characteristic of modernity: narratives of the self. Through a constant reflexivity or self-analysis, the modern individual seeks to control her/his own life and his sense of her/his own individuality (Giddens 1991). For Michel Foucault, on the other hand, sex is one of the privileged spaces for the exploration and construction of people's sense of identity in modern societies. According to the French thinker, we have come to expect sexual encounters to give us the truest idea of who we are (Foucault 1981). Romantic comedy, as one of the most popular cultural formations for the representation of sex and love in our society, seems an ideal place to link our modern sense of individual identity to our desire for the other, and therefore to bring together the theories of these two authors. Yet, my analysis of *Bridget Jones's Diary* has argued that Bridget's glorification of her own suffering and constant disappointments in love appears to be a necessary condition of her consolidation as a narrator, and consequently the happy resolution of her relationship with Mark significantly weakens the power of the narrator. Bridget's visibility as internal narrator and therefore as subject of the narrative in this contemporary 'chick-flick' is tied to her insecurity and help-lessness in love, much like the female subjectivity constructed by the 'woman's film' was, according to Mary Ann Doane (1987), tied to the characters' experiences of suffering, fear and masochism.

A different process seems to be at work in *High Fidelity*, one that appears to be related to the continuing inequality in the represen-tation of the sexes in our culture. In this film, the crisis of masculinity through the experience of love, which constitutes the starting point of the narrator's omnipresence in the narrative (the top five all time break-ups), becomes the source of change for Rob— an epiphany of sorts takes place while he is waiting for the inexistent bus after the funeral of Laura's father, just before they have sex in her car—who uses it 'wisely' to 'mature' without diminishing his control over the story as narrator. This may remind the film spectator of one of the most representative cultural icons of contemporary masculinity: the Woody Allen *schlemiel* hero, who often thrives in an atmosphere of beleaguered manhood and who, coincidentally or not, regularly doubles as film narrator. From a feminist standpoint, Kathleen Rowe criticises Woody Allen's comedies as examples of the way in which 'new men' use their melodramatisation—present themselves as victims—as a way to shore up their authority over women (1995, 196-200). Before Hornby's popular books of the 1990s, Allen had been using the format of romantic comedy since the early 1970s in order to explore the historical predicament of men (and sometimes women) in the face of important changes in cultural definitions of masculinity and femininity and the relationships between the sexes brought about by the sexual revolution and feminist movements of the 1960s and 1970s (Babington and Evans 1989: 152-78). In films like *Love and Death* (1977), *Annie Hall, Manhattan* (1979), *Hannah and her Sisters* (1986), *Another Woman* (1988) and others, Allen uses narrators in various ways to convey the experiences of these melodramatised men and women in similar if less ostensible ways to the two films that I have analysed here. A film like *Hannah and her Sisters*, for example, articulates a subtle struggle for control of the narrative between various men and women in which the character played by Allen himself makes his final romantic triumph coincide with a visible dominance over the other characters as narrator, in a way which may be seen as a precedent of *High Fidelity*. Allen has occasionally used younger actors to replace him as romantic lead, especially in the 1990s. Of these, probably the most successful was precisely John Cusack who, having already appeared in *Shadows and Fog* (1991), returns to play the protagonist of *Bullets over Broadway* (1994), a promising young playwright in the 1920s who, also acting as narrator, undergoes a similar personal development to that experienced by Rob in Frears's film. Like *High Fidelity*, this film uses the conventions of romantic comedy, and even the structure of the comedy of remarriage, as well as the device of the internal narrator, in order to convey what is essentially a male personal narrative of the self triggered by a crisis of masculinity disguised here as a crisis of creativity. John Cusack's presence in both films links the filmic Rob Gordon to Woody Allen as part of a wider cultural conversation about the contradictory position occupied by men in contemporary society. As in many of Allen's films, *High Fidelity* succeeds in appropriating the 'egalitarian' conventions of romantic comedy in order to reinforce the literal narrative of the self and manages to chronicle the romantic triumph of his protagonist without diminishing his position as narrator.[6] Frears's

---

[6] I am not suggesting here a cultural sexual determinism of the type entertained by

film consolidates Cusack as one of Allen's inheritors in the 1990s, as a contradictory yet far-from-helpless 'new man', and the film's outstanding use of a male character narrator emphasises, through its highlighting of issues of power, authority, subjectivity and desire, this line of cultural development.

Conclusion: Beyond Comparison

The literary narrators of these two films illustrate the cultural dimensions not only of the process of adaptation from novel to film but, more generally, of the complex relationships between film and literature. In a recent interview about *Dogville* (2003), Danish director Lars von Trier explains that through the radical stylistic approach used in his film he was trying to challenge what he considers reactionary attempts to cordon and limit film, theatre and literature. In *Dogville*, which is not an adaptation but based on an original script written by von Trier himself, and which employs an omniscient external narrator, he creates a fusion of the three arts. For von Trier, questions as to what is or is not filmic are irrelevant because in art everything is possible (Björkman 2004: 25). I have tried to prove that the figure of the narrator, indispensable in novels, but often employed in complex ways by both films and plays, is a good example of the potentialities of this artistic fusion and that, beyond predictable comparisons between the different ways in which this or that figure are used in the different arts, what is more relevant and more worthy of attention is its participation in cultural struggles for the construction of historically-specific identities and ideological discourses.[7]

---

traditional feminist film criticism: Bridget's loss of part of her control as narrator when the conventions of romantic comedy are activated is related to the fact that she is a woman and Rob's parallel preservation of his position in similar circumstances can be explained as part of the cultural representations of contemporary masculinity, but it is not impossible for female narrators to preserve a high degree of visibility after their encounter with the conventions of romantic comedy, as is proved, for example, by other contemporary films like *Clueless* (1995) or *The Opposite of Sex*. Therefore, rather than patriarchal inevitability, I prefer to refer to cultural tendencies.

[7] Research towards this chapter has been funded by the DGICYT project no. BFF2001-2564.

Bibliography

Babington, B. and Evans, P. W. (1989) *Affairs to Remember: The Hollywood Comedy of the Sexes*. Manchester: Manchester University Press.

Björkman, S. (2004) 'Lars von Trier: The Defects of Humanism' (interview with Lars von Trier), *Sight and Sound* 14 (2), 25-7.

Cavell, S. (1981) *Pursuits of Happiness: The Hollywood Comedy of Remarriage*. Cambridge, Mass.: Harvard University Press.

Chatman, S. (1990) *Coming to Terms: The Rhetoric of Narrative in Fiction and Film*. Ithaca and London: Cornell University Press.

Deleyto, C. (1996) 'Focalisation in Film Narrative', in S. Onega and J. A. García Landa (eds.), *Narratology*. London: Longman, 217-33.

Doane, M. A. (1987) *The Desire to Desire: The Woman's Film of the 1940s*. Bloomington and Indianapolis: Indiana University Press.

Faludi, S. (1992) *Backlash: The Undeclared War against Women*. London: Vintage.

Felperin, L. (2001) 'Thigh Society', *Sight and Sound* 11 (4), 36-7.

Fleishman, A. (1992) *Narrated Films: Storytelling Situations in Cinema History*. Baltimore and London: Johns Hopkins University Press.

Foucault, M. (1981) *The History of Sexuality, vol. 1: An Introduction*. Harmondsworth: Penguin.

Giddens, A. (1991) *Modernity and Self-Identity: Self and Society in the Late Modern Age*. Cambridge: Polity Press.

Internet Movie Database. On-line. Available HTTP: http://www.imdb.com (15 March 2004).

Kozloff, S. (1988) *Invisible Storytellers: Voice-Over Narration in American Fiction Film*. London, Berkeley and Los Angeles: University of California Press.

McFarlane, B. (1996) *Novel to Film: An Introduction to the Theory of Adaptation*. Oxford: Clarendon.

Naremore, J. (2000) *Film Adaptation*. London: Athlone.

Neale, S. (1992) 'The Big Romance or Something Wild?: Romantic Comedy Today', *Screen* 33 (3), 284-99.

—— and Krutnik, F. (1990) *Popular Film and Television Comedy*. London and New York: Routledge.

Rowe, K. (1995) *The Unruly Woman: Gender and the Genres of Laughter*. Austin: University of Texas Press.
Thomas, D. (2000) *Beyond Genre: Melodrama, Comedy and Romance in Hollywood Films*. Moffat: Cameron Books.

Filmography

Frears, S. dir. (1999) *High Fidelity*. Working Title Films.
Maguire, S. dir. (2001) *Bridget Jones's Diary*. Working Title Films.

Playing in a Minor Key:
The Literary Past through the Feminist
Imagination

Belén Vidal

The classic adaptation has been often dismissed as conservative, middlebrow cinema, on the grounds of the picturesque realism of the costume film and its association with past traditions of quality cinema. However, films like *The Luzhin Defence* (Marleen Gorris, 2000), *Mansfield Park* (Patricia Rozema, 1999) and *The Governess* (Sandra Goldbacher, 1998) challenge these notions, as they inflect well-known literary intertexts from the angle of postfeminist popular culture. This chapter proposes the term 'literary film' in order to expand the critical uses of adaptation, and explore how women's cinema engages with the literary past through contemporary modes of writing and address. I argue that these works adapt the 'major' idiom of the historical and the literary past to the 'minor' key of romance, allowing for a feminist revision whose strengths and limits need to be assessed through the framework of the visual and narrative pleasures afforded by the costume film.

Transgressive Gestures

In 2000, *The Luzhin Defence* was released to lukewarm reviews. With this film, Dutch director Marleen Gorris made her second English-language adaptation after *Mrs Dalloway* (1997) via another modernist author—this time, Vladimir Nabokov and his novel *Zashchita Luzhina/The Defence* (1930). The film takes place mostly at an Italian resort in the late 1920s, the chosen location for the world chess tournament. Alexander Luzhin (John Turturro), an obsessive chess player haunted by a troubled family past, is forced to choose between the normalcy of a bourgeois life with Natalia Katkov (Emily Watson), the woman who loves him, or his passion for chess, with the intolerable pressure that it puts on him. Unable to disentangle himself from its driving obsession and his memories, he commits suicide before completing a final and decisive game. The film, however, concludes with a twist that is not in the novel. Luzhin leaves behind a scrap of paper with a variation containing a brilliant winning move—a stroke of genius. It is left to Natalia to execute the move that makes Luzhin the posthumous world champion.

Like *Mrs Dalloway*, Gorris's version of Nabokov's *The Defence* somehow fell short of expectations in comparison with her celebrated written-directed *Antonia/Antonia's Line* (1995), which was received as a more personal, and therefore auteurist project. However, *The Luzhin Defence* was criticised not so much for its lack of truthfulness to what is, at any rate, a little-read literary classic, but for the inauthenticity of its reconstruction. Pointing at the inconsistencies of the eleventh-hour win, not to mention the misrepresentation of the world of professional chess throughout the film, novelist and chess specialist Tim Krabbé regretted that:

> The infantile plot makes you wonder whether the disrespect is greater towards the book or towards chess. It takes a sad sort of guts to turn a novel about the tragic enchantment of chess into a feminist pamphlet; man is too weak, woman must finish his work for him. (Krabbé 2001)

Krabbé's negative review is symptomatic of the resistance faced by many commercial films that bring to life worlds from the past through reference to literary sources. The period adaptation rides on a desire for the 'literary' that overlaps with the desire for authenticity—that is, the desire that takes its cue from the surface realism of period reconstruction. *The Luzhin Defence* not only changes the ending of the book, in which Natalia is just a marginal character ultimately unable to penetrate the fortress of Luzhin's obsession, but dramatises chess into a melodramatic metaphor for male genius and madness. Krabbé's critique is, nevertheless, more suspicious of what is really distinctive about Gorris's rewriting of Nabokov's novel: how the film narrative unfolds like an extended chess game which is finally given sense— and a sense of closure—by Natalia's invented gesture. Her intervention turns her into a sort of medium, guided by the genius of her dead lover. However, the inserts of her extended hand and the close-ups capturing her intense, expressive face as she executes the final moves of the game (and the film's final movement) reframe the moment as Natalia's personal triumph. Whereas Luzhin is unable to escape both his own personal history and the confines of a world defined by the implacable logic of chess, Emily Watson's spontaneous body language and insight make Natalia a timeless character. The shot that closes the film is a slow-motion close-up of her glowing face and confident gait, which self-consciously highlights the significance of the altered ending. Natalia's gesture both transcends and gives its full meaning to the romantic drama. Luzhin's failure is overturned by Natalia's moment of achievement.

Natalia's implausible yet exhilarating gesture mirrors the film's own idiosyncratic reading of the literary original in terms of the anachronistic 'gestures' of feminist revision. In this, *The Luzhin Defence* is not alone. Throughout the 1990s and early 2000s, a significant number of costume films—often directed by women—have reworked the past through stories focusing on female experience. Through the generic windows of the classic adaptation, the romance narrative or the biographical film, films like *Orlando* (Sally Potter, 1992), *The Piano* (Jane Campion, 1993), *Little Women* (Gillian Armstrong, 1994), *Sense and Sensibility* (Ang Lee, 1995), *The Portrait of a Lady* (Jane Campion, 1996), *Mary Reilly* (Stephen Frears, 1996), *Washington Square* (Agniezska Holland, 1997) or *Nora* (Pat Murphy, 1999) inflect familiar literary themes from the angle of postfeminist popular culture.[1] Although this is an extremely diverse cross-section, these films invite readings where the terms of the relationship with the past are not 'fidelity' and 'authenticity', but 'pastiche' and 'rewriting'. These costume films do not purport to offer definitive readings of canonical texts. On the contrary, they 'adapt' a major idiom—whether literary themes, historical records, or technological narratives—to the minor key of romance.

Rather than fitting traditional definitions of adaptation, these films transform and use the literary as a series of textual traces disseminated and recontextualised through the reflexive forms of the period/costume film. In this chapter, I focus on two of these 'literary films': *Mansfield Park* (1999), adapted from the novel by Jane Austen

---

[1] The list should not be restricted to transnational English-language cinema. The trend also includes films such as *Artemisia* (Agnès Merlet, 1997), *A los que aman/To Those who Love* (Isabel Coixet, 1997), *Marquise* (Vera Belmont, 1997), or *Esther Kahn* (Arnaud Desplechin, 2000).

and directed by Patricia Rozema, and *The Governess* (1997), an original script by Sandra Goldbacher about a Jewish woman in Victorian times. These films are invested in the reconstruction of feminine identity through disruptive gestures that rewrite a literary past in accordance with contemporary views and aspirations.

The dominant view on modern English-language period drama, the 'heritage' critique, has tended to pigeonhole the costume film into a category of intrinsically nostalgic forms and styles, which trades on reductive images of the national heritage.[2] However, the conventional realism of many of these literary films actively metamorphoses through the different modalities of desire underlying the retrieval of the past. In order to situate the points of (critical) inflection within the film text, this chapter looks at the ways these films transform certain intertextual motifs (such as the activity of letter-writing, or the birth of photography in the nineteenth century) into textual figures. The term 'figure' is redolent of the rhetorical and poetic functions of language. It helps establish a link between the literary and the film text, and between realist and poetic modes of representation. The figure participates in the structuring of textual meanings as a pre-condition for representation; it demands attention to the fragment versus the narrative whole. Reading the figure in the film text entails, therefore, reading against the dominant reality effect.[3]

Since 'desire alludes to texts—but in order to efface its own citationality' (Belsey 1994: 17), I use textual analysis in order to explore such mechanisms of citationality and how they articulate the desire for the past. The figures of the literary film lay out the narrative memory *in* the film text, identified by adaptation, through the palimpsest-like memory *of* the film text. Whereas, traditionally, the construction of the author as *adapter* has had to be negotiated through the dominant discourses on fidelity and authenticity, these films provide an avenue to rethink authorship in terms of the gestures of feminist revision. The strengths and limitations of such gestures need

---

[2] For a full account of the debates around the so-called 'heritage film' by one of its main proponents, see Higson (2003).
[3] See Mieke Bal's distinction between 'reading for the text' and reading 'realistically' (i.e. reading for wholeness, and therefore for the effect of the real) (Bal 1991: 216-46).

to be assessed through the framework of the visual and narrative pleasures afforded by the costume film.

From Major to Minor: Fantasy and Feminist Critical Strategies

The detours through the past staged by the literary film provide textual masks which, in many ways, are highly pliable to the politics and investments of women's cinema. From the 1970s on, both feminist theory and women's cinema have (re)turned time and again to the scene of History to retrieve marginal subjectivities erased from official accounts. Alison Butler cites the mainstream literary film *The Portrait of a Lady* along other international films that excavate women's past histories, such as *Daughters of the Dust* (Julie Dash, 1991), *Saimt el Qusur/The Silences of the Palace* (Moufida Tlatli, 1994) or the already mentioned *Antonia's Line*. For Butler, these films offer invaluable explorations of women's culture in ways that highlight 'the pleasures of specificity and of a systematized understanding of femininities ... they emphasize the historical presence of women rather than their theoretical absence, and ... resist dissolution into generalities' (Butler 2000: 77). The mainstream literary film contributes to putting women back into History by retrieving the past as an already textualised form that needs to be contested *from within* the dominant conventions of the narrative fiction film.

In this respect, the literary film has taken centre stage in the debates around women's cinema especially after the international success of *Orlando* and *The Piano*. In these films, gender and sexuality come to the fore not only in relation to the hidden histories of women, but in the light of prior feminine literary models, from Charlotte Brontë (whose *Wuthering Heights* is an oft-cited intertext for *The Piano*) to Virginia Woolf.[4] Stella Bruzzi has argued for two models of reclaiming the past used by women filmmakers, a 'liberal' and a 'sexual' model, which would work along the lines of the

---

[4] The association between *Wuthering Heights* and *The Piano* has been explored by a number of critics, who take their cue from Campion herself. In published interviews Campion has cited *Wuthering Heights* as one of her sources of inspiration (e.g. Bilbrough 1999). See, in particular, Bruzzi (1996) and Ken Gelder's argument about the 'literariness' of *The Piano* (Gelder 1999).

distinction, in literary criticism, between a feminist critique (focusing on the representation of women in canonical literature; posing woman as a political *reader*) and a gynocritics (dealing with the more self-contained and experimental practices of women as *writer*) (Showalter 1992: 1226). The liberal model coincides with the first wave of social feminism, with films like *My Brilliant Career* (Gillian Armstrong, 1979) bent on rereading the past in order to find 'a political and ideological affinity between the struggles of women in the present and figures from the past' (Bruzzi 1996: 233-4). The sexual model can be mapped most clearly onto the 1990s and the momentum generated by *The Piano* (central to Bruzzi's analysis), unearthing hidden aspects of feminine sexual identity.

As Bruzzi suggests, the sexual model complicates basic feminist narratives with representations of female sexuality that test the limits of liberal feminism. More importantly, *The Piano* but also *The Governess* or *Mansfield Park* engage in a complex dialogue with women's sexual histories, in which present-day consciousness is inscribed on the nineteenth-century narrative.[5] The embedding of a contemporary consciousness within the limits of historical representation transforms the romance narrative at the core of these films into a flexible frame of reference. In this respect, fantasy, as a psychoanalytical construct, provides a useful framework to investigate how the postclassical feminist film addresses the past in order to fulfil a feminist desire for critical agency *and* narrative pleasure.

The notion of fantasy has had a major impact on theories of film spectatorship, for it provides a psychological framework for the structuring of identity that translates well into the spectator's active voyeurism and participation in the decoding of the film text. Popular culture provides generative matrices of reading through the adaptation of social representations (public fantasies) into subjectivity and self-representation (private fantasies) (de Lauretis 1994: 285, quoted in White 1999: 196). Fantasy is, however, neither a straightforward decoding process, nor an eternal return of the Oedipal logic of

---

[5] Bruzzi argues that this duality becomes apparent in the use of clothes as a semiotic system. Whereas in the liberal model costume blends realistically with the background of period reconstruction, conveying information about country, class and period (e.g. *Sense and Sensibility*), in the films closer to the sexual model costume is a crucial instrument for the articulation of the characters' sexual personae.

sameness in the ideological work of narrative: it also involves an active encoding process that starts in the text itself, and in its mechanisms of writing and address. Accordingly, fantasy is not the object of desire as figured in the film text, but a true 'mise en scène of desire':

> The fantasy scenario always involves multiple points of entry which are also mutually exclusive positions, but these are taken up not sequentially—as in a narrative—but simultaneously or rather, since the unconscious does not know time in this way, to take up any one position is also always to be implicated in the position of the other(s). (Cowie 1997: 135)

This multiplicity of positions has facilitated both extensive critical reworkings of classical Hollywood narratives, and renewed possibilities of representability.[6] My point is that fantasy also offers a framework to investigate how postmodern adaptations of the past do their own work of revision. Repetition in the romance narrative cannot be separated from the films' self-conscious awareness of gender as a discursive strategy. In this respect, fantasy opens a door to potentially utopian meanings since 'the uncanny recurrence of phantasy [*sic*] always represents an attempt to restage the Oedipal drama of desire and identity, to rewrite it and to have it conclude differently' (Rodowick 1991: 94). Past and present cease to be stable, mutually exclusive points of reference; fantasy allows us to move into the wider possibilities of identity as a *composite*, hybrid entity, negotiated through competing and overlapping textual layerings—through the dissension, as well as the consensus, between past and present.

Nevertheless, potential readings are always already subject to the return of the historical as that which determines the textual limits of revision. The practice of adaptation would work as a fantasy scenario that tells us not so much about possible ways of thinking 'woman' historically, but about the historical as imagined stage for the struggle to access self-representation. Thus the critical act involved in the process of adaptation takes on the connotations of feminist film criticism as a *minor practice*—an expression adapted in turn by Meaghan Morris, from the work of Gilles Deleuze and Felix Guattari

---

[6] For example, Patricia White (1999: 194-215) argues for a notion of 'retrospectator-ship' in relation to queer viewing processes and practices that produces a different context for understanding the classic Hollywood text.

(1986 and 1988), to the needs of women's cinema and experimental
feminism. Women's film as a minor mode of filmmaking takes shape
as a practice of appropriation of the master's tools. As Morris points
out, the minor is a 'constructive concept':

> While it refers directly to the experience of immigrants and colonized
> people, this question is echoed obliquely in the concerns of early feminist
> criticism ... A minor literature is not 'marginal': it is what a minority
> constructs *in a major language*, and so it is a model of action from a
> colonized, suppressed or displaced position *within* a given society ...
> 'Minor' and 'major' are used in a musical sense: they refer not to essences
> or states but to different ways of doing something, 'two different treatments
> of language, one which consists in extracting constants from it, the other in
> placing it in continuous variation' [Deleuze and Guattari 1988: 106].
> (Morris 1998: xvii-xviii)

If the literary film represents in itself a minor variation of a major
idiom (the historical and literary texts inherited from the past), the
feminist literary film is doubly marginal: with regard to both the grand
tradition it adapts, and the normative frames of narrative cinema
within which it operates. Its specificity is located in its modes of
address and rewriting. Rather than staging a linear narrative
bookended by what woman was and what she has become, these films
set up the past as a complex scene of fantasy with fluid limits and
unpredictable outcomes: language in continuous variation, often
striving to articulate utopian meanings.

The literary film invites the question of how authorship can be
reimagined in relationship to literary culture, feminism and the
popular in order to enable the repetition and variation of
performance—and hence, the appropriation and 'authoring' of the
texts of the past. The retrieval of authorship in terms of *revision* and
dialogue (Doane *et al.* 1984; Fischer 1989) is highly relevant for the
reassessment of costume drama as a feminist practice. Feminism poses
as a 'critical reading of culture, a political interpretation of the social
text and of the social subject, and a rewriting of our culture's "master
narratives"' (de Lauretis 1987: 113). The author-figure, famously
deconstructed by Michel Foucault and pronounced dead by Roland
Barthes, is thus reborn in the figure of the adapter/rewriter posing as
reader.

Mansfield Park: **Reflexivity and the Scene of Writing**

The hugely successful 1990s cycle of Anglo-American film adaptations from Jane Austen's works is indicative of the transformation of a quintessential British product—the 'quality' literary adaptation and classic television serial—into the cross-over specialist film designed by the Hollywood studios (Higson 2003: 119-45). The cycle started with the transatlantic success of Ang Lee's and Emma Thompson's *Sense and Sensibility*, and the BBC adaptation of *Pride and Prejudice* scripted by Andrew Davies (both from 1995). Hollywood appropriated the commercial phenomenon via an adaptation of *Emma* (Douglas McGrath, 1996) and, indirectly, with the updated Austenian teen comedy *Clueless* (Amy Heckerling, 1995). Other notable 1990s adaptations include the startlingly sombre *Persuasion* (Roger Michell, 1996), a BBC film produced for television that enjoyed a successful theatrical release in the USA. Giving an unexpected edge to the realism of period reconstruction, *Persuasion* is the most openly critical film in the series in its depiction of the physical, economic and social yokes fixing woman's place in society.[7]

The decade closed with Patricia Rozema's *Mansfield Park* (1999). A box-office disappointment after the string of Austen hits, *Mansfield Park* represents the definitive internationalisation of the Austen franchise beyond the British heritage aesthetics.[8] It is also the most reflexive film in the Austen cycle. In *Mansfield Park*, the stylisation of the mise-en-scène articulates a discourse on the past that is divided between the reenactment of the pleasures of the romance narrative, and their ironic rewriting. The film sets to both evoke and reframe its literary intertext though the intertextual play suggested by the textures of the image.

Mansfield Park's opening credit sequence features a collage with the instruments of writing: quills, paper and ink are captured through the magnifying glass of textured close-ups, and juxtaposed with moving shots of hand-writing. The visual theme of writing is

---

[7] For a critical account of this cycle, see Pidduck (2004).

[8] *Mansfield Park* received funding from the Arts Council of England, but was produced by Miramax. For box-office figures and an analysis of the box-office performance of this and other 1990s Austen films, see Higson (2003: 86-145).

wrapped in a musical theme that progressively gives way to indistinct
voices, eventually dissolving to the first diegetic shot of two girls—
two sisters—sharing a dingy bed, where the elder whispers stories into
the younger's ear. The credit sequence alludes to the fragmentary
nature of the literary discourse as well as to the sensuous materiality
of writing. However, as the literary is transformed into film, it also
generates a metonymic chain in which image, writing, and voice
become disseminated traces interwoven into the fabric of storytelling,
an activity that the opening scene presents as an act of bonding and
resistance that is specifically feminine.

This visual investigation into the technologies of writing
continues in the first part of the film. Fanny Price (Hannah Taylor-
Gordon), the child from a deprived family, is sent away to live with
wealthy relatives at the estate of Mansfield Park. Trying to comfort
her after a cold welcome into the house, her cousin Edmund (Philip
Sarson) offers Fanny a ream of thick cloth-like paper to write letters to
the sister she left behind. Through a montage sequence of close-ups of
hands carefully preparing the paper and sharpening the quills, the film
text resumes the visual figure of writing established in the title
sequence while bringing to the fore the motif of the letter, a fixture in
the costume film that adapts the bourgeois literary tradition. As
Julianne Pidduck has argued (2004: 12-14, 53-7), letters and letter-
writing are part of the recurring tropes in the visual imaginary of
costume drama, presenting a series of discursive regularities in the
mise-en-scène of the costume film. The scene of writing performs as a
spatio-temporal image which, along the lines of the Bakhtinian
chronotope, facilitates the ongoing dialogue between past and present.
The affective duration afforded to the letter-image in *Mansfield Park*
gives visual expression to retrospective forms of bounded subjectivity,
evoking qualities of interiority, deep feeling and desire, as well as the
pure sensuousness and pleasure of letter-writing. The letter motif also
articulates contemporary discourses on gender, class, and individuality
through a characteristic moment in the mise-en-scène of the costume
film. The extended montage sequence in *Mansfield Park* thus presents
writing as a socio-economic activity: a pleasure reserved to those who
can afford the cost of the materials. The activity of letter-writing
figuratively encapsulates the broader economic and discursive context
of the Empire, which provides the foundation of social order, and,

implicitly, marks the complicit position of the white, middle class woman within it.[9]

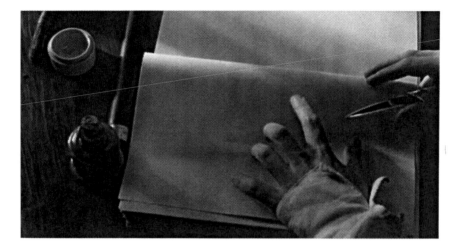

FIG. 7 The scene of writing in *Mansfield Park*

This sequence not only highlights the costume film's fascination with the rituals of the past, but opens up these cultural motifs with the performativity of the gesture. Letter/story writing is continued in a sequence that shows Fanny as a girl, then as a young woman (played by Frances O'Connor), engaging the spectator's look as she performs her own writings through time. Through the direct address to camera, the voice is deferred— 'written'—and writing is enacted as a gesture that lends itself to the variations of oral performance. The figure of the letter thus permits yet

[9] Rozema's film is distinctive as the only Austen adaptation in the 1990s that brings the subtext of colonial exploitation to the surface of the text. Pidduck points out the persistence of the colonial space as an *hors champ* or 'out-of-field' in the Austen adaptations: the structuring absence that provides the basis for a deconstructive critique of the films (2004: 35). Thus she tests the limits of the progressive gender critique in *Sense and Sensibility*, *Persuasion* or *Mansfield Park* against a broader discursive field touching on issues of class, race and sexuality (2004: 32-41).

another metonymic displacement: from fiction to History. The sequence of Fanny's letters condenses her maturing process in her garret at Mansfield Park. As Fanny grows up, the content of her writing changes from serialised Gothic stories to her sister into a very personal adaptation of History. The mise-en-scène of Fanny's writing blurs the boundary between the 'minor' activity of the storyteller and the 'major' activity of the History-writer, from the subversive viewpoint of a 'partial, prejudiced and ignorant historian', as she signs on the cover of her hand-written *The History of England*.[10]

FIG. 8 Adapting history in *Mansfield Park*

---

[10] Note that the mise-en-scène of the letter highlights the literary film as a citational practice: in true Derridean fashion, the film image exemplifies the dissemination of writing through new contexts of interpretation, 'fictionalising' Austen—the actual author of *The History of England*—and putting in Fanny's mouth the critique of History expressed by another Austenian heroine, Catherine Morland of *Northanger Abbey*: 'the men all so good for nothing, and hardly any women at all—it is very tiresome: and yet I often think it odd that it should be so dull, for a great deal of it must be invention' (Austen 1995: 97).

Although Edmund provides an invisible reader/audience for Fanny's writings/performances, in this sequence the letter works as a rhetorical figure addressed to an imaginary recipient beyond the limits of the diegetic space. As in *Orlando*, the look into the camera foregrounds the past as an intertextual space, mirroring the contemporary consciousness in the film text. The double consciousness of the literary film becomes apparent in the way that adult Fanny, as a fictional stand-in for Austen, 'adapts' History just like Rozema adapts Austen's works: as a fantasy space that makes room for a parody of Gothic novels, as well as for an ironic happy ending of the romance story.

The film closes with a free-floating, bird's-eye shot over the main characters and their houses. Mansfield Park turns into a theatrical décor where the actors freeze-frame as puppets whose strings would be pulled by Fanny's—Austen's—commanding narrative voice. Fanny's disembodied voice-over ('It could have turned out differently, I suppose ... but it didn't') and knowing glance at the camera as she embraces Edmund (the male hero eroticised into a suitable love interest) bring closure to the various strands of the story—which include her professional success as fiction writer, as well as her coming into love and property. *Mansfield Park* manages to bring together a compelling world of romantic fiction, only to reframe it by way of a reflexive performance orchestrated by a feminine wish-fulfilling author. The scene of writing comes through as a performative gesture that breaks the surface of narrative realism, pushing to the fore the playful intertextuality of the literary film. The result is a mise en abyme of writing: a game of mirrors in which Fanny Price becomes not only the reflection of 'Jane Austen, writer' but of 'Patricia Rozema, rewriter'. Whilst the film presents itself as based 'on Jane Austen's novel *Mansfield Park*, her letters and early journals', the scene of writing signals the continuity between all these intertexts and, more generally, between literary fiction, authorship, and feminine writing. The feminist gesture discloses the past as the scene of fantasy that permits the reconfiguration of modern feminine identity through imaginary models and inherited narratives.

The Governess: The Woman In/Behind Camera

The Governess establishes a further link between History and fiction through feminine writing. The film reportedly began as a journal that writer-director Sandra Goldbacher wrote from the point of view of the title character.[11] *The Governess* takes place in the mid-nineteenth century, and centres on Rosina da Silva (Minnie Driver), a Jewish woman living in a close-knit Sephardic community in Victorian London. After the murder of her beloved father, she decides to adopt a false name, Mary Blackchurch, and pass as Christian in order to take employment as governess with a wealthy family living in an estate on the Scottish Isle of Skye. While tutoring the Cavendishes' rebellious young daughter Clementina, Rosina grows increasingly fascinated with the experiments in photography conducted by her employer, Charles Cavendish (Tom Wilkinson). She starts working as his assistant, until she accidentally discovers the solution that makes possible fixing images on photographic paper, whose formula had been unsuccessfully pursued by Charles. This finding brings them closer and, as Rosina's passion for photography grows, the photographic apparatus becomes the instrument that mediates in their erotic and emotional attachment. Rosina poses for Charles in artistic portraits that she herself stages, but eventually steals a picture of him in the nude, while he is asleep. Charles grows afraid of Rosina's desire and aspirations, and when he publicly attributes their discovery all to himself, Rosina feels betrayed. She discloses their affair and her true identity to his family, and decides to return to London and become a professional photographer.

The Governess unfolds as a pastiche of themes and images from Victorian culture. Goldbacher's film offers a variation on New-Woman literature from the turn of the century, while falling back on canonical nineteenth-century referents. In particular, the motif of the governess evokes a range of literary intertexts from Charlotte Brontë's *Jane Eyre* (1847) to Henry James's *The Turn of the Screw* (1898), with Clementina and the adolescent Henry Cavendish taking up the

---

[11] The production notes on the film's official website (http://www.sonypictures.com/governess) state that Goldbacher was inspired by her desire 'to explore the two different influences of her own cultural heritage—her father is an Italian Jew and her mother came from the Isle of Skye'.

role of the Gothic 'corrupt' children. Visually, the film is clearly indebted to *The Piano*, with which it shares the theme of displacement (Skye replacing the untamed landscape of the New Zealand shores), and the strong-willed woman at the centre of a sexual triangle. However, it is the feminine viewpoint from the marginalised Jewish community and the central photographic theme that allow *The Governess* to establish its own distinctive minor variation within the major idiom of Victorianism.

Victorian culture constitutes a recurrent setting for postmodern rewritings of the past. The Victorian era has been rediscovered through commercial cinema and other forms of popular culture as a moment of both stability and change, which lends itself to the articulation of modernity. Its attraction resides in its imaginary status as a site of epistemological break, a place where the present can project its own narratives of origins:

> Rewritings of Victorian culture have flourished … because the postmodern fetishizes notions of cultural emergence, and because the nineteenth century provides multiple eligible sites for theorizing such emergence. For the postmodern engagement with the nineteenth century appears to link the discourses of economics, sexuality, politics and technology with the material objects and cultures available for transportation across historical and geographical boundaries, and thus capable of hybridization and appropriation … [T]he cultural matrix of nineteenth-century England joined various and possible stories about cultural rupture that, taken together, overdetermine the period's availability for the postmodern exploration of cultural emergence. (Kucich *et al.* 2000: xv)

The Governess's use of photography works within this fetishism of cultural rupture. Taking as main intertext the perfecting of the new technological medium and its professionalisation, the film locates the moment of emergence of a modern feminist consciousness alongside the imagined birth of portrait photography. While the letter scene in *Mansfield Park* interrupts the realist surface of the film with a multilayered mise-en-scène of writing, the 'photographic scene' in *The Governess* exploits the visual reflexivity implicit in the embedding of photography within a *filmic* narrative. Photography as a motif not only mediates a series of technological, cultural and sexual narratives inherited from Victorianism (Stewart 1995), but self-consciously foregrounds the gaze as a figure.[12]

FIG. 9 Rosina's look in *The Governess*

The figuring of the feminine gaze first appears in the opening scenes, as Rosina returns from the synagogue to the lively atmosphere of celebration at the family home. Upon crossing the threshold to the room where family and friends are congregated, a shot/reverse shot structure provides us with Rosina's viewpoint peering through a stained-glass screen. Rosina's look sutures the spectator's to her outsider position in English society, as we enter the unknown and 'exotic' world of Jewish culture. The view comes through the shot's double exposure and blurring colour filters, which provide a potent figure of 'difference' within the text. Whilst the coloured glass

---

[12] On the subject of the gaze as figure, see de Lauretis (1984: 142), quoted in Felber (2001: 32).

anticipates the photographic lens, the distortion effect in the initial images of the Jewish community already signifies Rosina's aesthetic eye—her ability 'to capture the beauty of her people' that will in the end define her as an artist-photographer, versus Cavendish's scientific practices.

The photographic theme contextualises the fictional story in the broader historical background, but the photographic *as figure* produces a web of meanings that stem from the characters' positions of power with regard to the photographic apparatus. The technologies of vision reflexively work as technologies of gender (de Lauretis 1987). Through the emphasis on framing and posing, the film articulates a series of binary meanings (voyeur/spectacle, artist/model, teacher/pupil, science/art, Self/Other) that come together in the all-encompassing dyad masculine/feminine. Rosina's progressive empowering is afforded by her appropriation of the technological means of production, which comes forcefully to the fore in the scene in which she moves behind the camera to photograph Charles while he is asleep. This scene has been criticised as symptomatic of the film's reductive vision of feminist politics, since it reverses the status quo but ultimately reinstates gender power relations (Felber 2001: 34). My contention is that this gesture has more complex consequences. It entails the transformation of the photographic scene into an open-ended scene of fantasy, where the terms 'posing' and 'framing' do not exclude each other but are complementary, marking the continuity between Oedipal romance and acts of resistance, repetition and difference in the fiction film.

The preoccupation with 'posing' has long been part of the deconstruction of gender in experimental feminist filmmaking. According to Mary Ann Doane,

> the subjects, whether male or female, inevitably appear to assume a mask of 'femininity' in order to become photographable (filmable)—as though femininity were synonymous with the *pose*. This may explain the feminist film's frequent obsession with the pose as position ... which we see as the arrangements of the body in the interest of aesthetics and science. In their rigidity (the recurrent use of the tableau in these films) or excessive repetition ... positions and gestures are isolated, deprived of the syntagmatic rationalization which, in the more classical text, conduces to their naturalization. (Doane 1991: 166-7)

Posing in *The Governess* is certainly naturalised by the plot, yet it acquires an ever shifting number of meanings (Felber 2001: 32). Rosina wilfully poses for Cavendish's camera on a number of occasions, and the rigidity of position demanded by the lengthy time of exposure in primitive photography transforms her mobile body into a reified image, the object of various 'tableaux vivants'. However, 'posing' also refers to Rosina's penchant for acting (at the beginning of the film she plays at being an actress with her sister Rebecca), and to her posing as the Christian Mary Blackchurch—with the added element of transgression signified by her 'passing' for the Other. Posing thus signifies the passive (masochistic) pleasure of the Oedipal romance narrative and the objectification of woman into image, yet at the same time it connects with the terms 'play', 'performance' and 'masquerade', resisting essentialist or 'fixed' notions of gender.[13]

This layering of meanings becomes apparent in the 'tableaux' scenes, in which Rosina stages her own gendered persona for the benefit of Charles's camera-eye, entering an erotic game that climaxes in a sequence in which Rosina dances and poses as Salome. In choosing to perform Jewish characters of biblical inspiration, the layers of her disguise multiply (in one scene she poses as Esther, herself passing for gentile in front of King Ahasuerus, in the Book of Esther). Rosina's hidden Jewish identity becomes an exotic mask, increasingly fetishised by the camera, but also a text that is already overwritten with the 'types'/citations she chooses to perform. The masquerade of femininity opens up the ironic distance between woman's body and her image, and this is what the photographic tableaux in *The Governess* achieve: the image not as naturalised representation, but as a framed textual space that deconstructs the reality effect with its palimpsest of citations.[14]

In the Salome sequence, posing momentarily brings the narrative to a standstill. The photographic produces a mise en abyme

---

[13] The posing/passing element in the mise en scène of *The Governess*, especially in the Salome fragment, invites the question of gender as a series of discontinuous performative gestures cemented in hegemonic historical narratives, as argued by Judith Butler (1990: 128-41). The popular postfeminist film, however, resists the more radical elements of Butler's critique (e.g. the deconstruction of the boundary between interiority and exteriority constitutive of the subject), as it asserts the search for self and identity underpinning the reenactment of the past.

[14] On film and masquerade, see Doane (1991: 17-43).

of cinema itself, yet it also functions as a rhetorical figure that literally stops the moving film image. In this set piece, punctuated by light flashes and edited to a soundtrack of orientalist music, Rosina is framed in different positions—including a classical 'Venus' pose, her back turned to the spectator and her naked body reclined over red draperies, offering itself to the viewer in a manner reminiscent of Ingres or Velázquez. The jump cuts constitute a mixture of high and lowbrow references: from painting to the erotics of the peep-show, underscored by the intercutting of masked shots showing Cavendish's eye peeping through the hole of the camera's viewfinder.

FIG. 10 The scene of fantasy from *The Governess*

The complexity of this sequence derives from the way it foregrounds the constructed space of the film frame by way of masking effects and superimpositions. In several shots, Rosina's wide-open eyes appear as a ghostly photographic imprint, hovering over her own immobile, blinded body. This collage is reminiscent of the fantastic, but it also recalls the dream-like images of the short film-within-the-film in *The Portrait of a Lady*, which playfully interrupts the realist surface with a self-standing fragment, grafting a metatextual commentary onto the narrative. The juxtaposition of two images, and therefore the projection of two different perspectives into the frame, destabilises the realist space with the 'compression' of exclusive and yet simultaneous positions: behind and on camera, artist and model, then and now. The fusing of Rosina's look and her own reified image leads to an uncanny effect: female subjectivity is inscribed over the spectacle of historical femininity; the body transcends the scene of its own objectification.

This sequence transforms Rosina into both the (narrative) subject and (visual) object of a fantasy scenario which, like Fanny in *Mansfield Park*, she is in control of. In both *Mansfield Park* and *The Governess*, the displaced feminist consciousness—woman as historical subject—is transcended through the textual identification of the woman artist with the artist-as-filmmaker. The figures of writing and photography are instrumental in the figuration of the double consciousness that aligns the heroine's eye with the contemporary 'feminist' eye, reconstructing feminine identity through the historical scene as reimagined by the romance narrative.

Mercurial Femininity and the Limits of Rewriting

In spite of their very different historical and literary intertexts, *The Luzhin Defence, Mansfield Park* and *The Governess* engage in a rewriting that endows their protagonists with the knowledge and self-expression of (post)modern femininity. This feminist gesture redefines the realist space of the literary film into a fantasy scene, which necessitates the backdrop of patriarchy as both transcultural and historically bound. Luzhin, as pointed out by Krabbé (2001), and especially Cavendish come across nearly as stereotypes, in contrast with the empowering of mercurial femininity. The melodramatic stance of *The Governess* transforms masculinity into an object of desire, but also into an obstacle. At the same time, Rosina's narcissistic expression through art is ultimately linked to the ghost of the lost father and her search for a sense of family and tradition. The father figure and, at the end of the film, the memory of family and community, become constitutive of her sense of self, anchoring her photographs in History.

In the context of the commercial costume film, the strategies of feminist criticism need to be adapted to address the varied responses offered by the contemporary imagination of period drama to our enduring fascination with both visual pleasure and narrative cinema. Within the conventional frame of romance, the literary film produces a narrative space poised between reconstruction and anachronism, which blurs the boundary between the two. Its textual work makes room for variation through reflexive figures that disrupt the continuity aesthetics of realism, revealing the workings of fantasy and desire. Through the active interventions of Natalia, Fanny and Rosina in the romance narratives, the films reimagine the past in order to construct 'an alternative imaginary for women, in which they might figure as historical agents' (Butler 2002: 13). In the process, the literary film self-consciously discards conventional notions of fidelity in favour of a dialogic retelling of the past, made possible through its transgressive reading gestures.

Bibliography

Anon. *'The Governess* (1998)'. On-line. Available HTTP: htttp://www.sonyclassics.com/governess (30 June 2004).

Austen, J. (1995 (1818)). *Northanger Abbey*. Harmondsworth: Penguin.

Bal, M. (1991) *Reading 'Rembrandt': Beyond the Word-Image Opposition*. Cambridge: Cambridge University Press.

Belsey, C. (1994) *Desire: Love Stories in Western Culture*. Oxford: Blackwell.

Bilbrough, M. (1999 (1993)) *'The Piano*: Interview with Jane Campion', in V. Wright Wexman (ed.) *Jane Campion: Interviews*. Jackson: University Press of Mississippi, 113-23.

Bruzzi, S. (1996) 'Jane Campion: Costume Drama and Reclaiming Women's Past', in P. Cook and P. Dodd (eds.) *Women and Film: A Sight and Sound Reader*. London: Scarlet Press, 232-42.

Butler, A. (2000) 'Feminist Theory and Women's Films at the Turn of the Century', *Screen*, 41 (1), 73-9.

—— (2002) *Women's Cinema: The Contested Screen*. London: Wallflower Press.

Butler, J. (1990) *Gender Trouble: Feminism and the Subversion of Identity*. London: Routledge.

Cowie, E. (1997) *Representing the Woman: Cinema and Psychoanalysis*. London: Macmillan.

De Lauretis, T. (1984) *Alice Doesn't: Feminism, Semiotics, Cinema.*
Basingstoke and London: Macmillan.
—— (1987) *Technologies of Gender.* Basingstoke and London:
Macmillan.
—— (1994) *The Practice of Love: Lesbian Sexuality and Perverse
Desire.* Bloomington: Indiana University Press.
Deleuze, G. and Guattari, F. (1986 (1975)) *Kafka: Toward a Minor
Literature.* Trans. D. Polan. Minneapolis: University of
Minnesota Press.
—— (1988 (1980)) *A Thousand Plateaus: Capitalism and
Schizophrenia.* Trans. B. Massumi. London: Athlone Press.
Doane, M. A. (1991) *Femmes Fatales: Feminism, Film Theory and
Psychoanalysis.* London and New York: Routledge.
Doane, M. A. *et al.* (eds.) (1984) *Re-Vision: Essays in Feminist Film
Criticism.* Frederick: AFI and University Publications of
America.
Felber, L. (2001) 'Capturing the Shadows of Ghosts: Mixed Media
and the Female Gaze in *The Women on the Roof* and *The
Governess*', *Film Quarterly*, 54 (4), 27-37.
Fischer, L. (1989) *Shot/Countershot: Film Tradition and Women's
Cinema.* Basingstoke and London: Macmillan.
Gelder, K. (1999) 'Jane Campion and the Limits of Literary Cinema',
in D. Cartmell and I. Whelehan (eds.) *Adaptations: From Text
to Screen, Screen to Text.* London and New York: Routledge.
Higson, A. (2003) *English Heritage, English Cinema: Costume
Drama since 1980.* Oxford: Oxford University Press.
Krabbé, T. (2001) 'Open Chess Diary 101-120 (10 March-30 May
2001)—22 March: Nabokov as a Feminist'. On-line. Available
HTTP: http://www.xs4all.nl/~timkr/chess2/diary_6.htm   (30
June 2004).
Kucich, J. and D. F. Sadoff (2000) 'Introduction', in J. Kucich and D.
F.   Sadoff (eds.) *Victorian Afterlife: Postmodern Culture
Rewrites the Nineteenth Century.* Minneapolis: University of
Minnesota Press, ix-xxx.
Morris, M. (1998) *Too Soon too Late: History in Popular Culture.*
Bloomington: Indiana University Press.
Pidduck, J. (2004) *Contemporary Costume Film: Space, Place and the
Past.* London: British Film Institute.

Rodowick, D. N. (1991) *The Difficulty of Difference: Psychoanalysis, Sexual Difference and Film Theory*. London and New York: Routledge.

Showalter, E. (1992) 'Toward a Feminist Poetics', in H. Adams (ed.) *Critical Theory since Plato*. Fort Worth: Harcourt Brace Jovanovich, 1223-33.

Stewart, G. (1995) 'Film's Victorian Retrofit', *Victorian Studies*, 38 (2), 153-98.

White, P. (1999) *UnInvited: Classical Hollywood Cinema and Lesbian Representability*. Bloomington: Indiana University Press.

Filmography

Goldbacher, S. dir. (1997) *The Governess*. BBC/Pandora Cinema/ Parallax Pictures.

Gorris, M. dir. (2000) *The Luzhin Defence*. Renaissance Films/Clear Blue Sky Productions.

Rozema, P. dir. (1999) *Mansfield Park*. Miramax/Hal Films/BBC.

Notes on Contributors

Mireia Aragay is Senior Lecturer in English literature and film at the University of Barcelona. She holds an MSc from the University of Edinburgh and a PhD from the University of Barcelona, where she teaches Shakespeare, Shakespeare and cinema, critical theory and literature and film. She has published essays on Harold Pinter and other contemporary British and Irish playwrights and on film adaptations of the classics.

Manuel Barbeito teaches English and Irish Literature at the University of Santiago de Compostela. He wrote his PhD on W. H. Auden. He has edited, among others, *Modernity, Modernism, Postmodernism* (2000) and *Feminism, Aesthetics and Subjectivity* (2001). He has written *El individuo y el mundo moderno: El drama de la identidad en siete clásicos de la literatura británica* (2004), and the forthcoming *The Brontës and their World*.

Deborah Cartmell is Principal Lecturer and Subject Leader in English at De Montfort University and has published on Shakespeare on film, literary adaptations, and Renaissance poetry. She is currently working, with Imelda Whelehan, on a *Cambridge Companion to Literature on Screen* and *Literature on Screen: An Overview*. She is also editor of the new journal, *Shakespeare*.

Celestino Deleyto lectures on English literature and film at the University of Zaragoza. He has published articles on film theory and history in various international periodicals, including *Cinema Journal, Critical Survey* and *Screen*. He is the author of *Ángeles y demonios* (2003), a book on contemporary Hollywood cinema, and co-editor of *Terms of Endearment: Hollywood Romantic Comedy of the 1980s and 1990s* (1998). His book on Woody Allen and the theory of comedy is forthcoming.

Karen Diehl holds an MA in Comparative Literature and a PhD on film adaptations of Marcel Proust from the Department of European History and Civilisation at the European University Institute in Florence, Italy. She is now part of the research project 'Immagini dell'Europa 1989-2006: per una storia culturale dell'Europa a traverso il cinema' at the University of Turin, Italy.

Lindiwe Dovey is currently a post-doctoral research scholar at Trinity College, Cambridge. She holds a PhD on African cinema and literature from Cambridge University. She founded and runs the annual Cambridge African Film Festival and Symposium on African Cinemas, and also works as a freelance specialist and African film programmer. She has made two short film adaptations, *Nina* (2000) and *Perfect Darkness* (2001), which have screened at international festivals, and has published fiction, poetry, film reviews, and academic essays.

José Angel García Landa holds an MA from Brown University and a PhD from the University of Zaragoza, where he teaches Shakespeare and literary criticism. He is currently editing an online *Bibliography of Literary Theory, Criticism and Philology*. He is the author of *Acción, relato, discurso: Estructura de la ficción narrativa* (1998) and has co-edited *Narratology* (1996) and *Gender, I-deology: Essays on Theory, Fiction and Film* (1996).

Thomas Leitch is Professor of English and Director of Film Studies at the University of Delaware. His most recent books are *Crime Films* (2002), *Perry Mason* (2005) and the forthcoming *Literature vs. Literacy: Why Adaptation Study Matters.*

Gemma López lectures in English literature at the University of Barcelona. Her research interests include English novels of the twentieth century, post-structuralist theory and gender studies. She is currently writing on the textualisation(s) of desire and identity.

Sara Martín teaches nineteenth- and twentieth-century English literature at the Universitat Autònoma de Barcelona. Her main research interests apart from film adaptations are Gothic fictions and the representation of masculinity in films and novels since the early nineteenth century.

Margaret McCarthy is associate professor of German at Davidson College, where she teaches twentieth-century German literature and film. She has published essays on Ingeborg Bachmann, Luc Besson, G. W. Pabst, Wim Wenders, and Doris Dörrie. She co-edited *Light Motives: German Popular Film in Perspective* (2003).

Pedro Javier Pardo García is Senior Lecturer in English Literature at the University of Salamanca. His main field of specialisation is comparative literature. His research interests include the Cervantean tradition in English, French and American literature, and popular narrative genres in literature and film.

John Style is Senior lecturer in modern and contemporary British literature at the Universitat Rovira i Virgili in Tarragona, Spain. He is the author of various articles on Martin Amis and Julian Barnes, and is currently researching musical/literary connections during the Modernist period.

Belén Vidal is the author of *Textures of the Image: Rewriting the American Novel in the Contemporary Film Adaptation* (2002). She has published in *Screen* and *Archivos de la Filmoteca* on film theory and images of the past in contemporary costume drama. She is lecturer in Film Studies at the University of St Andrews, Scotland.

Imelda Whelehan is Professor of English and Women's Studies at De Montfort University and has published on feminist thought, literary adaptations and women's popular fiction. Her most recent book, *The Feminist Bestseller*, will be published at the end of 2005.